RETURN

the RETURN

MIKE EVANS

THOMAS NELSON PUBLISHERS
Nashville • Camden • New York

Published in Nashville, Tennessee, by Thomas Nelson, Inc. and distributed in Canada by Lawson Falle, Ltd., Cambridge, Ontario.

Printed in the United States of America.

Unless otherwise noted, Scripture quotations are from THE NEW KING JAMES VERSION. Copyright © 1979, 1980, 1982, Thomas Nelson, Inc., Publishers.

Scripture quotations noted TEV are from the Good News Bible—Old Testament: Copyright © American Bible Society 1976; New Testament: Copyright © American Bible Society 1966, 1971, 1976. Used by permission.

Scripture quotations noted NIV are from The Holy Bible: New International Version. Copyright © 1978 by the New York International Bible Society. Used by permission of Zondervan Bible Publishers.

Scripture quotations noted TLB are from *The Living Bible* (Wheaton, Ill: Tyndale House Publishers, 1971) and are used by permission.

ISBN 0-8407-5501-5

Contents

To
Michelle
Shira
Rachel
Michael David

Preface

We live in remarkable times—disaster follows disaster and the world is in turmoil as its leaders seek solutions to the many problems that plague us on every side. Yet, in the midst of it all, a brilliant light of hope is beginning to shine, because the world is about to experience history's most climactic event—*The Return*.

I have purposely opened my book with a fictional dramatization of how the rulers of the world may one day have to face the startling evidence of the return. Although some might question the likelihood of such a dramatic scene as I paint, I urge them to keep an open mind, because I believe before they finish this book, it is highly likely they will come to the startling conclusion that they may well experience the return in their lifetimes.

So that nothing has been left to "blind" faith, I have also included an extensive compilation of footnotes, listing my sources for the more incredible of my assertions. Only in certain instances where I have thought that I might be endangering the security of a country, or someone's personal security, have I remained reticent about my sources of information.

To the enormous number of individuals consulted on this project, from world leaders to dozens of distinguished men in every field, I can only say thank you.

Readers of *The Return* must understand that this book does not necessarily reflect the views of any single individual interviewed.

1

Operation Global Probe

April 12, 2:35 P.M.

The intercom in the World Room buzzed, "Dr. Bradford, this is Madelyn. Dr. Chan is ready with your Global Risk and Perplexity Analysis."

Paul Bradford, director of the International Center for Multidisciplinary Analysis of the State of the World (ICMASW), turned his chair to view the wide computer screen. As he pushed the security clearance code, the words appeared:

PRESIDENTIAL GLOBAL ANALYSIS REPORT—PROJECTIONS THROUGH 1999

He hesitated a second before releasing the Phase II security code activating the computer's scanners. The code was released. Here it was—the report that was causing so much consternation both at the Center and at the White House. Before Bradford's deep blue eyes lay the great complexities of the world game—nuclear weapons, military strategies, environmental and world energy concerns, health and human survival possibilities. *There just has to be something in here besides these ominous projections we've been coming up with lately,* he thought to himself.

Bradford was deep in concentration when the phone rang again; it was his private line to the White House. "You've got seventy-two hours," said the voice on the other end of the line. "The president's not buying it, and he won't be embarrassed. We've spent six billion dollars on this project, and he wants some answers, not this malarkey about impending doom. Is that understood?"

"Yes, but—" The receiver clicked in his ear.

He pressed the intercom button. "Madelyn, tell each division head to be in the conference room in five minutes."

"Yes, Dr. Bradford." She paused, "Shall I tell them why?"

He could already feel the nervous perspiration forming on his brow. "Tell them we've heard from the White House."

Tension was in the air as he walked into the conference room a few minutes later.

"Our report is not acceptable to the president," Bradford blurted.

"Not acceptable?" said Michael Reinemann incredulously. "I couldn't care less if the president is an optimist or not. Facts are facts. Our Cyborg 9200 computer tells us that there is apparently no way to avoid world disaster!"

"Does he expect us to deny the fact that the planet is at a breaking point and write some sort of fairy tale?" questioned Alice Chan.

"Whatever happens, we won't stoop to that," Bradford insisted. "But we have to come up with a solution. He's given us seventy-two hours to find a different approach. I want you all to think of nothing else. Consider every idea that comes to mind, no matter how bizarre. Stay here all night if necessary. We'll meet here tomorrow morning at eight o'clock."

It was a sleepless night for Bradford, one of many he had had during the last few months as the ICMASW staff sought for a solution to the mounting crises around the world. *There has to be some end to this,* he thought. *There is more at stake here than simply gaining the president's approval. What a nightmare!* The future of the planet, not to mention his own children's, was on the line.

April 13, 7:21 A.M.

Bradford sipped his coffee and opened the morning paper. He stared at the front-page headline in shock:

APOCALYPSE IMMINENT, ACCORDING TO
PRESIDENTIAL REPORT

If the *Post* had the story, it would have been picked up by the major news services now. It would be on every newscast in the world.

Visibly shaken, Bradford reached for the phone and dialed the office of his old friend, Bob McPherson, the National Security Advisor. When McPherson came on the line, he said, "Bradford, you've no idea how far this has gone. The president is meeting with the Joint Chiefs of Staff. The Russians have used the hotline to the White House for the first time in over eighteen years. They think we're preparing for a major preemptive strike."

"What?!"

"They know we've been gathering data, and they've drawn the wrong conclusion. We'll issue a statement in a few hours, Paul. We have to tell the truth about the purpose of the Center."

Bradford was silent for a moment. Then he said, "I understand," and hung up.

Paul Bradford's wife Julia walked into the breakfast room. "What's the matter, Paul?" she asked. He handed her the paper, explaining the situation.

"What will this mean for you?" she gasped.

"I don't know all the implications yet, but the reporters will probably be here any minute. Don't answer the door today. I'll send security over to keep an eye on things."

He drew her into his arms. "What are we going to do, Julia?" he said. "If it were just one set of problems plaguing our world, maybe we could come up with some answers, but everything seems to be converging, coming to a head. I feel like a physician watching the vital signs on a dying patient."

Paul Bradford was forty-eight. He had always been an intense man, an ambitious man—but he was also a man of integrity.

He had been the director of ICMASW ever since it had been commissioned by the president twelve years ago to work in cooperation with dozens of pro-Western governments to find solutions to the problems threatening the peace and stability of the world.

A former chairman of the Atomic Energy Commission, Bradford had garnered two Nobel prizes, each in a different field, while he was still in his thirties. His widening interests included engineering, physics, biology, medicine, architecture, astronomy, psychology, and history.

Bradford's twelve colleagues, nine men and three women, were some of the finest minds in the world. They had been given a top priority task: to collect data from virtually every sphere of human endeavor. It had required the assembly of a mammoth international network of trained researchers and the most advanced technology available. It had taken more than a decade to accomplish. And it had cost a staggering six billion dollars.

Bradford still didn't know how so much money had been found for the research. The world economy was on the verge of total bankruptcy. Both of the "superpowers" had faltered under the crushing load of military spending, which had more than doubled between 1974 and 1984 with 25 percent of the 2.25 million scientists in the world working on military research and over 50 percent of all physicists and engineers working exclusively on the development of weapons. Bradford's research had proved without question that the U.S. Nuclear Utility Targeting Strategy Program, code named NUTS, which had cost over $500 billion, could even provide terrorists with the capability to unleash atomic blackmail on the great cities of the world.

Bradford, trying to find a way to justify the nuclear arsenals that now contained explosive power equivalent to one and a half million Hiroshimas, was perplexed. His access to NORAD's (North American Aerospace Defense Command) information had only confirmed his fears.

In the last twelve months, NORAD had had 431 major alerts because of the Soviet spy ring missiles, not to speak of the Russian's incredible military advancements in space. Bradford had become convinced that the planet was in the final countdown to a nuclear war.

Adding to this had been the environmental backlash, obvious symptoms of stress, including drought, pollution, deforestation, and the incredible depletion of the earth's nonrenewable resources that had left the world hungry and in pain—leaving no alternatives but violence, terrorism, and political unrest.

All the dangerous cracks in the world's management system were haunting Bradford like the plague. The list of global illnesses was almost endless. Conditions were so severe that the word *crisis* had lost its meaning. Suicide rates had soared in the face of a widespread sense of terminality.

But most people still clung to the hope that mankind had perhaps one last feeble chance to work together to solve its problems. And, in order to avail itself of this chance, it would have to get beyond its myriad of conflicting opinions.

Man would have to take a long, hard look at reality. And that could be done only with factual data evaluated by the most objective and detached use of universally accepted criteria.

That was where Bradford and ICMASW had come into the picture—to secure that data for evaluation. Isolate the problems and explore the relationships between the issues. Determine why the world had gone so terribly wrong.

As far as the public knew, that was the extent of it. But there was more. The Center had also been charged with finding solutions and making recommendations for action.

This element of secrecy had allowed the Center to carry on its work without undue external pressure. Media scrutiny, for example, had been occasional and casual. As far as the press was concerned, Bradford's Center was the largest data bank and ranked alongside the Census Bureau as a source of vital statistics.

In less than eight months from now, the president would be up for reelection. He was desperate to produce positive accomplishments for which his administration could take credit. That had caused him to seize upon ICMASW (in spite of the fact that it had been initiated under another administration) as the most significant achievement to which he could point—a possible ticket to a second term. This meant, of course, that it was essential for Bradford to come up with an optimistic forecast for at least the next four years.

But he and his associates had failed to do that. Just a month ago, the computer had completed its evaluation of the vast amount of data so painstakingly collected. The results had been finalized and sent to the president. Needless to say, the report was not what he wanted to hear. It painted a dismal picture, and the chief executive was furious, thus explaining the seventy-two-hour deadline.

Just three weeks before, Dr. Reinemann reported, "Our primary analysis models aren't working. Something is wrong. The data—stop and think about it. We are spending 20 percent more on weapons designed to destroy life than in health measures to preserve life. Four hundred wars are going on; 364 insects, 'superbugs,' are no longer susceptible to any known insecticides, over one hundred million babies have been aborted worldwide as we have endeavored to decrease the population growth. Yet, in the midst of it, there are over ten million refugees staring us in the face—hungry and violent. Fully one-third of the world's population is going to bed hungry. In America alone a million people may die of AIDS. The Pacific basin is on the verge of the greatest volcanic eruption ever, which will make Mount St. Helens look like a smoke bomb. That's only a sample. The list goes on."

Michael Reinemann, the institute's director of data analysis, was the world's acknowledged expert on advanced computer programming. But the program Reinemann and his team had written had been born in Bradford's mind. Actually, every member of the team, together with more than three hundred consultants and other experts, had contributed to its operation.

It was the most thoroughly encyclopedic system of analysis and evaluation ever devised. No possible angle had been left out. The program would weigh the political, economic, military, demographic, ecological, sociological, historical, and biological implications of the data.

But the biggest challenge facing Bradford and his team had been to devise a model or models (the ones Reinemann said weren't working) to use as a basis for finding solutions to the problems it was evaluating. They had debated long and hard about this. But recently they had managed to boil the choices down to two models: a techno-scientific model and a humanistic model.

According to the techno-scientific model, knowledge was foremost. Man would continue to ingeniously invent his way out of all problems. Thus he could always keep one step ahead of the apocalypse. If the earth became uninhabitable, for example, man could colonize outer space.

According to the humanistic model, the present evil plight of mankind could be solved by man's essential inner goodness. It was a belief in the upward progress of the human race toward perfection that had brought man out of the Dark Ages into the Renaissance. So, in the twentieth century, man should be able to once again find his way to a change of heart that would deliver him from this new age of darkness.

Yet it was precisely this program, using these two models, that had produced the apocalyptic scenario that so greatly distressed the chief executive. This had bewildered almost all of the scientists and scholars on the institute's team.

Reinemann had explained it quite concisely that day: "Maybe science and technology could have rescued us a few years back. Maybe we could have learned to get along with each other. I don't know. Anyway, it doesn't make any difference. It's too late. Let's face it. We have nothing hopeful to tell the president or anyone else."

And, with that, the staff had made the grim decision to send the results of the study to the president as their final conclusion.

April 13, 8:50 A.M.

As Bradford's car came within a block of the Center's sprawling grounds, he could see a crowd gathered outside the gate. A dozen or so of them held placards. On one was scrawled, "Bradford is a fascist." Another called ICMASW a temple of doom.

Bradford's driver turned down a side street to the service entrance. Bradford moved quickly into the building.

"The switchboard's been swamped with calls since we opened this morning," Madelyn said, following Bradford into his office. "Reporters with endless questions."

Bradford looked out the window toward the front entrance. The crowd had grown. The police had arrived, but had failed to keep the street cleared for traffic. "If only we had more time," Bradford sighed. He turned to his secretary. "I'm going over to the World Room to talk to Reinemann."

Bradford was out in the hallway when he saw Dr. Alive Chan, ICMASW's leading biologist and futurist coming toward him. "What are we going to do about the leak?" she said.

Bradford nodded grimly.

She went on, "The results could be disastrous if this thing goes any further."

He told her about the forthcoming White House statement.

"It's going to tell the whole story on the institute?"

"Yes."

"How will you control the press afterwards?" she asked.

Bradford paused. "I don't know. I may not be able to. When I saw the crowd out on the street, I knew we'd enjoyed our last day of obscurity."

The World Room, where Bradford was headed, was an enormous cavern in the heart of the Center's main building that housed an array of the most sophisticated and advanced computer technology available. This room was the Center's observation post, a front row seat on world events.

Bradford had always liked the World Room. He was strangely comforted somehow by the soft light of the giant screens and the low clicking and whirring noises all around him.

The Center's enormous mainframe computer, the Cybor 9200, was digesting raw data on the environment, political trends, nuclear proliferation, wars, population growth, food distribution, health, weather, economic patterns, geology, seismology, and so forth. Never before had the pulse of the planet been taken so carefully. But, then, never before had the world been in such a dilemma.

Reinemann was appalled by the turn of events. "Everything we've worked to accomplish here could be destroyed. The Center will be turned into a bloody scapegoat."

"Not if I can help it, Michael," Bradford said calmly.

"Paul," Reinemann said, "I did what you asked, but I don't have a single idea. Nothing came to mind."

Bradford frowned, "Nothing?"

"What else could there be?"

"I thought of something on the way over in the car this morning," Bradford replied. "We could just turn the computer loose and let it find its own model—whatever works."

Reinemann protested. "How is the computer going to find a model on its own?"

"Virtually all the great books, ideas, and philosophies of civilization are in our reference data banks, aren't they?"

"Yes, of course." Reinemann shrugged.

"Tell the computer to go through everything in the bank and

compare it with the information we've given it. If it finds something that fits, then go with it and see where it leads. Can it be done?"

"Yes, but—"

"How soon?"

"It'll probably take until tomorrow morning to revise the program."

"Do it!" Bradford commanded. "There are people out there on the street and a whole world beyond who need some answers before we all start killing each other for the last scraps left on the table. We've got to try it."

The president's announcement had the expected effect. Overnight the institute had become the focus of world attention. By midafternoon thousands had completely encircled the grounds.

The press was everywhere, even hovering over the building in helicopters. Bradford had no choice but to consent to media coverage of the experimental computer run scheduled for the following day.

April 14, 9:17 A.M.

The world was waiting. Pandemonium reigned in the World Room where camera crews had set up their equipment focusing on the enormous screen where the results of the analysis would appear first.

Bradford had hosted a press conference at which he, Reinemann, and Chan had fielded what had seemed an endless stream of questions. They had not had many answers except to explain their hopes about the computer's forthcoming analysis.

Reinemann was skeptical, but he admitted that, so far, the new program had taken shape with fewer problems than he had anticipated. It was possible that it would complete its run before noon if the loading from the data bank could commence as early as ten-thirty.

By eleven the computer was churning its way through the enormous data bank.

Chaos turned to quiet in the World Room as everyone became increasingly conscious that mankind's last hope was being considered by the computer. Would it find an ultimate answer to the problem of man's seemingly irreconcilable bent toward destruction? Or would it fizzle as had the two models they'd tried already?

The Center's research, as they knew, had represented a final economic gasp by the whole world. Scientific and medical research had been on the wane for over five years. No money remained anywhere to fund the projects that had once blazed a bold trail into the future.

Was there really any hope for mankind?

At eleven forty-five, Reinemann, weary with fatigue and a migraine headache, addressed the group: "All indications are that the computer is just a few minutes from reaching a conclusion."

The word on the screen had remained the same for the last two hours: "PLEASE WAIT, ANALYSIS IN PROGRESS." Suddenly, however, they vanished. Noises from the mainframe drives heralded the announcement. But, when it came, it evoked only a bewildered buzz in the room.

ANALYSIS COMPLETE
CONCLUSION: THE RETURN

Bradford and Reinemann looked at each other blankly. Reinemann turned quickly to an assistant. "Ask the computer some further questions. What does this conclusion mean?"

The assistant, perspiration lining his forehead, made a few quick strokes on the keyboard. Almost instantly, the screen fed upwards and, seconds later, began to fill:

OPERATION: QUERY CONCLUSION.
CONCLUSION: THE RETURN OF JESUS CHRIST.
BASIS FOR CONCLUSION: THE BIBLE.
ELABORATION: EXACT CORRELATION BETWEEN THIS DOCUMENT AND TOTAL DATA ANALYZED.
EXPLANATION: DOCUMENT CONTAINS SYSTEM OF FORECASTS THAT PROVIDE RATIONALE FOR EVALUATION OF DATA.

SUBNOTE: MANY FORECASTS IN THIS DOCUMENT AL-READY CONFIRMED AND VERIFIED.
PRESS RETURN FOR DETAILS ON CONCLUSION.

The private line to the White House began to ring. Bradford and Reinemann stood in stunned silence, staring glassy-eyed into each other's face in a state of shock.

II

Behind the News

"We think that mankind has perhaps only ten years or less to choose a course different from the present one—which is bound to end in disaster."

—Aurelio Peccei, President
Club of Rome

"Good morning. Topping the news this morning is a special report on the hijacking of TWA Flight 845 from Athens to Rome with 153 passengers aboard. At the present time, the plane is circling the Middle East. Shi'ite Muslims have threatened to blow up the carrier over Beirut if their demands are not met. Later in the program Marcia Lintner will give us an in-depth look at the Soviet Union's suspected involvement in the Middle Eastern turmoil. Soviet-aligned Syria and Soviet-influenced Iran may be the chief architects of a new terrorist organization.

"We'll also have a special report on a possible Soviet threat to Iran, where the Soviet Union has twenty-six divisions stationed on its border. And we'll spotlight Soviet concerns over losing so much military hardware to Israel. Ninety MiGs and twenty-five hundred SAM missiles have been destroyed by Israeli armed forces. There are even reports that Soviet pilots have been shot down over Israel's northern border.

"We'll have a special report from Dr. William Dinsley, our health and science expert, on the spread of AIDS. He'll tell us how over a million Americans have been infected with the virus at a cost to the country of over six billion dollars. If this trend continues during the next twenty-four months, more people could die from AIDS than died in Vietnam.

"An earthquake in Mexico City has left thousands homeless. Herb Atwood will be bringing us an up-to-the-minute report.

"Details on these and other stories coming right up. But first, let's have a look at the local weather..."

Appalling Facts

The headlines I have just given you are not fiction. They are reality. For example, over twenty-four hundred scientists from all over the world recently took part in the largest conference ever on AIDS. Many of them came up with just such sobering conclusions as those reported.[1] And there is a personal element to such tragedies. Consider the Burkes. Patrick is twenty-seven, a hemophiliac who contracted AIDS from blood clotting concentrates he was given. Not knowing he had acquired AIDS, he passed the virus on to his twenty-four-year-old pregnant wife, Maureen, who subsequently gave birth to their son, Dwight, and passed Acquired Immune Deficiency Syndrome to this newborn child.

Because of his illness, Patrick has quit his job. Mrs. Burke has now returned to work to help with the increasing flow of bills. she said, "I have got to have enough money to bury my son."

Israel *did* shoot down seven Soviet MiGs in 1972. The bodies of seven Russian pilots were shipped from Jerusalem to Moscow in caskets according to one of the top ministers of the Israeli government, Yaacov Meridor.[2]

Jack Anderson, the well-known Washington columnist, is my source for the twenty-six divisions. They sit just inside Russia's border with Iran. The enormous stockpiles of Soviet arms in the Middle East—fifty billion dollars may be a modest estimate—are common knowledge to those familiar with the region.[3]

Let me tell you I am angry! I am fed up with media-mind manipulators who smugly report "the news" but who actually conceal the truth from us. It's disgusting to watch them recount tales of death, destruction, and disease as if they were reporting a fashion show.

What they dispense, day after day, feeds an ever-increasing sense of hopelessness in any normal person. We become used to it—unaffected. We're like a frog placed in a pan of water. The water gets heated gradually, but the frog doesn't realize it until it's too late; by then he's boiled to death.

Newscasters are playing God to us. They tell us what's happening and how we ought to feel about it. And the way we're supposed to feel is not too alarmed or angry. Instead we should remain calm and aloof, as they do. For example, it would show an appalling lack of social grace and aplomb if a newscaster were to appear indignant while reading a report about a series of disgusting displays of affection during a homosexual rights parade.

So, like frogs in heating water, we become accustomed to hearing about worse and worse things. We begin to feel casual about things that should horrify us. We are, in effect, being lied to every day by God-playing newscasters.

In "Operation Global Probe," the first chapter of this book, I wrote a story designed to help you "jump out of the water" before it's too late. Even though the story was fictional, it indeed tells the truth. It should serve to alert you to the potential dangers ahead. If you are a pursuer of truth, then stay with me. I personally have done years of exhaustive research on the subject of what our world is coming to and have come to the conclusion that the events predicted in the twenty-fourth chapter of Matthew's Gospel are knocking at the door. The signs of the return of Jesus Christ are upon us.

Even Dr. Billy Graham agrees: "If you look in any direction, whether it is technological or physiological, the world as we know it is coming to an end. Scientists predict it, sociologists talk about it. Whether you go to the Soviet Union or anywhere in the world, they are talking about it. The world is living in a state of shock."

Many of the shocking statements made in the chapter "Operation Global Probe" are present-day, not futuristic, facts. Let me review them briefly:

1. Yes, 431 Soviet missiles did go off in the last twelve months. This is not fictional. This was told to me by Brigadier General Charles B. Bartholomew, the assistant deputy chief of Staff of Operations for NORAD in a recent interview I did with him in the Major Command Post of NORAD.[4] We will be discussing this in greater detail later in the book.

2. The superpowers have faltered under the crushing load of military spending. The amounts of money spent for military purposes in the Soviet Union and the United States doubled between 1974 and 1984. More than two million scientists around the world are doing military research. Over half of all the physicists and engineers in the world are currently working on weapons development.[5]

3. The U.S. government has a program, code named NUTS, which will cost over $500 billion. Opponents of this program claim that it will provide terrorists with the tools and expertise to use nuclear weapons in the great cities of the world unless it is carefully supervised.[6]

4. Suicide rates everywhere have soared in recent years.[7]

5. Suicide is now the leading cause of death among American teen-agers. A grim sense of terminality is spreading across the face of the earth.[8]

6. Spending for weapons to destroy life exceeds our spending for health by 20 percent.[9]

7. Four hundred armed conflicts are going on as I write these words.

8. "Superbugs," insects no longer susceptible to any known insecticide, now number 364.[10]

9. More than one hundred million babies worldwide have suffered death by abortion just since 1972. Almost 20 percent of those babies were American.[11]

10. Ten million refugees cannot live in their original homes.

11. A third of the earth's population goes to bed hungry.[12]

12. A million Americans are carriers of AIDS, and the experts say there isn't a chance in the world of a cure before 1990.[13]

13. Around the edge of the Pacific Basin sits a "ring of fire"— a violent circle of volcanic and seismic activity. The eruption of Mount St. Helens is thought by many experts to be but a small beginning to an upheaval that could change the entire planet in ways difficult to predict.[14]

Other startling facts confront us as well. Our divorce rate is fast approaching 60 percent of all marriages.[15] The experts say that we will be moving to a time of marriage contracts which will be negotiated and renewable.[16] Drug and alcohol abuse is common among almost one in every three Americans. Profits from the cocaine business in America are estimated to exceed $25 billion every year.[17] (That is three times bigger then the net income of the recording and movie industries combined.) Nuclear weapons are so plentiful that we could readily re-create Hiroshima 1.2 million times over.[18]

It is time to face these problems and to say boldly what they mean: they fulfill the predictions made by Jesus and the apostles about the evil things that would prevail shortly before His return. Jesus Christ is coming back soon. Laugh if you will, but I assure you, in my last sixteen meetings with presidents and prime ministers, and in hundreds of meetings with generals, intelligence leaders, and scientists, I have come to the startling conclusion that the prophecies of the Bible can be backed up and documented with today's newspaper. We are truly on the verge. The return is imminent.

In this book I am going to show that the moral condition of the world, which was predicted as a sign of the end of the age long ago in the Bible (see 2 Tim. 3), has come to pass with amazing exactness. The Bible itself predicted the things we see happening all around us—increased warfare, terrorism, civil strife in nations, increasing famines and earthquakes, amazingly widespread deception and falsehood, and an increase in lawlessness.

Some prophecies relating to the Lord's return date back almost three thousand years to Old Testament times. Among them, I believe, is Ezekiel's prediction that Russia would move toward the Middle East in one of the great final events of history. Everything is poised for that to happen soon. *It may be happening before your eyes.*

Time Machine

As I stood on the steps of the Capitol in Washington just before going inside to be on hand for the historic House vote on the prayer amendment, some reporters asked, "What are you going to do if you lose?" I told them that to put it that way was absurd. President Reagan once said, "The issue is not, is God on America's side, but is America on God's side?" Why, I asked, is there so much anger, resentment, and hostility against prayer? The proposed legislation didn't specify to whom school children ought to be allowed to pray. We really ought to be asking, "Will America win or lose?"

"The issue is not really prayer," I continued speaking. "It is much greater than prayer. The real issue is God. America has become dominated by God-players who refuse to acknowledge or submit to the God of heaven who created them. We've become too cultured for such foolishness as God!"

That same week I sat down with several CBS reporters and, later, with a bureau chief for the *Wall Street Journal*.[19] The meetings were so similar that I will comment on them as if they were one. As we went over current events and recent history, I began to tell them about the ancient biblical prophecies. I showed them how those prophecies helped to make sense out of our confusing times, and how they pointed to the nearness of the return of Christ. In doing this, my half hour with the CBS reporters stretched into two hours, and my hour with the bureau chief became, at his request, three and a half hours. All three of them were astonished to learn about the Bible's predictions. They had been completely unaware of their existence prior to those meetings. It was almost as if those ancient prophets had been put in a time machine and thrust thousands of years away from their time and into our own.

Journey to the Hiding Place

I am going to take you with me on a journey that will lead us out of the theater of the absurd and the festival of hypocrisy we've grown accustomed to in the way the news is dished out to us by the press and television. I will expose these God-playing mind manipulators for what they truly are: false prophets and deceivers or people who are themselves deceived. And, in the process, we will learn some of the shocking things they somehow manage not to tell us.

To be sure, it is an old story. When you look at the newspapers for months and even years prior to World War I, World War II, and the Vietnam War, you can see the signs that we were heading toward those major catastrophes. We needed to make strategic decisions at that time to avoid war or plan for the inevitable. But we didn't. Very little was done in that regard. The media certainly did not address those issues, nor did the national security advisors.

But one thing is certain, whether media people face it or not, the return will take place. All the signs of our time, as you will see in reading this book, are moving quickly toward that fulfillment. So you, as you read this book, will have a decision to make—either to ignore these predictions or to plan your life accordingly.

Yet as "Operation Global Probe" showed, this book is not a journal of gloom and doom. This is a book of hope—a book about the blessed hope of every believer.

Your life will never be the same after reading this book. The return of Jesus to set up His earthly kingdom of peace and righteousness and the prophetic events that will lead up to that great day are more certain than either death or taxes. There will be no place to hide from the things that are coming on the world. No place, that is, except one. To help you find your hiding place by trusting in Christ and His sacrifice on the cross for your sins is the chief purpose of this book.

Like Sheep to the Slaughter

A beloved rabbi once sat in my home and told me about thirty-nine members of his family who had perished in the Holocaust between 1935 and 1945. None of them, he told me, had ever believed such a thing would happen. They persistently ignored the signs that spoke clearly to them of what was coming. "Even when my father and mother, my aunts and uncles, were taken to the ovens of Auschwitz, they still believed that, somehow, they would escape," he told me. Let's not be like them in our day!

My Search

Because of my concern to get people ready for the end of all things, I have sought long and hard to find out what is really going on in our world. I have researched and written a number of books, including: *Marines, Middle East and Magog; Holy War; Jerusalem, D.C.; Israel, America's Key to Survival; Let My People Go;* and others. Let me give you some examples of how I think the media downplay the *significance* of the major events of our time.

The Iranian hostage crisis of 1980 is a case in point. We were getting our brains beaten out day after day, week after week, month after month. But not one news agency in America addressed the issue of why the hostages were released on Inauguration Day in 1981.

Yet, the facts were told to me six months in advance by Isser Harel, former head of Israeli intelligence and security (1947–63).[20] He told me that the Russians would orchestrate the release of the hostages through the assistance of Arab terrorist organizations trained in the Soviet Union. The release would help to swing public opinion away from President Carter. He stated that the Russians would do this because they always liked a new, inexperienced president every four years.

I challenged Harel on that. It struck me as unbelievable that the Russians were capable of arranging things so much to their liking. In fact, the release was delayed until well after the November, 1980, election was past. But when I watched those haggard hostages being released almost precisely at the time of President Reagan's inauguration, I became convinced that what Harel had told me may have had a grain of truth to it.

As a matter of fact, a military official has told me that through our embassy we had been guilty of attempting to manipulate who would succeed the Shah. Although we were making a big issue of human rights violations in Iran, our interference only increased the instability of that country.

But President Carter proceeded with his plans, and the Soviets sat back like the Cheshire cat with a big smile on its face, realizing that our game plan would fall right in line with their strategy, priming the country for revolution and overthrow by Khomeini.

Carter decided the most qualified man to rule Iran was the number two man in authority at that time. The strategy was implemented to encourage the Shah to take an extended vacation.

The Shah was assured that America would help stabilize the country in his absence. What a joke!

Needless to say, this story has never been told, and you may challenge its validity. However, the point I am trying to make is quite obvious—we are *not* being told *all* of the facts.

In a similar vein, I have learned a great deal about the aborted military mission to rescue the hostages from Teheran, code named OPERATION EAGLE CLAW, led by Charlie Beckwith. A dear friend of mine was included in that mission, and I know that it failed for more reasons than one. Some have even suggested that the Soviets learned about the mission and threatened to move in if we did not pull back. Such a possibility never got reported by the press.

Besides that we made so many foolish modifications to those helicopters—including removing the 201-pound air filters—that it is no wonder they crashed. Why in the world was not more emphasis put on these facts when the story was reported?

But there are countless other instances of possible Soviet involvement in the major events of our day.

Was it only a coincidence that Anwar Sadat was successfully assassinated exactly when he was? A top Israeli intelligence officer once told me of how many times the Israelis had managed to prevent Sadat's assassination by the Russians. "But," he added, "one day Sadat will make a tragic mistake." He did make that mistake when he closed down the Soviet embassy in Cairo just four weeks before his own death. Why has no one talked aloud about the truth of who was really responsible for Sadat's death?

Dag Hammarskjold, secretary-general of the United Nations (1953–1961), was a powerful voice for peace and stability in the world. However, he offended the Soviets by many of the things he said and did. Only recently has his mysterious death in a plane crash in 1961 possibly been linked to the KGB.[21]

This is not all. The most famous syndicated columnist in America told me in his office that the bombing of the U.S. embassy in Beirut was hardly a surprise. Twenty-four hours before it happened, information was available about the possibility of a bombing. This columnist told me that he personally knew there were classified documents in existence on this untold story.[22]

The Bible predicts that, in the last days, men's hearts would fail them for fear. I believe a lot of things, like the ones I have been talking about, are being shunted aside out of a desire to prevent panic. But Jesus said that the truth would set us free. Take courage from His promise—face the truth, proceed ahead.

AWACS in the Sky

As I sat in a room with generals and admirals and listened to the White House give what was considered the first major presidential foreign affairs security briefing, I could hardly believe what was being said. The purpose of the briefing, we were told, was to assure us that this decision to sell the AWACS plane to the Saudis would enhance the security of the United States. But what we were hearing was hype, not hope. I kept thinking to myself, *Where's the beef? When are they going to really discuss the issues?* I for one admire greatly and pray for President Reagan. But I thought to myself, *This is ridiculous. When are they going to stop all this hype and start getting to the real reasons?* What would it really do for the security of the United States if we sold our most sophisticated plane to Saudi Arabia?

One, I knew it would cause an escalation of the arms race in the Middle East, which would increase Israel's GNP and tear their country up economically. Defense spending already takes up over 40 percent of Israel's budget.

As I sat there, I calculated the speed of an F15 flying out of Iran at mock 2.2—one thousand sixteen hundred miles per hour. I realized that the speed of an AWACS plane is so slow that within approximately seven minutes of radar interception, that F15 could shoot an AWACS plane out of the sky. No Saudi crew could ground-interface F15s or F16s to protect an AWACS plane in seven minutes. The only true way these AWACS could be protected would be if Saudi planes flew alongside the AWACS. That would be highly unlikely in that the United States would want to protect its own interest and not allow the most sophisticated radar equipment in the world to go down the tubes.

What were the options? They certainly would not include U.S. planes alongside AWACS planes flown by Saudi crews. Giving

Saudi Arabia a ticket to fly anywhere desired with the most sophisticated radar equipment in the Middle East would be a nightmare. Saudi Arabia could very easily provoke an incident with
another hostile Arab country like Libya, not to speak of the fact
that these AWACS planes could end up being in the hands of a
pro-Soviet aligned country, like Libya.

And what about little Israel, the only democracy in the entire
Middle East? Who would make sure that Saudi Arabia, which was
in a state of war against Israel, would not do everything in their
power to detect every Israeli movement and turn that information over to hostile Arab countries, like they had in the past? Israel was doing an incredible job of policing the Middle East and
trying to provide some type of stability. If Israel's security was
jeopardized, America would have to spend more than $40 billion
a year trying to provide the same services in that region.

As I was meditating upon many of the facts, the Holy Spirit
nudged me to get up and ask some questions. They were embarrassing questions that would put the person doing the briefing on
the spot. I figured that once I began questioning, I would never
be invited to another briefing again!

But I got to my feet and asked the questions. I also made assertions as to why the administration was doing this, making it clear
that I did not buy the reasons being handed out at the briefing.
Instead of finding myself cast into outer darkness, I received an
invitation to come to lunch at the White House. I would be part
of a small group of leaders who would be meeting with the president himself.

The story behind the strange events at the security briefing had
begun in my office several months prior to the meeting. I had
been in the habit of meeting with several other men once a week
for prayer. During one of those meetings, I sensed that the Holy
Spirit was telling me that He was going to open a door for me. It
was the door of the White House, and it would open so that I
could speak the truth about the AWACS deal.

I told the other men what I sensed and invited their prayer and
comments. I also told my secretary to keep my calendar as open
as possible to allow for a trip to Washington when the invitation
came. It didn't matter that I knew little or nothing about AWACS

planes, or that I knew of no earthly reason why I might be invited to the White House.

The invitation arrived only five days later. Not long after that on a Tuesday morning, I found myself on a plane going to Virginia to appear on a television program called the "700 Club." I would go from there directly to Washington. Shortly before boarding that plane, I had asked the Lord to show me why America was selling AWACS planes to the Saudis.

Within moments of praying that prayer, some ideas came to me out of the blue: *Israeli jets flew over Saudi air space when they returned from blowing up the nuclear reactor in Iraq in 1981. The U.S. surveillance crew in the area saw this on their radar, but they neglected to inform the Saudis, who were helping to finance the reactor. This embarrassed the Saudis who felt they had been subjected to a great indignity. They protested vigorously to the American government and demanded that some planes be sold to them as a kind of compensation for their loss.*

"Lord," I prayed, "this is all news to me. Please show me if I'm really hearing You or if this is just the fruit of my lively imagination. In fact, I ask You to show me by allowing me to meet the AWACS crew that was flying the plane that detected the violation of Saudi air space."

It was something only God could do. AWACS crews are rotated every thirty days, and neither the Pentagon nor the State Department would ever give you specific information on that. I certainly had no time or authority to call or write anyone, as if it would have accomplished anything. But I did have time to write the request down on a piece of paper inside my Bible while on the plane.

As I was reading my Bible with the slip of paper containing the prayer request quite visible, the passenger next to me noticed it and asked me concerning my interest in AWACS. I told him only that I was headed for a briefing at the White House. I didn't mention my specific prayer request. Imagine, then, my astonishment when he told me that he was an AWACS crewman! When I questioned him further, I discovered that he was the precise answer to my prayer. He had been on duty in 1981 and had detected the Saudi overflight by the Israeli jets!

It turned out that the entire seventeen-man crew of which he was a part was sitting around me in that plane. I questioned him and some of the others about the things I felt God had told me. They confirmed the details. I also learned that only the most unusual circumstances had put these men on a commercial flight. Normally they would have been transported on military aircraft, but an urgent need to perform surveillance on Cuban flights off the Virginia coast had put them on this very flight with me.

Later, in the White House, I asked questions and made statements based on what the Lord had revealed to me and then confirmed through the testimony of those crewmen. Afterward, one admiral actually took me by the lapel and said, "Who in the world are you and where did you get that information? You've got the whole White House tap-dancing on the front floor."

As a matter of fact, I was also accosted by White House staffers who wanted to know the same thing.

When God leads in a matter, there's no hype in it. Just hard truth. The kind of truth that sets men free.

You're Weird

Last night I talked with a gentleman who confessed to me that he drinks too much and that he beats his wife and children. He was going to a counselor, but seemingly wasn't improving. I told him there was an emptiness in his life that only God could fill. As it was, guilt and anxiety were filling his life. These twin problems made him boil over with frustration. That frustration ended in the abuse of his wife and children, and that produced more guilt and anxiety. He was trapped and only God would get him out.

He looked at me as if I were weird. I'm used to it. I get that look a lot. Some people actually tell me that to my face, like one man I met in the asphalt jungle of New York. His disgustingly putrid breath told me he was a wino. He looked as though he had been living in trash cans for a year—more like a cockroach than a human being. But, as he leaned over to say, "You're weird," in my ear, he was, in a way, right, because I was kneeling on the sidewalk in plain sight at midday in New York City.

I had just come out of a big convention in the American Hotel. I had been inside praying with and counseling people in the plush circumstances the hotel afforded, but I had sensed the Spirit of God telling me, *Leave this place.*

I obeyed and found myself out walking on the sidewalk. Then I sensed the command, *Kneel.* I didn't want to do it. It would be so embarrassing. I got down on one knee as if I were about to tie a loose shoelace, but that wouldn't do. At last I knelt on both knees and put my hands in the air. Tears began to stream down my cheeks. Why was I crying? I was feeling the pain of the fact that millions of people, in that city and elsewhere, were blind to the truth. People without joy, peace, or hope. People sedated by alcohol and drugs. People bound in chains of immorality. People being swept out into a sea of pain and agony.

That was when the little cockroach of a man walked up to me and told me I was "weird." I smiled to myself because I could only agree with him. But I would never have seen and felt the pain of humanity as I did that day if I had not allowed myself to look weird. It was an experience that changed my life. For one thing, it prepared me to meet some people who were hurting in special ways.

Caught in a Trap

When I met her she lived in the same prestigious apartment house as Jacqueline Kennedy. Her husband was a world-renowned physician, a gynecologist. What more could a person ask for? Her position and lifestyle were something half the women in America dream of. But, when we met, she was weeping. Life had taken a nasty turn for her. The wonderful man she had married had turned out to be a monster. Filled with unresolved rage against his own mother, the doctor fulfilled his fantasies of punishing her and all women. As a surgeon, he did this by cutting into the bodies of his patients. He had not performed surgery on his wife, but he made her suffer for her womanhood in a hundred ways.

On the other side of the same coin were two lovely ladies from Houston who attended a crusade I was holding in that city. By looking at them, you would never believe in a million years that both had murdered their own husbands. I had been speaking to a large audience when I felt directed to ask for those who were experiencing tremendous bitterness and pain to come forward for prayer. Both of these women responded to that invitation.

I could hardly believe my ears when the first one told of her husband's bizarre behavior as a result of his practice of witch-craft. After she had shot him to death, she had cut his body into dozens of pieces, packed it into the back of their truck, and hauled it off to another state for disposal.

A little later I listened to the second tell me how she had mat-ter-of-factly emptied all the bullets from one pistol and half from another into her husband. To my shocked amazement, this very sick man, who served in a profession to assist and help women, had obviously lost his mind. He had subjected her to cruel sado-masochistic torture, using a closet full of paraphernalia.

Juries had acquitted both of these women, but they had not set them free from the anger and guilt that plagued their lives. Only Jesus could do that for the two who had killed their husbands, as well as for the one who would have liked to but had not. I'm glad to report that He has, in each of the cases I have just mentioned. It was for them and the millions like them that I was willing to do something weird like kneeling and praying on a sidewalk in New York. The tears I shed were in response to their pain.

Where's the Beef?

Our stay in life is short. As one person put it, "None of us is going to get out of this alive." I don't share that belief, but it makes the point. Each of us will experience the end of the world. It may come tomorrow, next week, next year, or in ten, twenty, or fifty years. But, if you are reading this book right now, you may indeed experience the end of the world before you finish this book. I am sure many will.

Your life on earth as you know it will end the moment you die, but not your life in the world to come.

The first time I had the privilege of sitting and talking with a man I have come to love very much, Menachem Begin, we spent over half an hour discussing eternity. He was thinking about his own problems with his heart. He told me about some of the won-derful advances in treating heart disease that had been accom-plished by Israeli researchers. Not long before our interview he had suffered a spell of faintness on the floor of the Knesset, Israel's parliament.

There was a Saudi prince who has spent over $20 million equipping his private jet with a complete life support system in case the dark cloud of death moves in his direction. It is nice to have enough money to do something like that. It creates a wonderful illusion that one can forestall the inevitable.

A lot of us endeavor to sedate ourselves by living in a world of lies and fantasy. It seems more pleasant than reality. It is pure hype, however, and I would rather have hope than hype. Life is fleeting, no matter how rich, famous, important, or good-looking we are. We need something more substantial to rely on than this fragile container known as our body.

The Signs of the Times

We are speeding toward Armageddon. But the God who created us is reaching out to us in love. His hands offer us hope, sanity, and peace, in this crazy world.

When some of the religious leaders in Galilee wanted to trap Jesus, they suggested that He perform a miracle to show that God approved of Him. "He answered and said to them, 'When it is evening you say, "It will be fair weather, for the sky is red"; and in the morning, "It will be foul weather today, for the sky is red and threatening." Hypocrites! You know how to discern the face of the sky, but you cannot discern the signs of the times' "(Matt. 16:2–3).

I'm going to take some headlines gleaned from the *New York Times* and interpret them on the basis of Bible prophecy. This will help us to see how to interpret the signs of the times in which we are living. It takes us to the truth the newscasters so consistently overlook as they downplay the significance of what is behind the news.

GULF TENSIONS RISE AS IRAN REJECTS U.N. CRITICISM

At this writing the bloody war between Iraq and Iran has been going on for several years. It is a grotesque war in which Iranian children are tied together in lines and marched across mine fields to clear them prior to infantry assaults.

IRAN IS IN THE GRIP OF MOSLEM FANATICS CALLED SHI'ITES

For the Shi'ites this is a *jihad*—a holy war. So, this ancient land of the Chaldeans, the birthplace of magic, sorcery, and the worship of demons, carries on as always. Its purpose is to destroy Israel and, ultimately, all who will not bow the knee to Allah.

The net result of this war is to bleed Iran to the point where it will be too feeble to resist when Russia moves south into Iran on its way to a long-awaited appointment in northern Israel at an event called Armageddon. The ancient prophecies of the Bible tell us this will be one of the events that marks the beginning of the end.

You would think that these things would have been unimaginable to anyone back in the nineteenth century when the Ottoman Empire was the Middle East and Israel was only a lingering memory among Bible readers. Russia, of course, even back then, eyed the region hungrily, but the czars were too inept to pose any serious threat. Amazingly, however, students of the Bible in the nineteenth century read Ezekiel's prophecies and concluded that someday Russia would come out of the north and attack a restored Israel.

Now that someday is now almost upon us. Russia dominates one-third of the Middle East and half of Africa, and these dramatic changes have taken place in less than forty years. Therefore, I believe we should expect the return of Jesus Christ in this generation.

CASES OF AIDS REPORTED ON RISE

A few years ago *Time* magazine surveyed the national epidemic of genital herpes. The article spoke almost lightheartedly about how it had come down like a divine curse on the sexual profligacy of the now generation, the sexually liberated boys and girls of the sixties and seventies. People, they reported, had actually become so fearful of contracting the nasty little virus that they had begun, in some cases, to abstain from sexual immorality.

Then came AIDS (Acquired Immune Deficiency Syndrome) and the lightheartedness went out of the public attitude toward venereal disease.

We are living in such a sick society today that it is almost unbelievable. We know, statistically, that 20 percent of all murders are family-related and one-third of female homicides are committed by the husbands or the partners. We know that reported cases of child abuse doubled from 1976 to 1981 and had gone up almost 400 percent by 1984.

Violence is so great that this year alone, we have had approximately thirty-five million victims of crime. As amazing as it might seem, only 464,000 people are in prison. I was told these amazing facts by Dr. Lois Herrington, Assistant U.S. Attorney General.

The Bible has long predicted that the last days would be marked by a casting aside of the restraints that have held human evil somewhat in check.

> For men will be lovers of themselves, lovers of money, boasters, proud, blasphemers, disobedient to parents, unthankful, unholy, unloving, unforgiving, slanderers, without self-control, brutal, despisers of good, traitors, headstrong, haughty, lovers of pleasure rather than lovers of God, having a form of godliness but denying its power (2 Tim. 3:2–5).

We get just a taste of this in newscasters who get choked up about the slaughter of whales and seals, but who remain unmoved by the murders of eighteen million Americans between 1972 and 1984 through abortion.

Today we can watch the idols of teendom—the singers, the comedians, the dancers, the punkers—portray almost precisely the lifestyle envisioned in the passage I just quoted from the Bible. They do it daily on television and radio. In fact, now, if you have cable television, you can watch endless video-music presentations that model recklessness, treachery, violence, lust—the list could go on disgustingly.

Boy George, as he is known to fans, loves to outrage the world by dressing in women's clothes and wearing make-up. He adorns the walls of his apartment with a myriad of bizarre items, including his large collection of crucifixes. He is the biggest thing to come out of Britain, entertainment-wise, since the Beatles.

Across the Atlantic is Prince, second only to Michael Jackson in popularity among teens. Prince was awarded an Oscar in 1985 for *Purple Rain.* When he went on stage to collect his trophy, he was clad in a long purple gown that descended from the top of his head to his ankles. Two punker girls accompanied him, rather in the manner of bodyguards. His espousal of homosexual styles and attitudes is notorious.

SEVERE DROUGHT HITS SOUTHWEST

Africa and other underdeveloped places, mostly in the Third World, have long been the province of famines. Are such things coming closer to home? I sat with a businessman who had made a fortune in the past growing oranges and grapefruits in Florida. He told me about the ruination of Florida citrus crops and the widespread problem of bankruptcies among the small farmers that could point to changes in our system of food production that will unexpectedly affect food supplies to American tables in years to come.

Famine and starvation are becoming a way of life on almost every continent. In southern Mexico the average family lives on a meager five dollars a week, virtually starving to death, while only a few hours away by plane, in Dallas, Texas, the average middle-class family thinks nothing of spending ten times that amount at a single sitting in a fine restaurant.

In the coming pages I am going to look much more closely at these sorts of things. In picking these three headlines, I have tried to show what I mean about interpreting the signs of the times." It also shows that there is nothing particularly fanciful about the story of "Operation Global Probe" and Paul Bradford.

Am I Bothering You?

There's a proverb that says, "All a man's ways seem innocent to him, but motives are weighed by the LORD" (Prov. 16:2 NIV). Most of us tend to divide people into two categories that, whatever we may call them, boil down to the good and the bad. But the Bible teaches something very revolutionary. It says *all* have sinned and no one is righteous.

Once, when I was on a flight to Los Angeles, I found myself in the company of the majority of the Dallas Cowboys football team. They were on their way to their training camp in Southern California. Before too long I found myself telling the group about Jesus and His love. I explained that I had once been quite athletic, having been a black belt karate instructor in Korea. Now I realized that even attaining great athletic goals could not bring peace to the human heart.

As I was anxiously talking about the wages of sin and God's free gift of forgiveness and eternal life, and how I had knelt to receive that gift by asking Jesus to come into my heart, the stewardess walked up. She placed herself squarely between me and the men I was talking to, with her back to me. "Is he bothering you?" she asked the men.

I chuckled to myself to think how much I must surely be bothering at least some of them. But all of them were gracious and assured the stewardess that I was not being a bother. In fact, what I was telling them was either the greatest hoax ever perpetrated or the key to life.

Fasten your seatbelt because we are going to move swiftly to examine the startling array of documented facts that are fulfilling biblical prophecy right and left.

III

The Beginning of Sorrows

"If changes are not made now, by the year 2000, there is doubt as to whether we will survive. By that time, there will be seven billion people in the world, and five billion of them will be starving, uneducated, and totally desperate."

—Dr. Albert Sabin

It is 2:00 A.M. and before my eyes I see the valley of the shadow of death. The roar of diesel engines, huge cranes, and generators is deafening. Right in front of me there had been buildings, some of them ten stories and some higher—now they are all flattened. The city is roped off with ambulances going off in all directions. Buses are filled with volunteers and vehicles with white sheets hanging out the windows with red crosses on them.

Soldiers everywhere. Police everywhere. There is no water, and because of the lack of electricity, it is dark in most of the buildings that are still standing.

People by the thousands are volunteering, taking the buildings apart, stone by stone, as the heavy cranes lift large pieces of concrete, and the people carry the smaller stones.

I am talking through a mask. Everyone in the city has his mouth covered with a medical mask or cotton soaked with alcohol strapped around his face. The stench of the dead bodies is unbelievable. It is difficult not to gag even with the mask because of the smell.

In the midst of all the dead, underneath these buildings are human beings that are trapped alive, men, women, and babies. One man was pulled out earlier in the morning. He was scraped and dehydrated but alive. He had spent sixty-five hours standing in a pool of water above his knees.

But the worst is yet to come because in San Lorenzo there is a ditch ninety feet long and nine feet wide. In this hole they are unloading plastic bags, bags filled with bodies or pieces of bodies that cannot be identified. These common graves can hold up to fifteen hundred bodies. No tears are being shed at these collective graves of those who are buried without identification. There are no flowers—just the silence of the dead.

No, what I have described is not fiction. It is the earthquakes in Mexico. There were thirty-eight tremors and shocks, and I was there in the midst of many of them. Matthew 24 predicts an acceleration of earthquakes before the return of Jesus. As we have already stated, there have been over one million measurable shocks in the last twelve months. As an example, look at the information from the National Earthquake Information Center.

Like enormous billboards beside the freeway, the dramatic prophecies of the Bible, found in the book of Revelation, in Matthew 24, in Ezekiel, Daniel, and Jeremiah, cry out to us declaring that the days in which we live are the beginning of the end. Millions of our fellow human beings are dying each year from the ravages of famines, earthquakes, floods, droughts, plagues, pestilences, pollution, torture, and drug addiction. Bhopal, India, where the leakage of poisonous gas from the local Union Carbide plant killed thousands of people and injured many thousands more, has become a grotesque symbol of the way we are destroying ourselves and are being destroyed. The gaunt faces of starving men, women, and children from Ethiopia and the Sudan stare out at us in hopeless despair from our television sets every night. Their starving never dwindles.

It definitely is not a coincidence that many of the prophecies of Matthew 24 describing the times we live in has become daily copy for the morning news. And, of course, there is plenty of copy for the weatherman, from hurricanes to typhoons as summer dwindles into autumn.

Listen to what Dr. Carl A. Von Hake, geophysicist at the National Geophysicist Data Center in Colorado had to say in my recent interview with him: "We estimate that there are as many as one million earthquakes a year around the world. Some of the largest earthquakes are many times greater than any bomb that has been set off. So, nature still seems able to create much larger energy releases than mankind."[1]

Hurricane Olivia claimed over 1,300 lives in Central America in 1982. In 1984, the fiercest typhoon in fifteen years hit the Philippines and killed about the same number of people. During just two days in April 1974, 148 tornadoes descended on thirteen states in the South and the Midwest. The injured numbered over 6,000; 329 were dead. Property damage stood at $540 million.

One million people died in 1939 when floods hit northern China. Not as many drowned during the flood as starved to death afterwards because of the destruction of crops. In Tulsa, Oklahoma, more than a dozen motorists were swept to their deaths by floodwaters on May 27, 1984.

A quarter of a million people died on July 28, 1976, when the strongest earthquake recorded since 1964 hit Tientsin-Tangshan, China. On November 23, 1980, a quake flattened 133 villages and left 300,000 people homeless in southern Italy. Funerals were conducted for 2,735 of the quake's victims.

How often do we keep national vigils, courtesy of television, at the openings of mines where fires have broken out or explosions have occurred? Or what of that horrifying night in Cubatao, Brazil, in 1984? There the poorest built their tiny shanties on poles over the water of a swamp. Late on the night of February 25, a nearby pipeline began to leak gasoline into the water of that swamp. Then came the explosion and the fire and the screams of more than five hundred people dying at once. That so many more survived was considered a miracle.

In 1975 a civil war broke out in the Portuguese colony on the island of Timor. The western half of the island already belonged to Indonesia, and the Indonesian government seized the opportunity to expand its territory and push the Portuguese still further out of the South Pacific. Indonesian troops entered the fighting on the side of the rebels. The former colony was formally incorporated as a province of Indonesia on July 18, 1976.

However, guerrilla fighting against Indonesian troops in east Timor continued into the 1980s.

More recently, some of the grisly truth about this seemingly inconsequential story of a faraway place came to light. In 1984 Amnesty International revealed that more than 150,000 people died in east Timor in 1975 during the Indonesian takeover. The two leading causes of death were violence and famine. The use of torture, said the report, had been particularly cruel and vicious.

In 1979 the Environmental Protection Agency banned most uses of the herbicides known as 2, 4, 5-T because they contained a highly dangerous substance, dioxin. High rates of leukemia and other gruesome disorders among the children in a little town in New York called Love Canal had helped them find out just how dangerous dioxin was. But it was too late for Times Beach, Missouri.

Then came the horror of what almost happened at Three Mile Island. If that were not enough, CBS exposed the fact that the incredible accumulation of cost overruns at the Shoreham nuclear plant in New York were directly attributable to Mafia control of the labor unions doing the actual work of construction.

Back in the 1970s, Jacques Cousteau, the famous French explorer who has done so many television specials for The National Geographic Society, began to report an equally troubling phenomenon. Everywhere he sailed in the *Calypso,* all the seven seas, he had found that the water was flecked with little bits of oil from all the spills that have occurred around the world.

Yet the Bible describes the trouble of the last days as only the "beginning of sorrows"!

The Bowls of God's Anger

In the sixteenth chapter of the book of Revelation, the last book of the Bible, we read of the seven angels who were sent to pour out the bowls of God's anger on the earth. What is described in that chapter sounds like the evening newscast or the morning paper. In fact, to read the words of this ancient oracle in these waning years of the twentieth century gives one an eerie feeling.

The first bowl was poured on the earth and produced terrible and painful sores. The second bowl was poured into the sea. The sea turned to blood and everything in it died. The third angel poured out his bowl on the rivers and springs of water, and they turned to blood. More death. The sun was the recipient of the fourth bowl, which caused it to burn fiercely and scorch the earth's inhabitants. Their response was to curse God. The fifth bowl brought such darkness that people bit their tongues because of their pain. The sixth bowl dried up the Euphrates River in order to prepare for the passage of numberless divisions of the "Kings from the east," perhaps the Chinese and other Asiatic soldiers on their march to Armageddon (about which I'll have more to say later). After that, it says:

> Then the seventh angel poured out his bowl in the air. A loud voice came from the throne in the temple, saying, "It is done!" There were flashes of lightning, rumblings and peals of thunder, and a terrible earthquake. There has never been such an earthquake since the creation of man; this was the worst earthquake of all! The great city was split into three parts, and the cities of all countries were destroyed. God remembered great Babylon and made her drink the wine from his cup—the wine of his furious anger. All the islands disappeared, all the mountains vanished. Huge hailstones, each weighing as much as a hundred pounds, fell from the sky on people, who cursed God on account of the plague of hail, because it was such a terrible plague (Rev. 16:17–21 TEV).

Earthquakes and Famines

Jesus predicted earthquakes and famines as part of the signs that His return would be near.

When Chaucer was writing *The Canterbury Tales,* in the fourteenth century the Europeans recorded reports of 137 earthquakes. In this century, seismologists sometimes record that many in a month. More than a million people have died as a result of earthquakes in this century. The damages have been estimated at 10 billion dollars.[2] The advent of the Richter Scale and scientific monitoring devices, together with a global communications system, have increased our awareness that this planet of ours is not the firm object Chaucer and his contemporaries thought it was.

The predictions of Jesus are true. In addressing the subject of earthquakes, geophysicist Von Hake said, "We estimate that there are as many as a million earthquakes a year around the world. Of course, there is a plus or minus factor in there. But that represents all size quakes from the very largest ones down to the real small ones. People have died from earthquakes. One earthquake in the past caused the death of 830,000 people in China. Another one in China killed 243,000 people.

"And earthquakes are expensive. In 1971 in Southern California, an earthquake took place that caused a half billion dollars' worth of damage. Earthquakes are definitely here to stay."

In a two-month period between mid-April and mid-June in 1984, the *New York Times* reported a dozen notable earthquakes from around the world. They occurred in Austria, Wales, New Jersey, California (three), Italy (three), Colorado, the Chinese seaboard, and the southwestern Indian Ocean. One in California hit late in April and registered 6.0 on the Richter Scale. It severely damaged the city of San José where a fire broke out from a broken fuel line. It was the strongest quake on the Calaveras fault since 1911. The one in China was even stronger, at 6.2. Another of the California three struck near the Diablo Canyon Nuclear Plant. Thousands of people were left homeless in Italy. That was almost exactly a year after the memorable earthquake that had struck Coalinga, California, in May 1983. More than ten thousand aftershocks were recorded during the twelve months that succeeded that shaker.

Scientists have devoted a lot of study to the large-scale physical makeup of our planet in order to learn more about the cause and nature of earthquakes. As a result, we know that the earth's crust is criss-crossed by a complex network of fractures, or faults. Geophysicists theorize that these faults mark the edges of six or seven large, rigid plates which, together with a dozen or so smaller plates, comprise the earth's crust. They further speculate that these plates are moving. On the basis of this theory, an earthquake occurs when two adjacent plates, each moving in the opposite direction, make a sudden slip in their respective directions. (This is what is happening in California along the San Andreas fault, which is part of the reason for the speculation that much of the state may separate from the continent eventually.) The amount of pressure that builds up along a fault line prior to such a slip determines the force of the consequent earthquake.

Sometimes this theory, known as the plate tectonics theory, is spoken of as if it were a fact, especially when some seismologist from Cal Tech is interviewed by a reporter for the evening newscast following a significant quake. But beyond the existence of fault lines and the evidence that earthquakes, as a rule, happen along fault lines, there is little in the way of hard facts to go on. According to the theory, the earth's crust sits atop a plastic or molten substratum. This is the source of volcanic activity which is also associated with fault lines. The continents, as we know them, are—again, according to the theory—drifting slowly about on this molten sea beneath us. That great sea is moving in convection currents which occur as a result of heating and cooling processes with the sea.

This matter of convection currents is hotly disputed among scientists. Never proven or demonstrated in any conclusive manner, the evidence for it is partial at best. As often happens with scientific investigations, the more we learn, the less we feel we know.

Students of the Bible can argue on the basis of the same facts that all these faults and unstable conditions are a remnant of the Genesis flood. In recounting that flood, the ancient biblical writers mention a phenomenon no one has ever understood. They report that "all the fountains of the great deep were broken up" (Gen. 7:11). What that meant or entailed is never explained in the pages of Scripture. One recent translation sought to make it a little clearer by rendering it, "all the outlets of the vast body of water beneath the earth burst open" (TEV).

The biblical writers made their point clearly. The sin of man had provoked the flood that was a cosmic cataclysm that changed the course of human history for all time—a return to the chaos out of which the world had been set in order by God's mighty power in the first place. Mankind's behavior affects the whole created order. When mankind goes wrong, the world is thrown out of joint.

Scientist after scientist has told me that the pollutants and acid rain will bring about the destruction of our plants. The biological balance has been tipped.

Scientists are saying that across Europe you will soon find that 85 percent of their forests are dead because of acid rain. If you look at the eastern United States and Canada, you will find the same thing. We will see similar effects on our plants within ten to fifteen years. And there are also pollutants that are destroying the layer of atmosphere that protects us from the sun, the ozone layer. It stops the ultra-violet rays from penetrating down and reaching us. This shield is being destroyed, letting in an increase of ultra-violet rays, changing the biological balance.

According to one scientist, carbon dioxide is causing a greenhouse effect. Sunlight cannot penetrate through but ultra-violet can penetrate. This causes the earth to get hotter and hotter instead of cooling off each night. What we are seeing is a steady global increase in temperature. Because of the burning of so much fossil fuel, we are beginning a trend which will increase the temperature of the earth. As the summers get hotter, the amount of ice melting increases the levels of the oceans and lakes. If we melt our arctic and antarctic ice caps, we are going to see the water levels rise all over planet Earth. You might see Houston under water.

It is not an accident that we are seeing an increase in the deserts on every continent on the earth. We have so modified the weather patterns of the world that you cannot predict the weather for the future based on previous years. We are flying blind.

These definitely are indications that some of the occurrences of the world may be irreversible. We have polluted the oceans to the point where we may never be able to restore them, and the oceans are our major source of food.[3]

Dr. John Firor, director of Advanced Studies with NCAR Laboratories, made this incredible statement to me in a recent interview: "The forests are now being cleared at a high rate, 1–2 percent per year. If it continues at this rate, there will only be twenty more years, thirty, or at the very maximum, forty more years with forests. After that time, there will be no more forests in the world."

"As the Days of Noah Were"

Jesus said the time just before the return would be like the days just before the Flood: "People ate and drank, men and women married, *up to the very day Noah went into the boat;* yet they did not realize what was happening until the flood came and swept them all away" (Matt. 24:38, 39 TEV; my italics). What Jesus did not mention about Noah's time, because it was so well known to his listeners that he did not need to mention it, was that the time was marked by widespread wickedness of unbearable proportions.

There is a persuasion, which has never entirely disappeared in the whole history of the human race, that sex can be a kind of religious experience which elevates one above the plane of mere mortality. The contemporary glorification of sexual pleasures, often in association with bizarre and cultic religious practices, is spreading precisely this lie with fresh vigor. In truth, we are only mortal, every one of us, and no matter how much glory attends our human pathway, it will end at the grave. That was the great lesson of the Genesis flood, and it will be reaffirmed soon by the return.

Jesus had all this in mind when He described the placid state of mankind prior to the Flood—life as usual: eating, drinking, and marrying with no sense of shame or alarm about the destruction of every moral standard that one could imagine. Unmarried men and women were living together, homosexuals brazenly displayed their lust in public, children and animals became common objects of sexual gratification. Violence was a part of everyday life. Babies, of course, weren't aborted. Pregnant women waited until babies were born to kill them if they were unwanted. Parents and children lived in worlds far separated from each other and with no communication between them. But it was unfashionable to raise objections to any of these things. People hooted anyone down who tried to do it. They certainly scoffed at Noah and called him an old fool. "After all, people should be allowed to do as they please, as long as it doesn't harm anyone else," they said.

In June 1983, the *New York Times* reported that a Census Bureau study showed that the proportion of American women who have a child before marriage or who are pregnant at the time of marriage has doubled, to 10.7 percent, since World War II. The study cited the lessening of social stigma normally associated with illegitimate pregnancies.

It was not long after the great eruption of Mount St. Helens in Washington that I was aboard an airliner that flew over the area. The pilot called our attention to the still-smoldering sight far below. As I looked down I couldn't help but reflect on the stubborn little man whose name is now indelibly linked with that mountain and its violent explosion on May 18, 1980. That man was Harry Truman, the caretaker of a recreation lodge on Spirit Lake, five miles north of the volcano. All that spring Harry had refused to listen to the warnings that had urged the evacuation of everyone for many miles in every direction from the smoking mount. Harry had smugly asserted that the mountain wouldn't dare blow up on him.

The eruption occurred at 8:31 that morning. What did Harry think in the brief instant of life that remained for him after that? Did he even have an instant? Harry is a symbol of our whole society. He waved his fist in the face of all those who warned him and said, "I'll be here until hell freezes over."[4] The rumblings of dreadful things to come are loud and clear, but we smugly refuse to heed their warning.

Sunshine

The time of reckoning is coming suddenly and unexpectedly. All around us we see evidence of this. For years the Florida citrus growers have made a handsome living off Florida's perpetually temperate climate. According to the *Annual Summary of Climatological Data,* the growing season lasts fifty-two weeks in most areas around Orlando. The shortest growing season, around Tallahassee, is thirty-eight weeks. But in recent years, Florida has been hit and devastated by unimaginable climatic changes as frigid storms have plummeted down from the Arctic Circle without respite. Charles Crisafulli, a wealthy citrus grower, gave me an engrossing afternoon one day as we discussed what was happening in Florida and how it might relate to biblical prophecy.

I remember well the day in Dallas, Texas, when I walked from my living room into the kitchen and thought I heard the sound of a freight train bearing down on our house. I was bewildered because no railroad tracks have been laid anywhere near our home. In a matter of seconds the sun disappeared behind black and menacing clouds. Hurricane-force winds beat against us and, in less than fifteen minutes, the temperature descended an incredible forty-five degrees (Fahrenheit). The Bible talks of the time when mankind will be confronted suddenly and dramatically with the reality of the Son of God and his prophetic return to the planet. Our changes in climate may portend the beginnings of the sorrows of the last days.

Mother Teresa

She was not a stranger to me. I had seen her face a hundred times, and as I walked around the corner of the counter at the Rome airport where I had to layover, I sat down next to her. She was Mother Teresa of Calcutta, a legend in her time. She had first gone to India after joining a Catholic religious order in Romania in 1928 at the age of eighteen. In 1948 she was granted permission to leave her convent in Calcutta and work among the city's poor people. She applied for and was granted Indian citizenship that same year. In 1979 she was awarded the Nobel Peace Prize for her work with the poor.

Her work had begun by caring for the indigents who lay dying on the streets of Calcutta every day. She picked these people up and took them to her hospice to die in peace. As others joined her in this work, she formed the Missionaries of Charity. They provide food for the needy and operate hospitals, schools, orphanages, youth centers, and hospices for lepers and the dying poor in fifty Indian cities and in about thirty other countries.

I took the seat next to her and quietly introduced myself. My heart broke as I listened to her tell me of the agonies caused by starvation and debilitating diseases in the people she had ministered to. Her dark and shining eyes are strong in my memory. I expect they always will be.

In a short while both our planes were ready for boarding. "Where are you going?" she asked me.

"To Jerusalem," I replied, "And you?"

"I am on my way to your country, Mr. Evans. Before we part, I will ask you to pray for the suffering poor people of the world."

"I do pray for them," I said, "and now that I've listened to you, I will pray for them even more."

"I will pray for the peace of Jerusalem, Mr. Evans."

"Thank you. Before we leave, why don't we pray for those things?"

"Yes," she said, "let's do it!"

After my meeting with her I recalled something I had once read. It said that neither war nor peace, nor world affairs, nor national affairs are of primary concern to most people today. The urgent questions in the minds of most people are, Where can I get food and How can I pay for it? A disaster more costly than all of World War II threatens us today—the disaster of severe food shortages in lesser-developed countries.

It may be difficult to realize that a hungry world stands just outside our doors, especially when 60 percent of us who are Americans or Europeans are overweight. Estimates have put American overweight at a billion pounds. Americans spend $15 billion a year on diet products in addition to the $22 billion we spend on cosmetics.[5] Less money than that would probably be required to relieve most of the world's hunger—certainly to prevent the deaths of countless millions of people.

The fact is that hunger is probably the greatest scandal of this century. Insofar as agriculture is concerned, the question of famine should be solved. America, Australia, and Canada have demonstrated a capacity to produce vastly greater amounts of grain than can be consumed within their borders. Hunger is not a matter of how much food exists, but rather a matter of how that food is distributed. Otherwise the U.S. Department of Agriculture would not be able to report that forty million Americans—more than one in every six of us—suffer from inadequate nutrition.

Most people who are in the business of growing food are motivated by the desire to make money and avoid going broke. They are not in business to feed the hungry. Most people are hungry because they cannot afford to buy the food they need, nor can they acquire it otherwise.

For example, take a typical scenario in South America. There a few people own most of the arable (capable of being cultivated) land. What do they grow on their land? Rice and beans, which, used together, provide a complete protein for normal human survival? No, they grow coffee, or bananas, or beef to export to the United States for cash. The poor people of many Latin American countries often have to buy pinto beans grown in Idaho to mix with rice grown in Louisiana in order to stay alive.

Some of the richest agricultural land in the world is in a region of Africa called the Sahel. It is the strip of land at the southern edge of the Sahara Desert and includes parts of Chad, Mali, Mauritania, Niger, Senegal, the Sudan, and Upper Volta. In the 1970s the Sahel was struck by a famine in which a million people died. But throughout the time of that famine, planes flew out of the Sahel loaded down with fresh fruits and vegetables for the winter market in northern Europe. The wealthy land owners in the Sahel, many of them Europeans, did not suffer from the effects of the famine. Instead their bank accounts were filled with German marks, Dutch kroners, Swiss francs, and Swedish kronas.

It is alarming to consider that probably half the world's population has to struggle to acquire a mere 5 percent of the world's income, while 15 percent of the population is raking in fully two-thirds of that income. In 1983 the 400 richest Americans had a combined wealth (that they would admit to) of $118 billion. Gordon Peter Getty, at the top of the pack, had an estimated net worth of over $2.2 billion. At the bottom of the pack the figure was $125 million. In the middle of the pack was one retailer who saw his holdings increase by the amount of one billion dollars in one year. That was equal to the average yearly income of 78,000 Americans, or nearly half a million Brazilians, 3.85 million Indians, or 9 million Chadians. But, of course, there are only about 4.5 million Chadians in existence.[6]

So, what are the main agricultural products of Africa? Food for the hungry? No. Delicacies for the rich, like cacao, coffee, tobacco, cloves, pineapples, citrus fruits, coconuts, cane sugar, grapes, and olives. All these provide cash for the wealthy few of the countries that produce them and that own most of the good land. The small farmers who want, at least, to grow enough to feed themselves and their families, have to subsist on marginal land that is available to them because the rich land owners have no use for it. The scandalous truth about famine in the twentieth century is that it can be attributed almost entirely to the greed of man, not to drought, overpopulation, poor planning, or anything else. No wonder an anti-God philosophy like Communism can grip the minds and souls of over one billion people almost overnight.

There is absolutely no question about it: The political decisions of life are based upon greed, primarily economic greed. One only has to study the history of wars, and you will realize that when a change in leadership is made during a period of great economic hardship, the way is generally primed for war.

Many economic experts have told me that America is heading for an economic collapse. When it comes, the government will be expected to end the depression. However, the government will not be able to end it. America will then be a breeding ground for terrorist-type groups to make demands or even to overthrow the government.

Those who analyze and study the problems we are experiencing worldwide are convinced that the primer for terrorism, at any given point, is hunger. If that is the case, we have big problems. The experts say that as many as 30 million children may be dying annually worldwide at infancy or the early stages of life from causes associated with malnourishment.

The Population Bomb?

We hear loud lamentations about the population explosion. What do they mean? They generally mean that the rich are alarmed that the expansion of the numbers of poor and racially different people will face an alteration in the distribution of wealth from that which prevails now. I can say that because vastly great numbers of people than are alive now could be supported at respectable nutritional levels if the world's available land were used to produce food crops instead of cash crops. Since it seems unlikely that the present system will change short of a cataclysmic revolution, we had better look at the sorts of pressures that are building up in terms of population growth.

India's population will achieve a billion before this century has finished its course. The population of the world will reach 7 billion by that time. It will have doubled to 14 billion by 2050.[7] Of course, the growing populations are those of the Third World—Africans, Latinos, and Indians and other Asians. Partly on the basis of prodigious Hispanic birth rates and partly because of enormous patterns of immigration, it is expected that the population of Los Angeles County may contain an Hispanic majority within the next twenty years.

Why do the poor have so many children? By our Western standards it seems hard to understand, but it's not. For a poor man in the Philippines, for example, there is no Social Security Administration, nor does he have an IRA or a retirement plan at the company where he works. Instead he may be trying to subsist on a little plot of land at the edge of the big banana plantation that employs him periodically. The bananas are for the Japanese market. He cannot live on bananas. He tries to grow food for his family, but the ground is poor. His only chance to avoid starvation when he and his wife become too old or feeble to work is to have several children. They may be able to support their parents in their "golden years" and are thus the best chance for survival in old age.

This being the case, do we have any reasonable expectation that the populations of the Third World will continue to do anything except grow exponentially? Can we expect that these people will not be almost entirely susceptible to Communist agitators?

The population growth goes on in spite of famine and the fact that the life expectancy of most Indians and black Africans is below fifty years. In Ethiopia the life expectancy of a male is thirty-eight. Ethiopian women can expect to live to be forty-one. More than four thousand miles west of Ethiopia, in Gambia—whence came *Roots* author Alex Haley's forbear, Kunta Kinte—the figures are thirty-nine and forty-three.

The population spirals ever upward in spite of the fact that twelve million newborn infants die of malnutrition every year.[8] Of those who survive only a minority receive adequate nutrition. This is especially significant because the brain of a human being achieves 80 percent of its cellular growth during the first three years of life. Any child deprived of hearty doses of protein and a full range of vitamins during pregnancy and those first critical years will suffer some measure of brain deficiency. Eighty percent of the children in India suffer malnutritional dwarfism.

The problem only promises to get worse. Almost half of the great tropical forests that once girded the earth in the vicinity of the equator are now lost. What remains is disappearing at the rate of a hundred acres a minute. What are growing instead are the deserts. All over the world men are creating them by improper farming methods. The Sahara, the Gobi, and the Mojave are all growing steadily.

No wonder that Dr. Albert Sabin, the developer of the oral vaccine against polio, has said, "If changes are not made now, by the year 2000 there is doubt as to whether we will survive. By that time there will be seven billion people in the world, and five billion of them will be starving, uneducated, and totally desperate."[9]

"Super Fly"

Before I conclude this chapter, I need to survey briefly two more problems that are but the beginning of sorrows. The first has to do with the bacteria and the insects that are developing resistance to antibiotics and insecticides respectively. There are now strains of typhus in Mexico against which all known antibiotics are ineffective. Medical specialists foresee the day when a large number of bacterial diseases may no longer be susceptible to treatment by any antibiotic. In fact, the relative freedom we have enjoyed from bacterial infections—among them strep, staph, and various sorts of pneumonia—will probably be a thing of the past, some time in the not-too-distant future.

In the meantime, there are those 364 insecticide-resistant insects in the world. They are devouring crops and bringing discomfort, disease, and sometimes death to millions of people. Plagues of grasshoppers have denuded millions of acres in fourteen states west of the Missouri River. In Maine, billions of tent caterpillars have been defoliating trees and even invading homes. Gypsy moths have stripped bare one-half million acres of Pennsylvania forest and are spreading south into the Blue Ridge Mountains. Colorado is losing two million Ponderosa pines each year on the eastern slopes of the Rockies due to pine beetle infestation. Locusts have swarmed across Africa and Asia eating everything from crops to wooden fence posts.[10]

The World Health Organization reports that eighty-four species of insects that carry dreaded tropical diseases are now surviving nicely in the face of every imaginable insecticide. In the United States we face a constant threat from mosquito-borne diseases that would make some of our southern states uninhabitable were it not for expensive, continuing control programs.

Acid

The most serious pestilence we face, however, is not from bugs but from the pollution of our environment. Acid rain, caused by acidic pollutants in the air, is damaging everything it falls on. Particularly hard-hit are farms, lakes, and forests in the northeastern United States and nearby areas of Canada.

The widespread elimination of forests (only a tiny percentage of these are replaced in spite of advertising to the contrary) is increasing the amount of carbon dioxide in our air because shrubs breathe carbon dioxide and exhale oxygen. We humans, of course, do just the reverse, so that we and the plants enjoy a sort of symbiotic existence. We need them and they need us.

The thing that has scientists worried about increased carbon dioxide levels, however, is not a shortage of oxygen for humans. There seems to be no immediate danger of that. Instead it's a matter of how the atmosphere affects the sun's radiation. Apparently more carbon dioxide is likely to cause a global warming trend which could be bad for farming and for the whole friendly environment of the world as it exists for us now.

When it comes to pollutants, America is the world's biggest contributor. We burn more gasoline than all the other people in the world together. This gives us high levels of lead in the air a lot of us have to breathe. When our children breathe that air, it inhibits brain growth. Sometimes it causes serious brain damage in our young.

For the first time in history, in July 1972, an entire town was declared unfit for human habitation because of air pollution. That was the village of Knapsack in the Rhineland of Germany.

Scandinavian scientists have made the alarming discovery that the Baltic Sea is dying. They have been unable to discover traces of oxygen at any point below two hundred feet. Down at the bottom nothing lives.

Pollutants threaten our lives at every level because the food we eat is not as nutritionally rich as it was only forty years ago. They contribute to all our health problems, but especially to the incidence of cancer. A baby born today has one chance in three of suffering some kind of cancer.

Conclusion

The headaches that plague us on every side are signs that point to the nearness of the return of Jesus Christ. Many of the things we have presented in this chapter are evidence of the judgment of God against a world gone berserk. The worst is yet to come. It is time to take warning and flee from the wrath to come. As it was in the days of Noah, so it will be in the days of the coming of the Son of Man. Do not be mistaken; my purpose is to alarm and to awaken you to the possibility of a whole new life.

You and I are doing our own Operation Global Probe. We're taking a hard look at the realities of life on our planet and we're learning to interpret them in light of the Bible. The seven seals of the book of Revelation are being broken open—war and bloodshed ensue, drought and famine, pestilence, earthquakes and floods, defoliation, the death of entire seas, the irretrievable pollution of a third of the world's fresh water, plagues of locusts, killer storms.

The prophecies of the Bible are telling us the return is very near. How can we know those prophecies are reliable? Stop and think with me for a minute. The Bible has a proven track record. Over sixty prophecies were fulfilled by the first coming of Jesus. Those prophecies foretold where the Messiah would be born, how He would live, how He would die, and how He would rise and then ascend to the place of all authority in the universe.

Take just one example. Both Moses and David (see Exod. 12:46, Num. 9:12, Ps. 34:20) said that none of the Messiah's bones would be broken and, indeed, none of Jesus' bones were broken. That may seem unremarkable on the face of it, but it's not. That's because breaking the shin bones of the victims of crucifixion was almost standard practice. You see, death by crucifixion was an agonizingly slow process. Strong and vigorous men were known to have survived for as long as three days on a cross.

The real cause of death from hanging on a cross was asphyxiation. The lungs of the victim gradually filled with carbon dioxide and he expired for lack of oxygen. The way to keep that from happening was to push up with one's legs, thus allowing the lungs to fill with fresh air. So, the process could be considerably shortened by breaking the victim's legs.

This was precisely what happened on the day of Jesus' crucifixion. It was Friday and the Sabbath would commence at sundown. The Romans did not want to offend their Jewish subjects needlessly, so Pilate ordered the guards to break the legs of the three men being executed. After that, death would ensue quickly, and the bodies could be taken down before the Sabbath started.

The guards carried out their orders with dispatch, but when they came to Jesus, they found there was no need. He had already died. They verified this by piercing his side with a lance (see John 19:31–37).

The fact that Jesus was already dead fulfills a prophecy that Jesus himself made about His death. He said, "No one takes my life away from me. I give it up of my own free will. I have the right to give it up, and I have the right to take it back. This is what my Father has commanded me to do" (John 10:18 TEV).

Just looking at one or two prophecies, as we have just done, gives dramatic evidence of the hand of God at work arranging events in accord with His special plan. But to stand back and contemplate the fulfillment of sixty such prophecies gives us overwhelming evidence of the reliability of the Bible.

According to the laws of probability the chances that one person could have fulfilled only eight such prophecies is one in a quadrillion. Jesus fulfilled not eight, but sixty!

When Jesus left his disciples after the Resurrection and ascended into heaven, two white-robed men came and stood among the upward-staring followers. They said to them, "Men of Galilee, why are you standing here staring at the sky? Jesus is gone away to Heaven, and some day, just as he went, he will return!" (Acts 1:11 TLB).

You can count on it. Jesus is going to fulfill all of the prophecies concerning Himself!

IV

Wars and Rumors of Wars

"The Soviet Union has twenty-six divisions on the border of one country, and believe me they are not customs officials...they are an invasion force."

—Jack Anderson

During a recent White House briefing, a high-level official confided in me that he is concerned about what is happening south of our border. He is concerned that the Soviet Union is involved in some of the trouble. "Mike," he said, "off the record, we're in serious trouble. Unless we can get control of the insanity that's burning throughout Latin America within the next two years, we may have to arm our own border. Do you know what that could mean?"

"Tell me," I replied.

"It could mean setting aside a considerable body of troops and materiel to protect a border that is three thousand miles long. That, in turn, could mean having to lessen our troop commitments in other critical parts of the world such as our NATO-aligned countries, the Middle East and Asia, not to speak of fanning the flames of terrorism in our own country."

Not long before that I had spent a day in Washington. First I visited the home of a high-ranking general.[1] He had served six U.S. presidents and had held one of the highest military intelligence positions of any man in the world. For hours he talked with me about wars and rumors of wars. He expressed his keen awareness that wars had escalated both in number and in intensity during the past sixty years. World War II, he explained, was the most costly war in all history. About fifty-five million lives were lost, and the financial cost of the war has been estimated at $3.5 trillion.[2] To divide that evenly among all the human beings on earth would amount to a little over seventeen hundred dollars for each person. That amount does not include the expense involved in the loss of lives and property.

As we talked I told him about Ezekiel's prophecies that Russia would invade the Middle East.

He stared at me in amazement. "Mr. Evans," he said, "I am one of 325 senior military officers who have appealed personally to the president, urging him to stand behind Israel because we feared a potential Soviet invasion of that country. If two Soviet divisions were introduced into the West Bank, it would mean World War III—a nuclear holocaust." Make no mistake about it, the Soviets are only a matter of minutes away by air, thanks to their Friendship Treaties with many of the Arab states surrounding Israel.

I had never felt more shocked in my life. But my day wasn't over. At noon I sat in the office of Jack Anderson, the syndicated columnist. That's when he told me about the Soviet divisions on their border with Iran—evidently in preparation for an invasion someday. Those twenty-six divisions, he told me, exceed the number of divisions the United States has placed outside its borders worldwide.

I told him what I had learned on a recent trip to Mexico and asked him what he thought about developments there. "You're right, Mike," he told me. "The Soviets are trying to bring America to its knees. They're pushing their anti-God ideology all the way through Mexico directly at our soft underbelly."

A few hours later, I sat in the home of another high-ranking general. I hoped I might hear some words of comfort and encouragement, but my hopes were dashed. He told me, "If America doesn't change its direction radically and soon, I doubt that we have a thousand days of freedom left." I understood him to mean that, in spite of our change in foreign policy, much more basic problems remained unsolved.

I had not expected these sorts of doomsday predictions from these men. Their closeness to the harsh realities of the course of world events made their declarations all the more alarming. They have to pay attention to those realities day after day. It's their job. We, on the other hand, are heavily insulated against those realities. No American has heard the sound of a true battle within the borders of this nation since the Civil War and the Indian Wars of the late nineteenth century. Like the ancient Roman emperor-philosopher, Marcus Aurelius (A.D. 121–180), we find "how easy it is to repel and to wipe away every impression which is troublesome or unsuitable, and immediately to be in all tranquillity."

But this is not true of the White House official, or of Jack Anderson, or of the generals with whom I talked. Nor is it true of Kurt Waldheim who served as Secretary General of the United Nations from 1972 through 1981. During his tenure he said, "We probably have ten years left to solve the problems that threaten our survival on this planet before it is too late."[3] He said that at least ten years ago.

Are we going to take seriously what these men are saying? Or shall we repel and wipe away these troublesome impressions? Those seem the only choices. But I doubt that the latter will really bring us to tranquillity. If we do endeavor to take these things seriously, we find quickly that the scope of things we can do that might really make a difference is exasperatingly small. The temptation to sink into a stupor of hopelessness is great.

But wait a minute. There is a third alternative. Jesus said, "And you will hear of wars and rumors of wars. See that you are not troubled; for all these things must come to pass, but the end is not yet. For nation will rise against nation, and kingdom against kingdom" (Matt. 24:6–7). We can choose to believe Him and refuse to be troubled on the basis of His word.

If you really know the Lord and have experienced His peace, then you can rest in the midst of the storm. The psalmist declares:

> The LORD is my light and my salvation;
> Whom shall I fear?
> The LORD is the strength of my life;
> Of whom shall I be afraid....
> Though an army should encamp against me,
> My heart shall not fear;

Though war should rise against me,
In this I will be confident.
One thing have I desired of the LORD
That will I seek:
That I may dwell in the house of the LORD
All the days of my life,
To behold the beauty of the LORD,
And to inquire in His temple.
For in the time of trouble
He shall hide me in His pavilion;
In the secret place of His tabernacle
He shall hide me;
He shall set me high upon a rock (Ps. 27:1, 3–5).

Record Breakers

Many of the great thinkers of the world during the nineteenth century believed in the humanist utopia similar to that which I have described in Chapter One. They believed that mankind was on a steady path of improvement and that democracy would truly solve the world's ills. England's parliament was slowly gaining more real power. Slavery was abolished throughout the British Empire by nothing more dramatic than an act of Parliament in 1832. At the same time, the industrial revolution and rapidly advancing technology, evidenced in things like steam-driven locomotives and ships, made the idea of progress seem inexorable. Darwin even developed a theory that portrayed the whole scope of biology as on an endless path of beneficial progress.

The sense of much of this was that man himself was improving, becoming more sensible, humane, and decent. Again, there was evidence to point to. Metropolitan police forces were emerging to supervise civilian public activities in place of soldiers, whose methods had long been notoriously harsh. Florence Nightingale's efforts to establish nursing as a profession were successful. Capital punishment was being handled in a less carnival fashion than had once been the case. There was much that could cause one to feel that mankind, as a whole, was improving.

Ironically, however, the developments of the twentieth century give dismal evidence to the contrary. The two world wars demonstrated two things clearly. One was the enormous advance of technology which enabled the belligerents to employ increasingly sophisticated weapons against one another. The other was that sin still plagues us. People around the world sat astonished and shocked, watching the newsreels of the bulldozers burying the heaps of emaciated corpses in the German concentration camps. This was the same culture that had given us Luther, Goethe, Bach, Beethoven, Handel, and so many more. The achievements of German culture and industry were legendary. How could these gruesomely repelling sights be coming from the same place? Never again would it be easy to demonstrate that the nature of man was on some steady upward course. Instead, philosophers had to consider solemnly the reality of the fact that man is, indeed, born in sin and in need of a Savior. The twentieth century has made the accumulated barbarism and savagery of the previous centuries of human history seem like child's play.

We read in our history books about the Hundred Years' War and the Thirty Years' War. The Crusades dragged on for nearly two centuries. The knights of Europe warred with each other almost incessantly. The same could be said about the Chinese war lords whose constant bickering kept China from being united until this century. These sorts of examples could be listed almost endlessly from all eras of history and all regions of the inhabited world.

So, how can we say that the twentieth century has been worse than previous centuries when it comes to warfare and bloodshed? First of all, we can say it because war is primarily a matter of economics. The increase in the wealth of the nations in the last two centuries has been astronomical. This, of course, is a result of the industrial-technological revolution. We see it happening before our very eyes today. Some years ago the first pocket calculators retailed for around three hundred dollars. Today you can buy one at a variety store checkout stand for less than ten.

When Napoleon crossed the Mediterranean to Egypt in 1798, his army numbered thirty-five thousand men. Today, in peacetime, the French Army maintains three hundred thirty thousand men on active duty. The point is that, with the increase of wealth and technology, armies and warfare have grown in size and scope as well.

As I discussed this subject with Dr. George Crawford, professor of Physics and co-founder of the Population Institute, he made this phenomenal statement. "Most people have no idea what the future may hold. Actually, most people don't even think about the future. They are so concerned about the here and now they forget that what they are doing now determines the future.

"For the first time, we are beginning to understand what would happen to planet Earth if there really were an exchange of nuclear weapons. If nuclear war starts, there is no life after nuclear war. There are literally hundreds of potential nuclear weapons unaccounted for. They could be in the hands of terrorists today of any group. We don't know *where* they are.

"And don't discount the possibility of a technological accident, a freak accident ushering us into a nuclear war. A simple computer decision—a malfunction—can produce nuclear war."

Dr. Crawford was sharing these incredible comments when the question was asked, "What would the planet be like after a nuclear war?"

Dr. Crawford said: "A nuclear exchange would create an intense cloud of dust and smoke which would block the surface of the earth from the sun's rays for at least one year...in some cases, it could be two years. That black smoke is a combination of all the things burned, including all the chemicals which are so dangerous and so highly radioactive. Now, during this time, the debris in the clouds will settle to the earth in the form of dust so that the surface of the earth and the waters will be covered with this debris. The debris is radioactive and toxic. The plant life, the animal life, and human life exposed to it will be destroyed.

"The temperatures will be below freezing when the dust settles out. The layers can be several inches deep, covering everything. The sun will then shine through. But it is not the same 'ole friendly sun' that we had before. We will be receiving the full blast of the sun's heat."[4]

With the words of Dr. Crawford ringing like a warning bell in my ear, I recalled the Scriptures in the book of Revelation that describe the earth in a catastrophic condition:

Then the angel took the censer, filled it with fire the altar, and threw it to the earth. And there were noises, thunderings, and lightnings, an earthquake....The first angel sounded: And hail and fire followed, mingled with blood, and they were thrown to the earth; and a third of the trees were burned up, and all green grass was burned up. Then the second angel sounded: And something like a great mountain burning with fire was thrown into the sea, and a third of the sea became blood; and a third of the creatures in the sea died, and a third of the ships were destroyed....Then the fourth angel sounded: And a third of the sun was struck, and a third of the moon, and a third of the stars, so that a third of them were darkened; and a third of the day did not shine, and likewise the night....I looked when He opened the sixth seal, and behold, there was a great earthquake; and the sun became black as sackcloth of hair, and the moon became like blood....Then the sky receded as a scroll when it is rolled up, and every mountain and island was moved out of its place. And the kings of the earth, the great men, the rich men, the commanders, the mighty men, and every slave and every free man, hid themselves in the caves and in the rocks of the mountains, and said to the mountains and rocks, "Fall on us and hide us from the face of Him who sits on the throne and from the wrath of the Lamb! For the great day of His wrath has come, and who is able to stand?" (Rev. 8:5, 7–8, 12; 6:12, 14–17).

How in the world could one not believe the Bible is true after hearing such a phenomenal statement?

You can be sure of one thing: destruction of this scope has never happened before. The armies of the ancient civilizations of Egypt, Babylonia, Assyria, Persia, Macedonia, and Rome would not have even conceived the possibility of what we are talking about. The battles of the Middle Ages were seldom engaged in by more than a few hundred thousand combatants. More often than not, the outcome of a military campaign was determined by which army managed to survive the smallpox, cholera, or some other plague with the greater number of soldiers.

The advances of technology and increases of wealth have also resulted in the proliferation of small-scale wars and enormous armed conflicts in this century. Significant small wars have occurred in numbers surpassing those of any previous century. The Boer War was fought between the British and the Dutch in South

Africa (1899–1902). Then there were the Philippine Insurrection (1900–1901), the Russo-Japanese War (1904–1905), the Mexican Revolution of 1910, the Chinese-Japanese War, the Spanish Civil War, the French-Indo-Chinese War, the Indonesian War of Independence, the Korean War, the Vietnam War, the Israeli-Arab Wars, and the Iran-Iraqi War. In 1984 the Center for Defense Information issued a study showing that over four million people were engaged in forty-two major wars, rebellions, and civil uprisings. Most of these conflicts, the study observed, are almost invisible beyond the field of battle.

Looking to the future, seven areas in the world threaten to see the outbreak of major violence before the end of the century. They are:

1. *The Sino-Soviet Border*—The largest single segment of China's three and a half million man standing army is stationed along its forty-five-hundred-mile border with the Soviet Union. The Soviets, likewise, maintain heavy troop concentrations in the same vicinity. In the event of an outbreak of hostilities there the United States would strive to remain on the sidelines. But a Soviet victory would shift the balance of global power drastically.

2. *Eastern Europe*—Any disintegration of the Soviet empire here, such as could happen in Poland, will be marked by unpredictable eruptions of violence. The possibility of spillover into Central and Western Europe exists.

3. *Western Europe*—Here NATO forces are faced off against Soviet and East German troops. If war ever broke out on this front, it could easily involve nuclear, chemical, and biological weapons.

4. *Africa*—Over half of Africa is strongly influenced by the Communists. I believe that the Communists will play upon civil unrest among blacks in South Africa and will eventually overthrow the government by playing upon the issue of human rights. This will seal the casket for Africa.

5. *The Middle East*—As I mentioned earlier, instability in this region, such as represented by the war between Iran and Iraq, will tempt the Soviets to intervene. The entire Middle East is on a short fuse. The Soviets have infiltrated every Arab country, and

leaders of military intelligence see the handwriting on the wall if there is not a radical change.

6. *Korea*—The second largest contingent of foreign-based U.S. troops is stationed in South Korea. The essential hostility between the Korean governments remains unabated.

7. *Mexico*—If a Marxist government comes into power in Mexico City, the present flow of illegal immigrants from south of the border will seem like a trickle compared to what would happen then. As discussed earlier, the U.S. would be faced with tough economic, political, and military decisions, not taking into consideration the terrorism problems we would encounter.

The Future in the Middle East

The phone was ringing. I cast a sleepy eye at the clock on the nightstand. Seven-fifteen in the morning. The year was 1982.

Carolyn called from the next room, "Honey, it's for you."

"Darling," I replied, "I'm exhausted. Ask them to call back later."

"Sweetheart, it's Dr. Reuben Hecht."

That woke me up. Hecht was one of Menachem Begin's senior advisors. I got out of bed and went to the phone.

"Mike," he announced, "Operation Peace for Galilee has begun. Our forces have crossed the border into Lebanon and our troops are moving northward with great speed."

I could hardly believe my ears. Only a week before I had sat in the cabinet room with Begin and Hecht and talked with many of Israel's top civilian and military leaders. I had little suspicion that such a thing was in the works. As a matter of fact, I encouraged the men in that meeting to take one another's hands and led in prayer. I asked God to anoint, protect, and strengthen the nation. I then walked out of the meeting to pray with Prime Minister Begin's military advisor.

Reuben Hecht went on, "The prophecies of the Bible are being fulfilled! Israel has shut down twenty-five hundred Soviet-made heat-seeking rockets. We have destroyed ninety Soviet MiG aircraft without losing one of our own! It is a miracle!"

In the days to come the world would learn of what I had

known for quite some time—that the Soviets had been stockpiling large amounts of arms and armaments in southern Lebanon. It would take Isreal two months, using a thousand soldiers and 150 ten-ton Mack trucks, to haul the Soviet equipment out of Lebanon into Israel. The stuff they hauled included over a hundred examples of advances in Russian technology that had never been seen first-hand in the West before.

Over the years, the Soviets have turned the Middle East into an incredible arsenal. MiGs in Damascus are only a few minutes' flight from Jerusalem. Amman, Cairo, and Tripoli have also long been bases for hostile flights. Israel has lived under the gun since the day it gained its independence. What could I say to Dr. Hecht? I was in a state of shock.

What Israel had done, indirectly, was administer the Soviet Union one of its greatest defeats. Since 1956 the Soviets had been aiding and abetting the Arabs in their attempts to break Israel's little back. But time and again Israel had thwarted their efforts. The stockpiling in southern Lebanon was a measure of the intensity of Soviet hostility toward Israel.

The truth of what Israel did in 1982 has never been told by the secular press in the West or anywhere else except, of course, inside Israel itself. And the failure of the press to publicize the extent of the arms pile in southern Lebanon has permitted Israel's neighbors, particularly Syria, to replenish their arsenals without attracting any international criticism.

As a result the military threat to Israel has grown rapidly. At this writing, when Israel faces her eastern neighbors—Syria, Jordan, Iraq, and Saudi Arabia—she is confronted by more than 9,000 tanks, almost 6,000 pieces of heavy and medium artillery, 7,700 armored personnel carriers, and more than 1,500 military aircraft. When Israel faces west toward Egypt, Libya, and Algeria, the tanks number 7,300, the artillery pieces 6,500, the armored personnel carriers 5,800, and the aircraft 1,400.

Russia's activities in the Middle East have become increasingly deceptive, mostly in response to the rise of Moslem fundamentalism. Muammar Khadafy, for example, has made Libya a major client of the Soviets in the Middle East while styling his regime as strictly Islamic. Marxist-Leninist doctrine is espoused openly by

Middle Eastern governments only in Ethiopia, the People's Democratic Republic of Yemen (South Yemen), and Afghanistan—all countries on the periphery of the region.

In general, the Soviets encourage extremism and tension, supply arms, and prepare their friends for possible war. It is important to realize that one of the largest Moslem populations in the world is *in* the Soviet Union. The Soviets are experts at penetrating the infrastructure of Moslem countries and developing Moslem-oriented "human rights" movements. Many times these movements are not aligned with the Soviet Union, but rather are unknowing puppets in their hands.

It is a very cunning chess game. The Soviets manage to continue pulling the bricks from under the building without anyone's realizing what is happening. The Soviets are hoping that Marxist-style revolutionaries might overthrow the present regimes of the United Arab Empires, North Yemen, and Oman. Their influence in Iraq, Iran, Syria, and even Egypt is a lot greater than many people realize.

The effect of this may have significance in terms of biblical prophecy regarding a Russian invasion of the region. Ezekiel prophesied that God would turn Gog (Russia) around, put hooks in his jaws, and drag him and all his troops away (38:4) and, again, "I will turn him in a new direction and lead him out of the far north until he comes to the mountains of Israel" (Ezek. 39:2 TEV). As Russian frustration grows over diminished Soviet political influence in the area, perhaps it will motivate them to think more in terms of direct military involvement. Afghanistan is a prime example, and leading intelligence experts have told me that the Soviets are having incredible success in penetrating the infrastructure of Saudi Arabia with their Moslem-coded human rights ideologies, priming Saudi Arabia for a revolution similar to Iran's within the next thirty-six months.

On-the-job Training

I sat in a flimsy wooden chair. My cup of tea rested on an equally flimsy table with a broken leg. Across from me was Saad Haddad, a lovely man in his forties. Dressed in khaki fatigues, he was the leader of the Christian militia in southern Lebanon. He was a likable and courageous man who had won the admiration and devotion of the people he was leading. He was a born-again Christian.

I opened my Bible and began to talk to Haddad about the prophecies. I asked him about his daily battles with Palestinian terrorists. I was thinking about how the warfare he was involved in was a part of the signs that the return was near.

But Haddad's reply took me by surprise. "Mike," he said, "the majority of my problems have nothing to do with Arab terrorists. Lebanon is the on-the-job training center for the majority of terrorist organizations throughout the world. I fight North Koreans, Cubans, Guatemalans, Nicaraguans, Czechs, people from all over the world, and most of them carry Russian weapons. The insanity of all of this is that they hate my guts because they think I am aligned with America, when, in reality, the United States is doing absolutely nothing to support me or my cause. Quite the contrary—they are using most of their influence to undermine it. The reason they think I am aligned with your country is that we believe the only principles that will make Lebanon whole are those biblical principles upon which your own country was established."

His words rang in my ear as I remembered the ancient prophecies of how the nations of the earth would form a devilish alliance against Israel and that this, indeed, would be a major prophetic sign of the nearness of the return. Later that week I would listen to some of the most brilliant intelligence personnel in Israel. Among them was Benzion Netanyahu, president of the prestigious Jonathan Institute. The institute, named for Jonathan Netanyahu, the fallen leader of the famed 1976 raid on Entebbe, tracks terrorism throughout the world. He told me that world terrorism is sponsored by the Soviet Union. The Soviets maintain twenty training schools for terrorists, and Lebanon is the graduate school of the system where the terrorists get on-the-job training.

On the eve of the Operation Peace for Galilee campaign, fully seventeen terrorist groups were represented in the various camps of the Palestine Liberation Organization. Among those seventeen groups were the Japanese Red Army, the West German Baader-Meinhoff gang, the Irish Republican Army, the Red Brigade of Italy, the MR-13 group from Guatemala, as well as personnel from Argentina, Brazil, Columbia, Uruguay, Turkey, Chad, Spain, France, Ethiopia, and Thailand.

How well I remember the trip I took to Beirut. I rented an Israeli vehicle with Israeli license plates. I drove it through Tyre and Sidon, all the way to Beirut. It was a harrowing trip. There were probably more than fifteen hundred terrorists in the hills along that road. No Israeli civilian vehicle had ever gone to Beirut and made it back to Israel at night on that road in several years, I was told.

Part of my reason for going to Beirut was to take Bibles and the message of the blessed hope of the second coming to the American Marines stationed there at Christmas time. I knew many of them were discouraged, and I wanted to encourage them. Standing in front of their compound, I explained the plan of salvation for any who might not have heard it and invited them to receive the Lord Jesus. One of those to whom I spoke was later killed in the enormous explosion that took so many lives on October 23, 1983.

Lebanon was a foretaste of Armageddon: buildings in ruins, children wandering the streets in rags, teen-agers heavily armed. Staring at me as I write this in my office is a 135mm shell casing made in China, fired by an artillery piece made in Russia which was manned by Central Americans who fired it at Israelis. The shell casing was given to me by a Lebanese doctor. The terrorists had used his home as a gun position because it sat atop a high ridge. Therefore, he had hundreds of them.

Don't think for a moment that terrorism is something that only exists nine thousand miles away. The Bible does predict there will be wars and rumors of wars. According to Dr. Kupperman, an expert on terrorism from the Georgetown Institute of Strategic International Studies, "Revolutionary guards have trained as many as fifty thousand people, many of whom are sufficiently committed to give up their lives in suicide bombing attacks or whatever.

"The majority of the terrorist incidents are against the United

States, and if we attack or counterattack, we may find that, for example, Iranian terrorists will infiltrate into the U.S. There is now in existence a large pro-Khomeini Iranian population in the U.S. I am certainly convinced that terrorism is going to come to the United States."[5]

If you doubt what Dr. Kupperman has to say, then listen to the words of Dr. George Crawford. "We have coastlines with which criminal elements penetrate with great ease. We can't stop narcotic traffic. We can't stop any of the smuggling that goes on. Now, translate that into terrorists—people who bring in nuclear weapons and use them for threats. We are totally vulnerable. We have no protection at all from a sudden explosion.

"We have developed so many nuclear weapons and have so poor control over them that there are literally hundreds of potential nuclear weapons unaccounted for. These could be in the hands of terrorists."

There is no question that terrorists could very freely cross from Canada or Mexico with no problem into the United States and, indeed, probably do by the hundred and thousands.

There is no doubt about it: Jesus' prediciton of wars and rumors of wars is coming true before our eyes. You may ask, "How can I not be troubled?" There is only one way. You must neutralize the power of fear, hate, and self with the power of God. Don't blame God for the darkness in this world. Recognize that it is Satan who has come to kill, steal, and destroy. Surrender your life to the Lord Jesus Christ. Repent of your sins and ask the Lord Jesus to come into your life as your personal Savior.

V

Red Hot Russia

"We will grapple with the Lord God in due season. We shall vanquish Him in His highest heaven."

—G.E. Zinoviver, former
Chairman of the Leningrad
Soviet.

"Our spy satellites have spotted fully twenty-six Russian infantry and armor divisions stationed on or near the Iranian border. That is a lot of troops. The U.S. has only nineteen divisions in all the world. Let me tell you, those Russians are not customs officials. They are an invasion on that border; they are a full-scale invasion force, awaiting the day the Ayatollah dies. With Iran in their hands, the Persian Gulf would be under their control. Most of the free world's oil flows out of that gulf, so the possibility of combined NATO response is strong. The Russians are going to need the Persian Gulf oil more and more urgently as their reserves in the Caucasus begin to run down. They, after all, have to supply for their own use and the entire Soviet bloc. This could be the big one."

Jack Anderson said this as I sat across from his desk in his office in Washington, D.C. Mr. Anderson has access to information that is not widely available. One of the things we talked about was the Soviet Union and its involvement in the Middle East and elsewhere. I asked him what they were trying to accomplish.

"Their first priority, according to the intelligence reports I've been seeing, is to test out their latest SAMs (surface-to-air missile systems). This is a matter of deep concern to them because of the ease with which the Israelis seem able to knock them out of action in Lebanon. The Russians had given the Syrians, who were positioned in Lebanon in the Bekaa Valley when the Israelis invaded and stood as the main obstacle to the Israeli advance, their SAM 6s and the Israelis knocked them out. So they rushed in SAM 8s, and the Israelis destroyed them.

"Then the Soviets brought in the best they had from their Warsaw Pact satellite countries: the SAM 9s. They brought in Soviet crews to man them. The Israelis destroyed them all in two strikes. Then the war ended.

"Now the Soviets have replaced what the Israelis destroyed with modified SAM 5s and the latest SAM 10s from inside their own Russian borders. Crack Russian units are on site manning these systems. They need to know if the Israelis can knock these out under battlefield conditions, because if they can it means Russia is vulnerable. In turn, that would mean a costly trip back to the drawing board."

"I understand," I interjected, "that the Soviets have installed satellite dishes to enhance communications between Moscow and Damascus [the capital of Syria]."

"Mike," Jack replied, "the Soviets control virtually the entire operation in Syria. They don't run the Syrian army, but Soviet advisors are very evident there, right down to the battalion level. We need to understand that they perceive this as their own and not as a Syrian task. It is for their military purposes. Syria's purposes are incidental."

"What about Khomeini and the Soviets?" I asked.

"Khomeini is a loose cannon," Jack replied. "He follows his own dictates. He listens only to Allah. He pays no attention to us or to the Soviets. He pays very little attention to his own advisors. He follows his whims, whatever Allah whispers in his ear.

"Khomeini's most evident goal is to undermine the corrupt Islamic regimes, as he regards them, of the Arab states, from Saudi Arabia to Libya. He stirs up the fanaticism of the Shi'ite Muslims, of which he is one, to enforce a revival of Moslem fundamentalism and to drive out the hated Sunni Muslims as well as the Jews. The Shi'ites make eager recruits. They firmly believe that to die while fighting the infidels is a one-way ticket to heaven.

"Now this suits the Soviets well enough. Their goal has long been to destabilize and weaken the region so that they could eventually take it over. As far as they are concerned, for example, the longer the Iran-Iraqi war drags on the better. In the meantime, they stay out of the way of Khomeini. There's no way they can win his favor. Their policy is to outwait him and, at his age, time is on their side.

"This policy makes even more sense because the Ayatollah is so jealous of his supreme power that he has allowed no one to share even a fragment of it. There are no successors. When he dies, chaos will reign. The country will split into warring factions, and the best organized, the most tightly organized and disciplined faction will be the Iranian Communist party. They might have enough strength, in all the confusion, to seize control of Teheran.

"That would set the stage for them to claim, somehow, to be the legitimate government. Then, Afghanistan-style, they could invite the Soviets to come in and help them bring stability to the country. We know the Soviets are prepared to do that."

"Where do the terrorist organizations fit into this?" I asked.

"The Soviets have always had close ties with the terrorist movements throughout the world. By funding and supplying the terrorists they run a low-cost, low-risk, low-profile, underground war against the West. What they do is go into the various free-world countries and find the most charismatic malcontents. They recruit them and then train them. The training camps are primarily inside the Soviet Union, but they've got them in East Germany and Hungary too. I've talked with graduates from some of these camps. They get as much as four years of indoctrination and training in how to overthrow governments.

"Once they graduate, they're sent back home to begin to form cadres and liberation movements, as they like to call them, which exploit and capitalize on the discontent in a given country. Often that discontent is founded on legitimate grievances that may affect a wide range of people. The graduate of a Communist training camp does not care what sort of people he recruits. They can be of any ilk—non-Communist, anti-Communist, fascist, Christian, Jewish, atheist. It matters not. They never divulge their own Soviet indoctrination and background, except insofar as all these revolutionary movements employ the same Marxist buzz words, follow the same tactics, and use the same techniques."

"Do these sorts of programs have much of a foothold in the United States?"

"The foothold is small, but it's going to get bigger. We have better police methods, and our general population is less restive, less divided than in most countries.

"The Soviets are aiming terrorist activity at us from the south. Only 20 percent of the Sandinistas that forced Samosa out of Nicaragua were Communists, but once the coup was achieved, those 20 percent were ready. They knew what to do in the power vacuum. The others did not.

"Now they hope to accomplish the same thing in El Salvador and, after that, in Guatemala. After that, possibly Mexico. If that happened, our soft underbelly would be exposed.

"It wouldn't mean that we would be invaded and overthrown by way of Mexico, but it would give us a taste of what life is like in Israel where terrorists are just across the border. One can imagine terrorist raids into San Diego, Tucson, El Paso, Laredo, and Brownsville. Imagine their commandeering a Greyhound bus full of our citizens and then blowing the whole thing up after some harrowing ordeal."

"That's just the sort of thing that's happened in Israel," I observed.

"Precisely. It's not a happy thought, is it?" Jack replied.

"No."

"We'd keep the lid on it, of course. Most of the time, anyway. Its real purpose, in Soviet eyes, would be to keep us preoccupied, less free to respond to their moves in faraway places like the Persian Gulf."

"Hmmm," I murmured, "Shades of Pancho Villa's raid into New Mexico in 1916. Except today it would be with a lot more than six-shooters. It needs to be stopped long before any of that can happen."

"It can," Jack commented. "The Soviets and the Arabs understand one thing: physical power. Moral power carries no weight for them. Stalin was at one time concerned about the Pope and the power of the Catholic church. Therefore, he sent several of his aides to come back and report to him how many divisions the Pontiff had at his disposal. Nobody attacks the Soviet Union, certainly not Poland or Afghanistan. They know what would happen if they did. If you're big enough, nobody picks a fight with you."

"In the Middle East," I commented, "Israel is the one with the strongest punch. It's taken everyone a while to find that out and to be willing to leave them alone at least in a measure. Without that punch, Israel would have been annihilated long ago."

Jack nodded his agreement. "Strength is what counts. I wish it were otherwise. But history has taught us that unpreparedness actually tempts one's enemies to attack. I remember a story Dean Rusk [secretary of state under both Kennedy and Johnson, 1961–1969] told about a time when he was a young student in Germany, back in the twenties. One day he rented a canoe. Later in the afternoon, it was stolen from where he beached it so he could take a nap in the park. He reported the theft to the police and they caught the culprit, but they also laid a fine on young Dean Rusk for tempting the thief by not guarding the canoe well enough!

"Rusk said it was something he never forgot, but that our nation has a habit of forgetting it repeatedly. Andrei Vishinsky, who was the Soviet foreign minister during the last Stalin years [1949–1953], told Rusk that everything we had done in Korea had indicated that we were pulling out. 'You tempted us,' the Soviet diplomat had told him.

"That's what appeasement amounted to in the thirties when Hitler was gobbling up bits and pieces of Europe. Britain and France just stood by and let him get away with it. They kept tempting Hitler to take bigger and bigger bites. They finally drew the line at Poland, but it was too late to prevent the Second World War.

"You tempt them when you are weak, when you have no resolve, no strength, no will. You tempt them when you pay the price, and we have always had to pay a steep price for being weak. We know our country and its traditions. We are not going to start a war, and nobody is going to start a war against us, as long as we are strong. Not many people pick on Muhammed Ali, do they?"[1]

Old Prophets

The ancient prophet who spoke most clearly about the role of Russia in the last days was Ezekiel. He was just a lad when the Babylonians laid siege to Jerusalem. It was the end of the last vestige of Israel's independence. The young king of Judah, Jehoiachin, had surrendered at last. He and his family and roughly ten thousand others were deported to Babylonia. Ezekiel was among them.

In Babylonia Ezekiel lived with other Jewish exiles by the irrigation canal Chebar, which connected the Tigris River with the Euphrates above Babylon. Five years after his arrival there, he was called to prophesy to the inhabitants of Jerusalem who had not gone into exile. During the first years his messages were warnings of coming judgment with stern denunciations against the sins of the people and especially of their leaders. But once his warnings had been fulfilled in the fall of Jerusalem and the destruction of the temple, Ezekiel began to speak of the more distant future. He promised that God's people would one day be restored to their land and that the kingdom of God would come at last to Israel.

Prior to the final establishment of the kingdom, the full power of the Gentile kingdoms would be unleashed against an unsuspecting Israel. Many of the earlier prophets had focused more on Israel's immediate neighbors like Moab, Edom, and Philistia when foretelling the judgment of God on Israel's enemies. But Ezekiel's vision was on a grander scale. The Gentile attack on Israel in the latter days would be truly international in scope. Israel's attackers would come from much further away, particularly from much further north than Mesopotamia.

Except for three of them, the names of those attackers are strange, unfamiliar to modern readers. The prophecies speak of:

Gog, chief ruler of the nations of Meshech and Tubal in the land of Magog…Men from Persia, Sudan, and Libya are with him. All the fighting men of the lands of Gomer and Beth Togarmah in the north are with him.…He will invade the mountains of Israel, which were desolate and deserted so long, but where all the people now live in safety. He and his army and the many nations with him will attack like a storm and cover the land like a cloud (Ezek. 38:1–9, selected NIV.)

The names Gomer, Magog, Tubal, and Meshech were names in the family of Japheth. Japheth was the third son of Noah. In the same genealogical list in Genesis, we are told that the people of Togarmah were descendants of Gomer. The list (see Gen. 10:2–5, part of the Table of the Nations) is really a map in literary form which depicts Japheth as the forebear of those ancient peoples who lived to the west and north of the Hebrews, primarily those dwelling in the vicinity of the Aegean, Black, and Caspian seas.

Magog, Meshech, and Tubal

The Japhethites who descended from Magog, second son of Japheth, apparently became the dominant tribe. Their migrations carried them around the shores of the Black Sea and up into more traditional Russian territory. Meshech and Tubal were long located in Asia Minor. Ancient Assyrian documents refer to Tabal, and the Greek historian Herodotus listed the Tabaleans and the Mushki in that region. The last we hear of them in ancient sources is a sketchy record of an unsuccessful conspiracy against the Assyrian emperor Sargon which involved the Mushki. This may have resulted in a northerly migration in order to escape the emperor's avenging sword.

In any event, without doubt, the majority of students of prophecy and experts in the original language associate the name Moscow with Meshech and Tobolsk with Tubal. Tobolsk is a town on the western edge of the West Siberian Plain about two hundred miles from the foot of the eastern slopes of the Ural Mountains. It takes its name form the Tobol River, which flows north and slightly east from the southern end of the Urals, about five hundred miles from the northernmost point of the Caspian Sea.

I believe that Tobol derived its name from the ancient people of Tubal. When we consider that the Hebrew language uses an alphabet of consonants only, it strikes one as even more likely.

Tobolsk's population is small, less than fifty thousand. It sits at the point where the Tobol flows into the Irtysh River. From there the waters continue to flow northward where they merge with the Ob and finally empty into the Arctic Ocean. The city's longitude is close to that of Moscow. Tobolsk sits near the fifty-eighth parallel; Moscow near the fifty-fifth. Thus the two cities, quite different in most ways, sit opposite one another so that, in the eyes of a person reading the map, they somehow encompass that vastness that is known loosely as Russia.

The origins of the Russian people is a phenomenal, prophetic adventure. The land is so vast and open that its history has been a series of tugs of war between east (Asia) and west (Europe) and between north (the Vikings) and south (the Slavs). The origin of the Slavs is not even shrouded in legend; it is entirely unknown. Some historians speculate that they were farmers in the Black Sea region from before the time of the Scythian invasions (ca. 700 B.C.). That would accord with the biblical indications that the nations of the world emerged from the sons of Noah and the intimations that certain of the Japhethite tribes may have eventually moved on north from their original locations in Asia Minor.

The earliest signs of national life centered in the south around Kiev (where my grandfather was born), which would indicate the possibility of migrations northward from around the Black Sea. Only after the arrival of the Viking conquerors in the ninth century A.D. did the focal point of Russian culture begin to move farther north toward present-day Moscow. It may be also from the Vikings that the name Russia was derived.

Gomer and Beth Togarmah

Gomer's descendants were called *Gi-mir-ra-a* which the Greeks translated into "Cimmerians." A fair amount of ancient data exists regarding these Indo-European nomads who were eventually driven out of Asia Minor northward through the Caucasus and into the steppes of southern Russia. They, like the descendants of Meshech, may have formed part of the nucleus of the Slavic race. However, in contemporary Hebrew usage, the term *Gomer* is used for Germany. So, today we may associate them with central and southeastern Europe, the Warsaw Pact nations of Hungary, Czechoslovakia, Romania, East Germany, Bulgaria, and Poland.

Beth Togarmah means "House of Togarmah." The Assyrians

called them *Til-Garimmu,* a name derived from the Hittite Tegarama and carried into classical times as Gauraena (modern Gueruen in Turkey). The city was destroyed in 695 B.C. by the Assyrians, good evidence again for northerly migrations. Because they were known for breeding and trading horses and mules in ancient times (see Ezek. 27:14), it is customary to associate them with the Cossacks of the Ukraine in southern Russia, who are world-famous horsemen.

When Ezekiel foresaw that these ancient tribes would one day attack Israel, he had no way of knowing where their subsequent migrations would lead them, although in his time the preliminary migrations brought on by the Assyrian invasions had already taken place. From his perspective these people were at the remote edges of the world as he understood it. The incredible point on which to reflect is that, through the swirling changes of fortune that twenty-six intervening centuries have brought since Ezekiel penned those words by the Chebar canal, the thing he prophesied seems now to be reasonably lined up for a long-awaited fulfillment. Ezekiel probably had no idea what was meant when he was prompted to write that all this would happen after many years.

"Let's Be Friends"

Who, then, will be Russia's allies in the great invasion of Israel? According to Ezekiel 35:36 they will be Persia, the Sudan, Libya, the Warsaw Pact nations, the Ukraine, and men from many other nations. Are these plausible candidates in terms of today's political realities? Let's examine these possible would-be Soviet allies one at a time.

Persia

With the understanding that this name is interchangeable with Iran, Jack Anderson's comments at the beginning of this chapter are pertinent. With the Ayatollah out of the picture, the potential for a Communist takeover in Iran is great. Russian interests in Persia/Iran are much older than the Soviet regime that took over in 1917. Even before oil achieved its present status in the world economy, Russia eyed Iran hungrily because it could afford them access to even better warm water facilities for a fleet than did the Crimea and the Black Sea. That was because any fleet stationed in the Black Sea could be easily holed up by the simple act of blockading the Dardanelles, the straits between the Black Sea and the Mediterranean. The problem was doubled by the British presence at Gibraltar.

At the end of World War II Soviet troops had penetrated Iran as an ostensible part of the war effort against Germany, but after the war, those troops were not withdrawn. President Truman was compelled to call their bluff and issue an ultimatum. At that time America held a strong upper hand because of its demonstrated ability to deliver an atomic bomb. The Russians had no such capability. The Soviet divisions pulled meekly back into their own country.

Today the balance of power is much more even. The combined might of NATO roughly matches that of the Warsaw Pact nations. In the Middle East the Soviets are more highly motivated to win Iran than even the Czars were. The same problems exist for their southern fleets. The Turks are at the Dardanelles, the British are at Gibraltar, and the air over the Suez clearly belongs to the Israelis any time they want it. Added to the need for oil is the still undiminished strategic advantage of Iran's coastal exposure to the Indian Ocean. This time an ultimatum from the president of the United States would carry much less weight, not only because the Soviets have nuclear capability but also because a strong grip on the Persian Gulf would give the Soviets an unexcelled bargaining position.

The Sudan

This ought not to be confused with the nation of the same name. The biblically prophesied Sudan is an enormous geographical region that encompasses much of Ethiopia, Sudan, Chad, Niger, Upper Volta, and Mali—the sub-Saharan region. The word in the Hebrew that Ezekiel used was *Cush*. Because of the abundance of evidence, scholars have long agreed that this takes in an area larger than just today's country, Sudan. Sometimes the same word is translated as *Ethiopia*. Neither of these is incorrect so long as we understand them as regional terms not restricted by the arbitrary boundaries of twentieth-century geo-politics.

We also need to be aware again that Ezekiel's perspective at the time he prophesied these things made him perhaps only dimly aware of the extent of the African continent. To him Cush was that distant land south of Egypt. What lay beyond that horizon was uncertain at best.

At the time of this writing, the government of Ethiopia is solidly in the Marxist camp. Sudan is stridently Islamic, having even invoked such Moslem laws as those requiring hand amputations for convicted thieves. Chad is in chronic Moslem-Christian civil war which Muammar Khadafy of Libya fuels regularly. Niger is solidly in the Islamic camp, Mali and Upper Volta less so. All three of these nations are extremely poor and, like their neighbors to the east, hard hit by the droughts of the 1970s and 1980s. They are ruled, by and large, by military dictators. It would be easy to imagine them being recruited for a big invasion of the Middle East if some material inducement were offered. It would represent a happy adventure, a distraction from the dreary realities of life in "the Sudan."

Libya

Ezekiel used the term *Put*. Again, we need to sense the way in which biblical prophecy is a living thing, not limited to the perspective of the writer-prophet, although guided by it. Put was the third son of Ham (who was the second son of Noah). Put's descendants populated the regions west of Egypt. So, today, we see it applying not only to modern Libya but also to Algeria, Tunisia, and Morocco.

Modern day Libya, under the notorious leadership of Muammar Khadafy, has become like a gang of juvenile delinquents in the international community. As mentioned earlier, he is claiming to be ardently Islamic while at the same time sucking steadily on the Soviet breast. The stockpile of Soviet arms in Libya is enormous, much more than could be used if every Libyan man, woman, and child were put under arms. Khadafy is violently antagonistic toward Israel and would love nothing more than to drive the Jews into the sea.

Algeria, Tunisia, and Morocco have various political complexions, but their Islamic solidarity is something they are all pledged to maintain. They could be counted on to join in the fun, if ever a sure-fire invasion of Israel were being planned.

The Warsaw Pact

This is how we have already identified the forces of Gomer that Ezekiel envisioned as part of the great invasion force that would come against Israel in the last great battle of history. The Warsaw Pact is a treaty that brought the Communist nations of Europe under a unified military command. Russia, Albania, Bulgaria, Czechoslovakia, East Germany, Hungary, Poland, and Romania signed the treaty in May 1955. It was the Soviet response to the formation of NATO, the North Atlantic Treaty Organization, in 1950. (NATO is comprised of Belgium, Canada, Denmark, France, Great Britain, Greece, Iceland, Italy, Luxembourg, the Netherlands, Norway, Portugal, the United States, Turkey, and West Germany.) A Russian army marshal serves as supreme commander of the Warsaw Pact Forces. The command headquarters is in Moscow. Further comment about the likelihood of their compliance and cooperation with a Soviet military adventure is needless.

The Ukraine

This is the name of the region in the southwestern corner of the Soviet Union. Through the centuries this area has been overrun by Mongolian Tartars, Lithuanians, Poles, and finally, Russians. The Ukranians themselves are a slavic people with their own language and customs. Kiev, on the Dnieper River, has been their capital since before the Middle Ages. The Cossacks have long been associated with the Ukraine. It was they who resisted both the Tartars and the Poles, thus allowing the Ukraine to survive into modern times.

The greatest threat to the survival of the Ukrainians in this century has been the Russians, particularly under the leadership of Joseph Stalin. His repressive measures seemed to reflect a determination to exterminate this hearty race, millions of whom died in the 1930s. So great was the hatred of the Ukrainians for their

Russian overlords that, when the Germans invaded and passed through the Ukraine on their way to Stalingrad in 1941, the Ukrainians welcomed them as liberators. When the Germans evacuated the Ukraine after their defeat at Stalingrad in 1943, many Ukrainians fled back toward Germany with them.

Today that sense of separation from Russian culture persists in the Ukraine. But there is no danger of serious revolt. It would be crushed mercilessly. The Ukraine is squarely in the Soviet sphere and its soldiers, the descendants of Togarmah, will be on hand for their appointment at Armageddon.

Before I finish with this list of Russia's allies in the great Middle East invasion, I want to bring one other item to your attention— Egypt. Egypt, notably, is missing from Ezekiel's list of Russia's allies. Any political scientist would have scoffed at such a notion until 1977.

Britain granted independence to Egypt in 1922. After World War II Egypt became a charter member of the United Nations and of the Arab League. The monarchy of King Farouk toppled after the debacle of Israel's war for independence. In 1954, a young army colonel named Gamel Abdel Nasser emerged victorious in the struggle for power that followed Farouk's ouster.

Nassar was, in many ways, the leading figure in the Arab world while he held power. In fact, he came as close as anyone ever has to unifying the ununifiable Arabs under one flag. Egypt and Syria and Yemen merged briefly into the United Arab Republic. It didn't last. No one thought it would, but it did help establish Nasser's position of leadership.

In the 1960s Nasser concentrated on achieving Arab unity by loudly announcing freedom from the hated influence of the West throughout the Arab community. Thus he aligned himself increasingly with the Soviets who became his major sponsors. With their backing, he promoted socialism, Arab unity, and the struggle against Israel and the West.

Nasser's prestige was dealt a terrible blow during the Six-Day War with Israel in 1967. Egypt lost the entire Sinai Peninsula in that fracas, but the blow to Arab pride was much worse. Nasser submitted his resignation after that, but the national assembly refused to accept it. He died, suddenly, unexpectedly, but naturally, in September 1970. His vice president, Anwar Sadat, succeeded him. Then came the Yom Kippur War in 1973, which now stands as the final concerted Arab effort to drive the Israelis into the sea by direct military confrontation. It almost succeeded, but only almost. Four years later, Sadat made a move that won him a Nobel Peace Prize by going in person to Jerusalem to talk peace with Manachem Begin. Thus did Egypt evaporate as the chief Soviet client in the Middle East.

After Sadat was assassinated on the eighth anniversary of the Yom Kippur War, in 1981, the warmth between Egypt and Israel grew a little tepid. Mubarak did not introduce any major contradictions to his predecessor's policy. There was certainly no renewal of the romance with Moscow.

I spent a day discussing the subject with Muhammed Hakki, at that time the former minister of communications for the Camp David accords for Egypt. He expressed to me his great concern about Soviet purposes. He went on to say that their aggressive intentions certainly have not changed in regard to Egypt or the Middle East.

As I mentioned in the second chapter, Isser Harel, the former head of Israeli intelligence, told me that Israel had been able to intercept and defuse two assassination plots against Sadat.

Although the men who fired the weapons that killed Sadat were Moslem fanatics, Harel assured me that Libya stood behind them—and the Soviet Union stood behind Libya as the prime mover of the plots, both the ones that failed and the one that succeeded.

A Forty-yard Dash

Russia emerged from World War II bloody but victorious. Her contribution to the final Allied victory, in fact, cannot be underestimated. The amount of Russian blood spilled in fighting with the Germans dwarfed the losses of the Western Allies. Probably only the Japanese suffered more drastic losses. Military analysts agree that the course of the European war turned not at El Alamein, the beaches of North Africa, Sicily, Anzio, nor Normandy, but at Stalingrad. Stalingrad cost Hitler almost half a million of his finest soldiers, including twenty-four general officers. After Field Marshal Friedrich von Paulus, German Sixth Army Commander, surrendered on January 31, 1943, the German army never again held any significant initiative in the war.

Russia's sacrifice was tarnished by the greediness of her leaders, especially of Joseph Stalin. Once his troops had set foot on the soil of eastern Europe, they were destined never to leave. As far as Poland and the others were concerned, Stalin simply took over where Hitler had left off. Nothing had changed.

In the forty years that followed the end of World War II, the advances that the Soviets have made all over the world have been so spectacular that I call it a forty-yard dash. The strange thing is that many don't seem to have noticed. Here's how it happened.

President Harry Truman stood up to Stalin in Iran, Greece, and Berlin. Weary of war, however, the allies thought little could be done to help the nations of eastern Europe gain their freedom. The Iron Curtain had fallen. But surely the land-hungry Soviets must be allowed to go no farther; thus was born the policy of containment. NATO was formed to contain the Soviets in Europe and the Middle East. SEATO, the Southeast Asia Treaty Organization, was organized in 1954 to contain Communism—the Chinese brand more than the Soviet brand, of course—in that region of the world. SEATO was comprised of Australia, France, Great Britain, New Zealand, the Philippines, Thailand, and the United States. The failure of India, Indonesia, and Japan to join SEATO, however, led to its ultimate dissolution in 1977.

But the die was cast in the 1950s so that the Soviets eventually began to resort to the kind of tactics Jack Anderson was describing at the beginning of this chapter. Those tactics have worked admirably for them. Whereas, at the end of the Second World War, the Soviets had virtually no direct influence on affairs much beyond their borders, they have become a full-fledged shaper of world events.

They have made dramatic gains in the Middle East which have already detailed to some extent. In Africa they have gained significant influence in a score of nations. Some of their most notable African clients are the Congo, Libya, Ethiopia, Angola, and Mozambique. In Asia they have become the patrons of Vietnam and the owners of Afghanistan. Most dramatically, they have gained a significant foothold in the Western Hemisphere through Castro and probably through the Sandinistas in Nicaragua.

The Soviets have five major objectives in Latin America. They are:

1. To sharpen economic conflict between Latin America and the U.S.
2. To create trade for their benefit while denying the same to the U.S.
3. To strengthen Communist parties in the hemisphere.
4. To check Chinese influence in the region.
5. To maintain and enhance their relationship with Cuba.

The big Soviet efforts have been aimed at the Middle East and Africa. Soviet aid to countries of the Middle East and Africa totaled a little over $3 billion between 1965 and 1974. That figure more than doubled in only four years between 1975 and 1979. Soviet technicians of all sorts in these countries numbered about 8,000 in 1970. By 1979 that figure had risen to over 21,000. However, we are not including such countries as Afghanistan, where there are over 115,000 Russian military personnel.[2]

According to a recent 1985 Department of Defense document, over nineteen major countries have experienced substantial Soviet arms transfers in the last ten years. A large number of these countries has received Soviet military aid that would be calculated literally in billions of dollars. There are better than forty-five countries aligned with Russia through treaties of friendship, Soviet military personnel lining their borders, or Soviet mutual defense treaties.

When one looks at the Soviet navy operating in access areas and airfield access areas surrounding the United States, there is no way in the world that you will not believe that Matthew 24 is knocking at the door. The Pacific Ocean, the North Atlantic bordering North America, and above all South and Central America have become a virtual playground for Soviet military aircraft and submarines.

The Russians, obviously, are on the move. Ezekiel 38 prophesied it thousands of years ago. Only thirty years ago they had virtually no power at all, certainly not in space or nuclear power on the ground. Militarily, they were not a threat and had little control over the countries of the earth. As a matter of fact, only ten years ago the Russians were supplying arms in support of twenty-two countries, but that number, as I have already mentioned, has more than doubled.

The most spectacular form of Soviet involvement in the Middle East and Africa has come when Soviet arms as well as Soviet personnel have been engaged in combat. This took place in Egypt between 1970 and 1975. Soviet personnel worked closely with the Cuban troops that went into Angola in 1975–76. High-ranking Soviet officers were on hand when Cuban forces helped Ethiopia push the Somalians out of the disputed Ogaden region.

Perhaps the most strategic accomplishment of the Soviets has been to secure control over the Straits of Bab el Mandeb, which guard access to the Red Sea and the Suez Canal from the Indian Ocean. They have done this through their deep involvement with Ethiopia and South Yemen. In the event of war, Soviet troops and their allies in those two countries could easily blockade this critical passageway. They have achieved a similar advantage through their support of Vietnam. From air bases there they could easily reach and interrupt shipping through the Straits of Malacca, a major route for oil tankers on their way to Japan from the Persian Gulf. The only piece of the puzzle left for the Soviets to fit into place is at the Strait of Hormuz that stands at the mouth of the Persian Gulf where it joins the Indian Ocean. Already, from bases in Afghanistan their planes have only 550 kilometers to fly to reach Hormuz.

Let whoever has ears hear what these facts are saying. The ancient prophecies are coming to life after centuries of apparent dormancy. Never before in history have international conditions allowed for the uncanny arrangement of things that accords with the visions of Ezekiel by the Chebar canal.

Israel Loves Russia

One of the great ironies of recent history is the role Russia played in the establishment of the political state of Israel after World War II. We are so accustomed to the fact that Israel and the

Soviet Union waste no love on each other today that these facts are startling.

It happened because the Soviets saw an opportunity for themselves in the British decision to allow the U.N. to decide Palestine's fate in 1947. By supporting the motion to partition the Holy Land between the Arabs and the Jews, the Soviets saw the best possibility of ending the British Mandate that had existed since the end of World War I. Of course, to the Soviets, any British retrenchment was their opportunity to move in and gain influence, if not control.

Russian diplomat Andre Gromyko worked skillfully to assure partition at the U.N. Meanwhile, the Soviets sold Czechoslovakian aircraft and arms to the fledgling Israelis, recruited and trained Jewish displaced persons in Poland who wanted to serve in Israel, and generally did everything they could to assure that Palestine would not fall back under British influence. In return, the Israeli government pledged itself to follow a neutral foreign policy. That was more than the Syrians or the Lebanese had done for the Russians in return for Soviet support in securing the withdrawal of French and British troops from those countries.

But the honeymoon stopped there and never went any further. To make a long story short, it was simply a matter of the longstanding tradition of anti-Semitism in Russia that caused the falling out. They had been persecuting Jews longer than anyone could remember—long before the Bolshevik Revolution—and they just weren't able to purge anti-Semitic attitudes from their system. Before long, Israel was curled in the friendlier lap of the United States, and the Soviets were busy seeing new opportunities in Egypt and Iraq who were both eager for help to rid themselves of the British.

The divorce was final by 1956. That was when Israel was engaged in what they call the War of Attrition. It was essentially a long, drawn out artillery duel with the Egyptians across the border. The Egyptian artillery was, the Israelis discovered, being maintained by Russian technicians. Since that time the Israelis have been in the forefront when it comes to the number of casualties inflicted on members of the Soviet armed forces. They have been as nice as they could about it. The Israeli attitude might be summed up in these words: "We're a small nation and we don't want to arouse the wrath of an enormous nation needlessly, but neither will we back down or be intimidated."

During the American conflict in Vietnam, the Israelis were in control of the Suez Canal. In that capacity they refused passage to any freighter bearing supplies, usually from Russia, intended for the Viet Cong or the North Vietnamese. Consequently, Russian arms and supplies had to circle the entire continent of Africa to get to Hanoi.

Then there was the big haul of Russian arms captured by the Israelis in southern Lebanon in 1982. Much of that loot was vital to Western intelligence, giving us our first good look at some of the latest examples of Soviet technology. In the years since then, whenever I have visited Israel, it has been commonplace to see Russian equipment sitting about in various open storage areas, especially large vehicles and weapons. They're all over the country.

Someday, when that final battle comes, the Soviets and their allies will find themselves confronted by Israeli soldiers using some of the most fascinating and phenomenal equipment imaginable, comparable in capability only to Star Wars weapons. In addition, Russia will also be confronted with much of its own equipment captured and modified by Israel.

"It's Cool in the Furnace"

Never before in history has there been a nation like the Soviet Union whose government has made an essential tenet of atheism. But Marxism is a religion, and it wouldn't do to have two religions competing for supremacy. So, the Soviets shake their fists at the Creator of heaven and earth who has, thus far, been very patient with them. I believe that patience is growing thin because of the way the Soviets are deceiving the poor people of the world with half-truths that lead them into paths of violence and destruction.

One morning I was jotting some notes to myself in the lobby of the Santa Maria Isobel Hotel in Mexico City. I had spoken shortly before this to a business convention in the hotel. As I was writing, a man approached me. I looked up and smiled.

"My name is Carlos Alvarez," he said, stretching out his hand. "I heard you speak and I wanted to talk to you."

"Go ahead, my friend," I said.

"I am a Christian man," he said. "I love God very much."

"Wonderful," I replied

"You see, I have a Bible with me."

"Yes," I said. "But what is that other book?"

"It is a book that exposes the evils of capitalism."

"Oh?"

"Yes, you see, I am also a Communist. Communism is the wave of the future. It is God's plan for the whole world—the wave of the future. God has special love for poor people, true?"

"That's true," I nodded, "the Bible teaches it."

"Well, then, whoever would love and serve God must become a Communist because it is the only salvation for the poor."

I told him he was being deceived. I could never believe that Karl Marx and Stalin were prophets of God leading people to the light.

My heart was broken that day with the realization that there are many more people throughout Latin America who are deceived like Carlos Alvarez. Millions of frightened, hungry, afflicted people whom God loves are walking in darkness, marching down a pathway to destruction.

Later that day I dined with a Mexican businessman who told me that Mexico is being strongly influenced by Castro. He said Mexico is selling oil to Castro at bargain prices because it supports his aims for Latin America and adamantly opposes the United States' policy in the same area. He told me that the school books Mexican children grow up with have only kind things to say about Russia, while only scorn is reserved for the "Yankees."

"Mexico," he said, "is a time bomb with a short fuse."

I shuddered to think that the prophetic train had already moved a lot farther down the tracks than most people realized. But ironically this fact can also be a source of encouragement. We can live in anticipation that the return of our Lord is near.

VI

Earth—Planet of Destiny

"We see around us today the marks of a terrible dilemma, predictions of doomsday. Those predictions carry weight because of the existence of nuclear weapons, and the constant threat of global war...so much so that no president, no congress, no parliament can spend a day entirely free of this threat."

—President Ronald Reagan

Secret cameras were in every direction. Farther and farther we proceeded down through solid granite, well over one third of a mile, until my eyes glared into a pair of steel glass doors with over three feet of steel in them and a swing weight of twenty-five tons each, set fifty feet apart.

Behind those doors were eleven of the most unbelievable buildings in the world. They were suspended by flexible walkways and did not touch the walls or ceilings. All of the buildings were placed on rows of huge steel springs designed to protect the delicate equipment. There were over thirteen hundred springs made from three-inch diameter steel rods, each weighing approximately one thousand pounds. Unbelievable shock absorbers supported the springs to hold down the amount of bounce and sway that could result from an outside nuclear explosion.

No, I was not having a dream. I was in the midst of the nuclear nerve center of North America, NORAD, monitoring aircraft, missiles, and space systems that might pose a threat to North America.

I was given a briefing of the entire complex, including the warning center, space surveillance center, the defense operations center, and most importantly the command post.

As I sat in the command post realizing only moments before that I had beheld with my own eyes on screens Russian planes flying across the outer border of North America, I heard the startling word that within the last seventy-two hours two Soviet satellites had gone up into space and that the Soviets, indeed, have the ability to destroy satellites orbiting there. I thought to myself, *What in the world am I going to hear next?*

But my interview with Brigadier General Charles W. Bartholomew, the Assistant Deputy Chief of Staff for Combat Operations, was even more startling.

"General Bartholomew," I said, "does the planet really have anything to worry about?"

"Mr. Evans, the United States has no direct defense against a Russian nuclear attack. We are literally sitting ducks if the Soviets move their Bear-H Cruise missiles in our direction. The Russians can hit our nation with nuclear weapons in thirty-five minutes from the ground and in eight minutes from their subs.

"We have had more than 500 Soviet missile launches last year along and more than 450 of them were without warning."

I interrupted that statement to say, "General, do you mean that any one of those could have literally been directed toward the United States and could have, indeed, been the beginning of Armageddon?"

The general looked at me with sober eyes and said, "Yes, any one of them could have. However, fortunately, they weren't. Mr. Evans, we have the most complex computer system in the world here at NORAD. We are tracking 5,603 satellites. In the last seventy-two hours, the Soviets have fired an additional three satellites into space and four others have gone from other countries. As a matter of fact, in the last twenty-four hours we were on alert because of a missile launched from Moscow."

I turned my eyes to the left. As I looked at the command post with the incredible stacks of classified folders, something caught my eye more than anything else there—a clock that said MOSCOW on it.

I asked, "General, why is that clock up there with MOSCOW?"

"Mr. Evans, that is the most important time in the world. You see, if the Russians ever do launch a nuclear attack, we need to know the precise second. Believe me, they will launch everything they have."

I turned in total amazement and said, "General Bartholomew, is there an acceleration of Soviet military hardware?"

"You've got to be kidding, Mike! The Soviets were virtually no threat at all thirty years ago. Almost everything we are dealing with, militarily, either on the ground or in space, that is of consequence has taken place in the last thirty years."

It is awesome. Into my hands General Bartholomew handed a red book with white letters reading "SOVIET MILITARY POWER—1985." This 140-page department of defense document was staggering. The facts were worse than I could have ever conceived. As I scanned the document, I looked in his face and said, "General Bartholomew, I believe in Jesus Christ. What hope can you give to those who do not believe in Jesus Christ?"

General Bartholomew turned to me with piercing eyes. Behind him I could see the most sophisticated command post in the entire world. As he hesitated for a moment, getting ready to speak, I glanced down at my notes. The notes read: "According to this society of international law at London, there have only been 268 years of peace in the last 4,000 years of human history, despite the signing of more than 8,000 separate peace treaties. It has been calculated by a former president of the Norwegian Academy of Science, aided by historians from England, Egypt, Germany, and India, that since 3600 B.C. over 14,531 wars have been waged in which 3,640,000,000 people have been killed. This figure is over seven times the population of the United States."

Suddenly I looked up as General Bartholomew said, "Hope? Without Jesus Christ? There is no hope because we will all be dead."

The Big Bomb

The story of the first atom bomb stretches back into the nineteenth century and the work of the Curies, Roentgen, and Becquerel. By the early 1900s scientists had discovered how an atom was structured. Then Einstein's special theory of relativity gave researchers a basis for understanding nuclear energy and showed that the atom contained vast energy.

By 1939 a number of physicists had succeeded in splitting atoms of uranium by bombarding them with neutrons. They found that a split atom emitted released neutrons and energy. Enrico Fermi, an Italian scientist, reasoned that those neutrons that emerged from a split atom could produce a chain reaction.

The military possibilities of atomic energy were plain to see. Einstein addressed his letter to Roosevelt that summer to sketch the possibilities and to describe the need for further research on this chain reaction idea of Fermi's. The first funds for this research were in the hands of scientists by early 1940. By 1942 it was clear that Fermi had been right and that a bomb could be produced.

The Manhattan Engineer District of the Army Corps of Engineers (the Manhattan Project) was organized to accomplish the job. On December 2, 1942, Fermi and his coworkers at the University of Chicago succeeded in producing a real chain reaction. After that the Manhattan Project went into full gear. Huge plants were built to produce plutonium from uranium and to separate two different sorts of uranium, U235 and U238, from each other. This provided the raw material needed to build a bomb. This raw material was shipped to Los Alamos, New Mexico, where the weapons research laboratory of the Manhattan Project had been established. It was there that the scientists and technicians worked out the elaborate techniques needed to detonate an atomic explosion.

On July 16, 1945, a terrific flash lit the early-morning darkness near Alamogordo, New Mexico. Robert Oppenheimer and others watched from a distance inside a concrete bunker as a mushroom-shaped cloud ascended into the sky. Twenty-four days later, on August 6—the date of the ancient Feast of the Transfiguration—a B-29 bomber named the *Enola Gay* flew over a city few people had ever heard of before: Hiroshima, Japan. Captain Tibbets and his crew turned their eyes from the blinding flash. A moment later the shock wave hit the plane and gave it a nasty jolt. Then they saw the cloud. Below, ninety-two thousand people were dead or dying. Four and a half square miles in the middle of the city had been obliterated.

Three days later, a second bomb was dropped and exploded in the air over Nagasaki. This bomb used plutonium instead of the uranium that had been at the core of the weapon that destroyed Hiroshima. Its design was an improvement over the first, and its destructive power was more controlled. It only destroyed one and a half square miles and killed seventy-four thousand people. The injuries in both cities were roughly the same in number as the fatalities. But the war was ended quickly. Prior to the dropping of the bombs, it had been estimated that it would require at least two more years and the loss many of hundreds of thousands of American lives to finally defeat Japan on their home islands.

A year after the war, in July 1946, the United States tested two more bombs at Bikini Atoll in the Marshall Islands of the South Pacific. Each bomb was equivalent to twenty thousand tons of TNT in explosive force. These tests were made to determine the effect of the explosions on military and naval equipment.

In the spring of 1948, the United States exploded three atomic weapons at the Pacific Testing Grounds on Enewetak Atoll. These bombs marked big advances in nuclear technology. They used their nuclear material more efficiently and were thus more powerful than their predecessors. One of the three was six times more powerful than the bomb that fell on Nagasaki.

The Russians made their first successful test of an atomic explosion in August 1949. In 1951 the United States detonated twelve small nuclear devices, four large ones, and the first hydrogen bomb (it required an atomic explosion to trigger it). The Russians exploded two atomic bombs in 1951.

On the first of November 1952 the United States detonated the first megaton-class hydrogen fusion weapon Enewetak Atoll. (*Fusion* means "joining" whereas *fission,* the process employed in the previous bombs, means "splitting.") It had the power of 10.4 *megatons* or 10.4 million tons of TNT. It was also in 1952 that Great Britain first tested an atomic weapon. The Russians duplicated the megaton-class hydrogen bomb in 1953.

In 1954 American scientists carried out six nuclear explosions on the Pacific Test Range. One of those set the new record at fifteen megatons. The British caught up with a hydrogen-fusion weapon in 1957. After 1955 so many tests were carried out that most people lost count. But alarm over the effect these bombs were having on the planet rose in their face so that the United

States, Russia, and Britain called an informal halt to all testing in 1958.

France got into the picture in 1960 by exploding a nuclear bomb in the Sahara. China did it in 1964 in Sinkiang, its most remote and thinly populated province. Nineteen sixty-eight saw France detonate a hydrogen bomb, and India exploded its first atomic bomb in 1974 in an underground test.

Russia resumed conducting tests in 1961. The United States and Britain followed suit in 1962. In 1963 the nuclear test ban treaty was composed. It banned nuclear explosions anywhere except underground. By 1965 more than 130 nations had signed the treaty. The only important exceptions were France and China. China continued to conduct atmospheric tests all through the 1970s.

The U.N. approved a treaty to halt the spread of nuclear weapons in 1968. It took effect in 1970, but by the 1980s both Israel and South Africa were strongly suspected of having developed nuclear weapons. Furthermore the capacity to produce nuclear weapons existed in every European nation, Canada, Mexico, Brazil, Argentina, Libya, Egypt, Turkey, Iraq, Iran, Pakistan, the Philippines, Taiwan, South Korea, and Japan. Among those nations eight are considered very likely to join the ranks of nations with nuclear weapons: Brazil, Argentina, Libya, Iraq, Iran, Pakistan, Taiwan, and South Korea.

Late in the 1970s it became known that the United States had developed a neutron bomb. It had the distinction of being able to kill large numbers of people by radiation without doing much damage to property. The public was so appalled when the news got out that not much has been said about it since.

Current stockpiles of nuclear weapons are so great—it is estimated there are at least sixty thousand hydrogen bombs—that the earth could be destroyed about twenty times over. If they were detonated all together the fireball would achieve 130 million degrees—a temperature so phenomenally high it is unspeakable to even think about what it would do to planet Earth.

When President Reagan addressed the British Parliament—both Commons and Lords in uncommon joint session—in 1982, he said, "We see around us today the marks of our terrible dilemma—predictions of doomsday." Those predictions carry weight because of the existence of nuclear weapons and the constant threat of global war—so much so, he said, that "no president, no congress, no parliament can spend a day entirely free of this threat."[1]

Friend, nuclear war is no joke. According to Richard Nixon in an interview with *Time* magazine, "Eisenhower probably considered using a nuclear bomb in Korea in the war."

Nixon went on to say that Lyndon Johnson told him that he was seriously considering using the bomb in Vietnam. He continued, "In 1956 we considered using the bomb in Suez, and we did use it diplomatically. The Russians called us to join them in sending a combined force to drive the British and French out of the area. Eisenhower's response was that that was unthinkable. We were trying to use diplomatic leverage, but he wasn't about to join the Russians against our allies." Eisenhower made sure the word got out "that if Khrushchev carried out his threat to use rockets against the British Isles, Moscow would be destroyed 'as surely as day follows night.' "

Nixon went on to say that in the Berlin crisis that the Russians became very well aware that if they kept pushing, it "could lead to a general war with the Soviet Union and 'nuclear weapons have to be used.' "

Further in the interview, Nixon talked about three different instances when he considered using nuclear weapons. One was during the 1973 war "when Brezhnev threatened to intervene unilaterally in the Middle East. We could not allow Israel to go down the tube. We could not allow the Soviets to have a predominate position in the region. I sent that message very strong to the Soviet Union by putting our nuclear weapons on alert. They, indeed, backed down.

"A second time involved China. There were border conflicts. Henry Kissinger, National Security Adviser, was concerned about the Soviet Union jumping the Chinese. We had to let the Soviets know we would not tolerate that.

"Finally, there was 1971, the Indo-Pak war. We were concerned that the Chinese might intervene to stop India. We didn't learn till later that they didn't have that kind of conventional capability. But if they did step in, and the Soviets reacted, what would *we* do? There was *no question* what we would have done."[2]

In the fourteenth chapter of the book of Revelation, we read about an angel with a sharp sickle that was commanded,

> Then the angel took the censer, filled it with fire from the altar, and threw *it* to the earth. And there were noises, thunderings, lightnings, and an earthquake. So the seven angels who had the seven trumpets prepared themselves to sound. The first angel sounded: And hail and fire followed, mingled with blood, and they were thrown to the earth; and a third of the trees were burned up, and all green grass was burned up (Rev. 8:5-7).

Jesus said, "For then there will be great tribulation, such as has not been since the beginning of the world until this time, no, nor ever shall be. And unless these days were shortened, no flesh would be saved; but for the elect's sake those days will be shortened" (Matt. 24:21–22).

It has only been since August 6, 1945, that passages like these in the Bible have not stretched a person's ability to believe. They are easy to believe, horribly easy. Estimates of the death toll in the event of a nuclear exchange, such as was depicted in the television movie *The Day After*, fluctuate wildly and are never small. Conservative estimates place the toll at a quarter of the population of the entire globe.

Of course, the death tolls would likely be highest in North America, Europe, and the Soviet Union. The survivors would be concentrated in the Third World nations of Africa and South America and, perhaps, India and China.

Speaking of *The Day After,* that film had an effect on many people's lives, including Peter Engle. Peter over the years has been is one of the most celebrated producers in Hollywood. Peter sat with me and shared that after watching *The Day After,* he stayed tuned in as Kissinger and several famous leaders came on to talk about the movie and analyze the facts.

Peter saw the look on Kissinger's face and realized that those with him said nothing but that which confirmed his greatest fear: the planet was doomed. Peter then made up his mind that life was not worth living.

Peter was an agnostic. Through a series of incidents, he experienced a glorious vision in which Jesus of Nazareth stood before him and said, "I am the Messiah." Needless to say, today Peter Engle is an extremely committed believer in Jesus! He truly experienced the real "day after" and can say like the apostle Paul, "For I am persuaded that neither death nor life, nor angels nor principalities nor powers, nor things present nor things to come, nor height nor depth, nor any other created thing, shall be able to separate us from the love of God which is in Christ Jesus our Lord" (Rom. 8:38–39).

Ancient Prophecies

The book of Revelation in Chapters 8 and 9 describes a period of time when catastrophic changes will take place in the atmosphere and on the structure of the earth, and the sun and the moon will be darkened.

Who would have ever believed these strange doomsday predictions in this ancient book, the book of Revelation?

Now listen to the fulfillment of this. According to the Scripps-Howard News Service on September 5, 1985, as reported in the *Ft. Worth Star Telegram,* the International Council of Scientific Unions met on nuclear war and declared that possibly 4 billion people would starve to death if the United States and the Soviet Union have an all-out nuclear war. This would cause catastrophic climatic changes making it impossible to raise food crops for one or more years.

The study says that nuclear war could cause enormous fires that would shroud the world in smoke, prevent sunlight from reaching the earth, and produce a bone-chilling "nuclear winter." Farmers would be unable to produce crops in the Northern Hemisphere for one and possibly several growing seasons. The war itself would massacre several hundred million Americans and Russians but starve to death up to 4 billion innocent bystanders throughout the world. "There would be more starvation in India than war deaths in the United States and the Soviet Union," according to Cornell University ecologist Mark Harwell, "and more people would die in Africa than in Europe."

This study was compiled by three hundred scientists from thirty nations. They said a nuclear exchange would explode twelve thousand nuclear warheads, obliterate more than one hundred American, Russian, and European cities and cause raging firestorms that would consume 20 to 30 percent of all the buildings and structures in the Northern Hemisphere. The warheads' detonating would clog the atmosphere with several hundred million tons of black smoke. The pall would reduce sunlight by 90 percent and initially cause a 36-to-72 degree temperature decline on the entire planet. The fires would turn the world's atmosphere upside down. It would be hot in the upper atmosphere and cold at the surface. The climatic disruption would sharply reduce the planet's rainfall, and experts say it would be virtually impossible to grow food from one-to-four years.

Short Fuses

The most frightening possibility regarding nuclear power is that nuclear weapons may come into the hands of irresponsible people. The chief candidate I have in mind when I say this is the Middle East's bad boy, Muammar Khadafy of Libya. But the whole Arab world is suspect when it comes to nuclear power. Both the United States and the Soviet Union include the Arab world among those countries upon which they seek to place strict limitations regarding nuclear acquisition, due to fears regarding possible military use. But if the U.S. and the USSR are reluctant to sell nuclear hardware and information to the Arabs, several other vendors have stood ready to serve their needs. These are France, China, Brazil, Pakistan, and India.

In all, nine Arab countries are engaged in some nuclear activity: Egypt, Iraq, Libya, Syria, Jordan, Algeria, Morocco, Tunisia, and Saudi Arabia. Egypt is in the midst of preparations for entering the industrial nuclear age across a broad front by the year 2000, with massive Western help. Although this activity is basically oriented toward peaceful purposes, it is nevertheless liable to promote its ability to develop military applications.

As Iraq's nuclear program developed (with the help of France) through the 1970s, experts soon could see that it could give Iraq nuclear weapons under the cover of a seemingly innocent research program. This alarmed the Israelis who had to expect that such weapons would be used against them. Their intelligence gathering indicated that Iraq's Osirak reactor was about to become operable in the summer of 1981. The Israelis knew they had to destroy it then, before the reactor became "hot." If they didn't, any damage they might do to it would release radioactive waste which would endanger the civilian population in the Baghdad vicinity.

The raid was carried out by Israeli jets in June, 1981, with complete success. The Israelis knew that it would only constitute a setback to the Iraqis by about three to four years. Indeed, Saudi Arabia quickly pledged the money required to repair the damage, about $350 million. Its chief accomplishment, from the Israeli perspective, was to make the Israeli position crystal clear. It also served to create a controversy between the French and the Iraqis. After the raid, the French told the Iraqis they would help them rebuild only if the Iraqis would agree to accept low-grade enriched uranium (in place of the high-grade, weapons-quality uranium previously supplied) and to allow much stricter French supervision of the operation to guarantee compliance with the nuclear nonproliferation treaty. The French believed these conditions would satisfy the Israelis and thus prevent a second attack, but the Iraqis were having none of it. They insisted that the French abide by the terms of the original contract.

But it is Libya's Muammar Khadafy who has represented the shortest fuse of all. Throughout the 1970s Khadafy was busy trying to find a shortcut to nuclear weapons capability. He hoped he might get a complete unit capable of producing a bomb from the Pakistanis. Thus he supplied a great deal of funds to Pakistani research and development projects. He was also instrumental in arranging for the delivery of uranium from Niger to Pakistan.

In the meantime, Libya made substantial progress in its efforts to train nuclear students abroad, particularly in Sweden, the United States, and the Soviet Union. As a matter of fact, in the United States, 10 percent of all Libyan students are enrolled in special physics courses, specializing in nuclear energy. But, so far, both the Pakistanis and the Soviets have remained reluctant to hand over a bomb to Colonel Khadafy. His quest goes on.

Arab states have demonstrated chronic instability since the collapse of the Ottoman Empire at the end of World War I. Israel is the only viable parliamentary democracy in the entire Middle East. Any Arab who becomes a head of state lives in daily danger of assassination. King Hussein's grandfather, Abdullah (the first king of Jordan) died by an assassin's gun in 1951. Sadat, of course, is fresh in our memory. Lebanon's debacle gives vivid evidence of the Arab propensity to break into warring factions at the drop of a hat. Nothing, not even the Islamic religion, truly unifies them for any length of time. It is this volatility in Arab culture that makes their control of nuclear power a source of trembling to the whole world.

It is bad enough that nuclear weapons are possessed by any nation, however. For all men and women are, to put it kindly, *only human.*

If we could see international repentance, nations turning to God with love and trust rather than fear and greed, then and only then could we hope that nuclear war might truly be averted and that our children and theirs could live in a peaceful and secure world. Sadly, however, the Bible itself tells us that it will not be so. Instead, just as our civilization is doing now, so it will do in the future. It rejects God's ways. It scoffs cynically at those who revere the Bible and its teaching. When trouble comes, our culture trots out the appropriate scientist—be he a psychologist or a physicist or a chemist or a systems analyst—to perform the cure. In the end, our culture will turn to a superexpert who will give every indication that he can solve and, in fact, *is solving* the world's ills. The world will worship him, but not the God who made us.

Only a small percentage of us will be ready for the return. For most it will be as the Bible says: "For when they say, 'Peace and safety!' then sudden destruction comes upon them, as labor pains upon a pregnant woman. And they shall not escape" (1 Thess. 5:3).

In the years of the great nuclear arms race, a concept evolved to explain why the arms race was needed. Of course, the idea was to prevent nuclear war. The obvious way to do that was to get everyone to agree to put down their weapons, to discontinue nuclear arms production, and to throw away what has already been manufactured. However, it was equally obvious that getting "everyone" to agree to something like that was a big order. Something, in fact, that had never happened before in the history of the nations. Besides, we have the Bible's assurance that just as the poor will always be with us, so will wars.

So, what to do? The answer became couched in an acronym, MAD, which stands for Mutual Assured Destruction. According to this concept, nuclear warfare can be prevented to the extent that the major opponents maintain roughly equal armories of weapons together with sophisticated early-warning detection systems. Then each side would know that, if they decided to launch their weapons, it would surely bring down an equally devastating retaliation. Mutual destruction of the warring parties would be assured. The possibility for emotional tension and frayed nerves under this arrangement is enormous, but it did seem to keep the arms race from achieving the frenzied levels of the 1950s.

MAD was the accepted doctrine of all the administrations in Washington from Eisenhower through Carter and Reagan. But, by Carter's time, it was obvious that the doctrine was wearing thin. Ronald Reagan's distaste for it was obvious. To him it amounted to nothing more than two men pointing cocked pistols at each other.

Reagan listened sympathetically to Edward Teller, the renowned physicist who is the father of the hydrogen bomb and was long associated with the Lawrence Livermore Laboratory in Livermore, California, a center for developing nuclear weapons. Teller argued that new defense systems could be erected on the basis of the incredible technological advances of recent years— systems that would, as it were, place a protective barrier between the two men with the cocked pistols.

Teller's idea was largely opposed in both the state and the defense departments as being impractical and unfeasible. But a few advisors, notably National Security Adviser Robert McFarlane and Chief of Naval Operations Admiral James Watkins, gave Reagan the encouragement he needed. To the president, this idea gave birth to a "vision of the future that offers hope." On March 23, 1983, he unveiled the concept for strategic defense weapons in a televised address. American strategic thinking would never be quite the same again.

The program that emerged from Reagan's decision is called the Strategic Defense Initiative, but it has been popularly dubbed "Star Wars." This is partly because the idea involves intercepting Russian rockets and warheads before they strike their targets in the western hemisphere. It is also because the technological thinking behind some of the ways proposed to accomplish this interception is so heady that former defense secretary James Schlesinger called it "half Buck Rogers, half P. T. Barnum."

The best practical expectation for the system is that it will be able to wipe out enough Soviet missiles to make the odds for the success of an attack not worth it. Thus it would not erase the deterrent concept. Instead, it would reinforce it. It is merely a new stage in the arms race.

A Soviet warhead goes through four distinct stages in the thirty minutes it would take to travel from its launch site in Siberia to its point of detonation atop a Minuteman silo in North Dakota—or above the Hughes aerospace plant in Canoga Park in Southern California. The first stage is its ride atop a large rocket that carries it up through the atmosphere into space. That requires about five minutes. The second stage happens there on the edge of space when a device called a bus detaches from the spent rocket and maneuvers for about five minutes before releasing as many as ten warheads, each of which is independently targeted for some specific site. The bus may also release up to a hundred decoys, like aluminum-foil balloons. During the third phase, the warheads and decoys cruise for about ten minutes through the emptiness of space. Reentry is the fourth stage when the warheads descend on their targets while the decoys are burned up by the same passage through the atmosphere.

The best time to intercept this system, obviously, is during the first and second stages before the individual warheads are released. After that the targets are smaller and more widely dispersed. Intercepting a missile after reentry is better than nothing, but not much because of the radioactivity a nuclear explosion in the atmosphere would rain down on the population below.

American scientists are looking at several different sorts of technology that might be used to intercept Soviet missiles. In one scenario a mountaintop laser station would send beams to a relay mirror on a satellite orbiting high above the earth. The mirror reflects the beam to a second mirror on a much lower orbit which is sighted in on a soviet ICBM rising out of Siberia.[3]

Another method would involve putting a laser-generator directly into space in a low orbit. A computer would aim it and it would fire directly on missiles. The same concept would be employed for firing particle beams at oncoming missiles. This concept is simpler than the one with the mirrors, but the technology of lasers and particle beams is not ready for deployment. One problem, for example, is that a laser would have to lock on its target and stay at precisely the same spot on the side of the missile for as long as seven seconds. In that time a missile could travel twenty miles.[4]

X-ray lasers are the most promising candidates, and thus the most shrouded in secrecy. It has been known for a long time that, in the millisecond before detonation, a nuclear device emits powerful X-rays if rods are attached to and project from the device. This laser is so powerful that it requires no "dwell time" on the skin of the missile. Any contact would mean an instantaneous knockout.

But deploying X-ray lasers would mean putting as many as fourteen hundred satellites, each loaded with an atomic bomb, in low orbits that would constantly crisscross the Soviet Union, not to mention the rest of the world. That would not be politically acceptable. The solution is to employ a "pop up" deployment. This means putting the devices aboard submarines stationed near the Soviet Union and firing them up into space on first sign of an attack. Of course, getting the message from Washington to the submarine, assuming the Soviets had not found and destroyed the sub, would be tricky at best.

The most immediately feasible Star Wars devices are called kinetic energy weapons. They are easier to understand because they are simply rockets or other objects which would be fired at missiles and destroy them with the force of the collision. The technology is at hand to employ devices like these right now. Their main drawback is their slowness when compared to beam weapons. It might require keeping twenty thousand such devices in constant low orbit to stay within effective range of Soviet launch sites twenty-four hours a day.

If any such defense systems got much further than the research phase we can be certain that the Soviets will not stand around with their hands in their pockets. They would counter by strengthening and enhancing their attack system so that it would be less vulnerable to interception. And so, the stage would be set for one countermeasure to follow another. In the end the Soviets and the U.S. might simply bankrupt each other in this sort of contest. Perhaps that would preclude the need for armed hostility altogether.

Star Wars is the right name for it. It is a further escalation of the nuclear arms race. It means the fuse will be trimmed even shorter. No longer content with fighting our battles on earth, we have turned our attention to the heavens. Now the prospect of polluting not only the earth, the sea, and the air with radioactive fallout but also polluting the reaches of outer space is before us. Is there no end to our insanity? When will we realize that, more than anything else, it is God we are fighting?

Nearly two thousand years ago a man named James asked, "Where do all the fights and quarrels among you come from? They come," he answered, "from your desires for pleasure, which are constantly fighting within you. You want things, but you cannot have them, so you are ready to kill; you strongly desire things, but you cannot get them, so you quarrel and fight" (James 4:1–3 TEV). There could be more truth than we realize in those words of the Bible. They are painful because they make ignoble the high-sounding pretensions men employ when the time comes to declare or make war. If we are realistic, those words apply not only to our domestic spats but to the nations of the world.

It was General Douglas MacArthur who warned us in 1945:

"We have had our last chance. If we will not devise some greater and more equitable system, Armageddon will be at the door. The problem basically is theological and involves a spiritual recrudescence and improvement of the human character that will synchronize with our almost matchless advances in science, art, literature, and all material and cultural developments of the past 2000 years. It must be the spirit if we are to save the flesh."[5]

More than a generation has passed since he uttered those words, and as of this writing, no detectable improvement of the human character has been reported. Armageddon is knocking at the door, loudly.

The bulletin of atomic scientists' "Doomsday Clock"—a symbolic expression of urgency—is set at three minutes till midnight. Five years ago it was seven minutes away from nuclear holocaust.[6]

Richard Garwyn, a physicist, conservative, and consultant to the Department of Defense for thirty years, believes escalating Soviet/U.S. tension indicates a 50 percent chance of nuclear war before the end of the century.

There is no question about it. Everyone is rushing like madmen to get in on the action. The most amazing thing about it is that it has all come into existence in the last forty years, and now 115 nations are racing to build atomic bombs. For what?

Barry Maguire wrote a song in 1967 that describes for what: "The Eve of Destruction."

You may feel like you are on "the eve of destruction," and perhaps you are facing a personal Armageddon right now, in your marriage, your job, with your children, or even in yourself. Perhaps you are near to being overcome by anger, rage, frustration, hostility, or fear because you don't know Jesus Christ.

Jesus of Nazareth has good news for you! He is standing at the door of your heart and knocking. If you'll hear Him and open the door, He will come into your life right now (see Rev. 3:20).

VII

Dungeons and Dragons

"Our culture is breaking down, and if any confirmation is needed, go to the films, read the books of today, walk around a modern art gallery, listen to the music of our times."

—H.R. Rookmaaker

POLICE FEAR CULT KILLED SEVENTY-FIVE

"Animal bones and a twelve-foot cross were unearthed Thursday by sheriff's deputies tracking down reports over several months of up to seventy-five ritual killings of humans by a satanic cult. Lucas County Sheriff James A. Telb ordered the search fearing that more killings could occur this weekend since the slayings supposedly mark the cult's observance of changing seasons.

"The digging in abandoned shacks and fields also yielded a headless doll wearing an armband with the satanic symbol, two-inch faces, a knife, and hypodermic needles. The excavation to continue today was prompted by tips by three residents that cult meetings involving human sacrifices occurred in nearby fields."[1]

This incredible article appeared in most of the major U.S. newspapers only a few months ago. As I recall that article and write these words, I turn my head to the left with tears streaming down my cheeks. I behold two photographs. One photograph is of a lovely young lady, attractive, with bright eyes shining happily. The other is of a haggard woman with tatoos. Her sullen expression reveals a person bound in darkness, shackled by chains of deeply evil things. Once this haggard woman showed up at my front door with a suitcase full of books. She insisted I look at them. The first one I looked at was called *The Everlasting Gospel,* but it was very different from the gospel with which I was fa-

miliar. The first chapter gave instructions on how to become
Jesus Christ. Another chapter was devoted to similar instructions
on how to become God.

The other books in that suitcase were about things like reincarnation, extrasensory perception, magic, spiritualism, transcendental meditation, mind control, and psychic phenomena. The
haggard woman's name was Sherry. She practiced witchcraft and
had become so proficient over a period of twenty years that she
had begun to teach others.

Sherry firmly believed that she had lived six previous lives.
Only a week before coming to my door she had called her sister
to tell her she was getting married. "He's the same man I was
married to in my six former lives," she explained matter-of-factly.
"I am at perfect peace about this marriage because I am from the
planet Venus. I know what real love is because I have had sex
with Jesus Christ Himself."

Her sister was appalled and worried for Sherry's sanity. She
called me to report the conversation and commented frantically,
"Mike, this is wild! This is like something out of *The Exorcist!* I
don't understand much of what she was saying, but one thing I
know: that wasn't Sherry, not the Sherry I know, talking to me on
the phone. Mike, is it possible? Do demons really get into people
and take them over like that?"

I assured her that it was possible, and that very likely that was
what had happened to Sherry.

"What can be done!?"

"A lot," I answered. "Jesus died and rose again to break the
power of demons. Sherry can be set free in Jesus' name. In fact,
we can already see signs that God is working in Sherry's life."

Sherry's brother, Bobby, spent eleven hours straight praying
over her. As he prayed, the Holy Spirit gave him insight and dis-
cernment. Using those gifts, he would address the demons that
were living in Sherry and command them to come out of her. Ten
came out of her one by one, screaming horribly. It was like something from another world.

Bobby was well equipped to deal with such alarming phenomena because he had participated in many of the same sorts of
things Sherry was doing. In fact, years before, when Bobby had

been so involved in occultism, it seemed that he would call me at least two to three times a month reporting that demons were crying, through him, "Bless you, Lucifer." He was tormented to the point of attempting suicide many times.

I had prayed over Bobby in much the same way he later prayed over Sherry, and with much the same results. In the name of King Jesus I had cast seven demons out of him. After that Bobby was never tormented again. Instead, he turned his life over to Jesus. Now God's peace rules his life.

I keep Sherry's two pictures to remind me of the power of Jesus. I also keep them because she is my sister. We are only a year apart. For the first seventeen years of my life, Sherry was closer to me than any other person on earth. Because of my closeness to Sherry and Bobby, I have experienced the battle between darkness and light in a way that will never allow me to doubt it again.

Reflecting on this bizarre story makes me more grateful that the Lord Jesus revealed Himself to me when I was only eleven years old. He changed my life entirely. Twenty years have elapsed between the night I met him and the night I sit writing this. Throughout those years I have enjoyed, in the face of some hard trials and Bobby's and Sherry's cruel bondages, the peace of God which is far beyond human understanding and which has always kept my heart and mind safe in union with the Messiah, Jesus (see Phil. 4:7).

Dungeons and Dragons

Occultism is a term that refers to a large range of beliefs and practices involving magic or forces beyond the natural realm. It includes astrology, fortunetelling, magic, and spiritualism. The term *occult* means hidden or secret. People who believe in occultism regard it as based on hidden knowledge that ordinary people do not possess.

On the day before Halloween, 1985, "Good Morning, America" had a special report on Detroit. A night is celebrated called "Devil's Night" and on that night before Halloween, they reported over two hundred fires throughout the city as some individuals absolutely went insane setting fire to buildings. But as amazing as it might sound, only thirty days before, *Newsweek* had reported:

Ten-year-old Michael Nokes told it—he and twenty other children from Bakersfield, California, were taken to the "bad church" by forty adults who disrobed and encircled them while chanting prayers to Satan. A black-robed leader called: "Arise, devil, and worship us so we may worship you." Michael said he and a little girl were than forced to throw knives at "Baby Jonathan," and soon Michael's parents and their friends joined in. "Baby Jonathan cried," said Michael. "Once all the knives were thrown by the adults, Jonathan's head looked like the ring that was around Jesus' head." The adults then dismembered the baby's body, Michael said, and forced the kids to drink his blood. Finally, the adults allegedly began to molest the children, beginning with their own kids....In Mendocino County, near San Francisco, several children claim they were forced to chant, "Baby Jesus is dead," before being raped at a preschool. In Pico Rivera, an East Los Angeles suburb, twelve boys charged they were sodomized by four male neighbors during Satanist rituals.[2]

Although many scientists have rejected occult practices as outlandish and unscientific, in recent years we have seen researchers in some of our major universities lending new respectability to occultism by establishing centers or departments for paranormal studies. I can't say whether the stories from *Newsweek* are true, but they do prove that the topic has come out of the closet.

Belief in occultism is most often found in remote or isolated areas in nonindustrial societies. At least that's the way it used to be, but since the midpoint of this century, at roughly the same time that Israel was reestablished as a political state, there has been a widespread revival of occultism throughout the Western world. This is another sign that tells us clearly that the return of Christ to establish His kingdom is at hand. Let me explain why.

Biblical scholars trace the origin of occultism to Satan's being cast out of heaven. In his perversion of the earth, there is a very special example of a man named Nimrod, "the world's first great conqueror...At first his kingdom included Babylon, Erech, Accad—all three of them in Babylonia. From that land he went to Assyria and built the cities of Nineveh, Rehoboth Ir, Calah, and Resen" (Gen. 10:8–12, selected TEV). Babylon is the name of Satan's kingdom on earth in the book of Revelation, at least partly because the whole realm of occultism seems to have emerged and developed from ancient Babylon. They were the original soothsayers, magicians, necromancers, astrologers, and clairvoyants.

And from very early on, God gave special warning to His people about those who practiced the dark arts. They were, he said, an abomination to him (see Deut. 18:9–13). That meant they were particularly loathsome to him, more so than most of the evil practices of mankind. These practices were and are most closely linked to Satan. Their whole design and purpose is to lure men, women, and children away from the one true God and to bring them into union with the devil.

Other sins, like theft, false witness, murder, covetousness, and sabbath breaking, were grievous enough to warrant the death penalty under the law. They owed their origin to human perversity alone. The seemingly harmless practices of occultism, on the other hand, owed their origin in a peculiar sense to the prince of darkness. Through these practices he beckons and lures the unsuspecting into his clutches. We read the sobering words near the very end of the Bible that tell us that, at the end, those excluded from the heavenly city will be "sorcerers and sexually immoral and murderers and idolators, and whoever loves and practices a lie" (Rev. 22:15).

An Angel of Light?

One day I was sitting in a restaurant with Carolyn having lunch. Two charming little girls—I guessed their ages at around ten—came by. When we smiled at them, their expressions brightened. "I'm a Leo," announced one of the children.

I must have looked very puzzled because the second little girl quickly responded without Carolyn's or my having to say anything. "Yes, and I'm a Gemini. Those are our signs under the zodiac. You see, in astrology, we learn that the heavenly bodies influence our lives and everything that happens. You can learn a lot about yourself and how your life will be by having a horoscope cast for you. It shows the position of the planets in relation to the earth and the stars when you were born.

"My sign, Gemini, is symbolized by twins. It is ruled by the planet Mercury. Mercury was the messenger, and Geminis make good teachers or salespeople; sometimes they are good writers and work for magazines and newspapers, or they can be politicians. There're two sides to a Gemini. We change moods fast, and we can usually see both sides of an argument."

Her discourse went on a while longer. When she was winding down, I asked her a question. "Do you know Jesus?"

"Oh, yes!" they both responded. "We received our signs from Jesus. Astrology is from God—the Bible says so."

"Did you read that in the Bible for yourselves?" I asked them.

"Well, not exactly, but that's what the lady who cast our charts told us."

"Well," I tried to speak very gently, "sometimes people think something is in the Bible because they've heard other people say so. It's that way with you, and it is also that way with the lady who told you that. Would you like to know what the Bible really says?"

The little girls nodded.

"The Bible says that all the magical arts, including those that seek information from the stars, are demonic."

"Really?" little Carol was impressed.

"Yes," I said. "Tell me when you met Jesus."

"Well, we're Christians. Our families are Christian, you know."

"But you can't tell me about a time when you know you met Jesus personally?"

Both the girls lowered their heads a little.

"Well, then," I said, "let me ask you another question. Did either of you ever turn into a car by standing around in a garage?"

They giggled, "No!"

"Just so," I smiled, "you can't become a Christian by being in a certain family or having certain parents. Each of us has to make a personal decision to ask Jesus to come and be the Lord of our lives.

"Do you believe that the Bible is the Word of God?" I asked.

"Yes, we do," they said.

"Well, here, I'm writing down a passage for you to look up in your own Bibles. It tells us that a thing called *divination* or "observing the times" is wrong. *Divination* means trying to find out something, especially about the future. Astrology is one way of performing divination, and it has especially to do with observing the times, don't you think?"

"Well, it sure is about where the planets are at a particular time," Carol answered.

"That's right," I said. "So, when you go home and read that for yourselves in your own Bibles, do you know what you should do?"

"No, what?"

"Well, if you see that it's something God doesn't want His people doing, then just pray and tell God you're sorry. He knows you didn't know. And He'll forgive you through the blood of Jesus. Then throw away your horoscopes and other stuff, and get several Christians to pray with you that the power of Satan will be broken along with the curses associated with these things."

After I jotted some more notes for them on some cards, little Carol and Sandy went their ways. I turned to Carolyn as soon as they were out of earshot. "Isn't it amazing? Millions of Americans are just like them, aren't they?"

Carolyn nodded, "It's scary to see little kids like those two, completely deceived. They don't realize that the power of Satan is real and strong."

After that Carolyn and I recalled the humorous story of a man by the name of Sherman Reynolds we had led to Christ. Sherman was an ex-convict who had served time in San Quentin, California.

We remembered the time Sherman had been giving his testimony to a group of gang members who called themselves "Hell's Angels." As he was sharing, one of them began cursing him. Sherman lost his temper and yanked the guy out the window. All of a sudden, Sherman realized what he was doing and apologized. "Mister," he said, "I'm sorry for losing my temper. I was just about to kick your face in on the sidewalk when I realized that

God has forgiven me, and I need to forgive you for what you just said. You see, in my past, I was so filled with anger and hatred that I would have killed you for no better reason than looking at me. That's how full of darkness I was, but now I am filled with the light of Jesus. His peace, love, and joy rule my life." Those gang members were so touched that the whole group of them came to the meeting that night, and several came to the altar to accept Jesus Christ.

Sherman's story also brings to mind that of Tommy Rawlings. Tommy was the former Grand Imperial Wizard of the Ku Klux Klan. I invited him to give his testimony at one of my crusades. That night both he and Cheryl Pruitt, a former Miss America, sat on the platform, she to sing and he to talk. That crusade was attended, as all my crusades are, by people from all walks of life. Tommy Rawlings stood before them to confess that his former life of racial hatred and bigotry had resulted from his deception by and enslavement to demonic powers. He had called out to Jesus who had touched him and set him free. Then he told his audience, "God loves each one of you, and so do I! All the hatred is gone from my heart. It left with the darkness that was driven out by the light of Christ."

God has the power to do the same great things in your life if you will let Him!

Selling Satan's Wares

In 1983, a writer in *U.S. News & World Report* commented that "even in an age of science and reason, a surprising number of Americans still are willing to spend money to learn the secrets of their 'psychic souls.' "[3] With its emphasis on things supernatural or paranormal, the occult is big business. People from all walks of life are paying top dollar to consult with readers, seers, and other self-proclaimed visionaries. Millions are spent on movies, books, magazines, and cassettes that which deal with these subjects: alchemy, astrology, clairvoyance, divination, ectoplasm, extrasensory perception, fortunetelling, graphology, hypnotism, magic, mind reading, numerology, Ouija boards, palmistry, parapsychology, phrenology, psychical research, spiritualism, superstition, telepathy, and witchcraft.

Conventions and lectures about these sorts of things are constantly available. I even heard of one that purported to deal with "vampirology." Don't bother to look that one up in the dictionary. It's not there. The proper word is *vampirism*, but I suspect the speaker wanted to sound more scholarly than that term would have allowed him to sound.

Spurring all this interest are some six hundred thousand practitioners of the occult. Many of their followers are sincere people for whom occultism amounts to a religion or a body of knowledge that will eventually be proved correct through scientific procedures. Efforts to debunk these practitioners are numerous, backed by clear reasonable evidence; but they fall on deaf ears among the Americans who are daily flocking to the doors of palm readers and other consultants. Psychologists suggest that we do this because we're afraid of dying, or because we've had some eerie experience like a premonition that something was going to happen that did, indeed, happen. Another motivating factor is the widespread treatment of these topics, especially in their more violent and sensational forms, in books and films.

Thirty million readers regularly consult horoscopes printed in their daily newspapers. For more detailed and personalized service, about ten thousand astrologers are available for fees ranging from thirty dollars to whatever the market will bear. They will cast a horoscope for a client and then offer advice based on it regarding important decisions. Many professional astrologers see as many as thirty-five clients a week.

New York stock analyst Arch Crawford began his career using conventional means, but later he switched to astrology. It is a basis for his newsletter for which subscribers pay $250 a year. He consults individually for an annual fee of $2,500 and receives $3,000 for a lecture.[4]

Computer enthusiasts have an array of astrological programs to choose from, one or more of which will be usable on their home or business computer. The Astrion System 80 is a portable computer dedicated to casting horoscopes. Digicomp Research of Ithaca, New York, manufactures and distributes them.

Shirley Ann Tabatneck directs the Psychic Fair Network which conducts fairs in shopping malls. She has about three hundred psychics on her staff who charge shoppers ten dollars for a fifteen-minute session. Spiritualist camps across the country bus clients in for a vacation weekend devoted to seances and demonstrations of other psychic phenomena.

The big names, Jeane Dixon and an Israeli named Uri Geller, reportedly have earned millions. Dixon is basically a fortuneteller who sometimes uses a crystal ball. Geller claims to control objects with his mind.

Laurie Cabot was named the official witch of Salem, Massachusetts. Cabot actively practices witchcraft. She's a member of the chamber of commerce and earns a healthy income teaching classes, giving lectures, counseling, doing a daily radio show, and casting "good" spells for corporations.

Children for Sale

The important thing to notice about the visible occultism of American commerce is the innocent, light hearted ambiance that accompanies it. People with nonspecific religious sentiments would find little, if anything, to offend them in the things I've just recounted, but we may be sure that the face of occultism belies its heart. There is a dark side to the occult that can only be ignored at our peril.

One of the occult practices most commonly mentioned in the Bible had to do with the sacrifice of children to the god Moloch. The practice was called making one's children pass through the fire (see Lev. 18:21; 2 Kings 23:10; Jer. 32:35). Human sacrifice was practiced by the Moabites, the Ammonites, the Assyrians, and a number of the other nations of the ancient Middle East. Its most hideous form involved roasting infants alive above flames leaping up from the lap of Moloch's image.

The Hebrew prophet Zephaniah associated Moloch worship with the cult of the host of heaven or astrology (see Zeph. 1:5). Neither he nor any other biblical author explains how or why this association is made. In light of that biblical association, it is uncanny to trace the emergence of pornography and child abuse with the rise of occult practices since the end of World War II. I believe this revival has served to provide an atmosphere in which pornography has flourished; and pornography has in turn spawned a flood of cruel and wicked violence that, in the end, is visited on defenseless women and children.

Calendar Girls

After World War II the calendar girls whose partially clad bodies had graced the back rooms of service stations and machine shops gave way to the centerfolds of *Playboy*. From there things moved rapidly downhill. *Penthouse, Hustler,* and *Screw* each came in their turn. We began to behold new levels of gynecological accuracy in those full-color photos. Furor rose and furor faded. Eventually they were safely ensconced on our neighborhood newsstands, part of the accepted scene.

But once that had happened, a vacuum was created just beyond the outer limits of what society considered acceptable. So, in a sociological rendition of the second law of thermodynamics, the producers started coming up with increasingly outrageous stuff: hardcore porn, x-rated movies with lots of close-up shots of sexual intercourse between men and women (magazines followed suit). Next came group sex, oral sex, anal sex, homosexual sex, sex with pregnant women, sex with crippled women, sex with animals, child pornography, and sadomasochism. In this last category we find a series of increasingly bizarre subcategories: black women bound and struggling against their tormentors; Asian women bound and hung from various objects; and white men bound and masked, typically with an unpleasant contraption attached to their genitals.

In sadomasochism especially, but in all categories of pornography we find, according to a report by UCLA psychology professor Neil Malamuth, "the eroticization of violence." His study found that viewers were more often aroused by depictions of sex with violence rather than without it.

This pornographic violence includes rape, beatings, whippings, dismemberment, and the "snuff" movies, which involve the murder of one or more of the film's subjects. According to a *Newsweek* report, these murders, "as best as can be determined," are simulated. Maybe, maybe not.[5]

But even these obscenities give indication of achieving acceptance. Fashion magazines feature ads with models striking each other or using sadomasochistic props like a whip. Rock videos, especially on cable TV, depict fantasies in which women and men are caged or chained. "Even the otherwise wholesome Jacksons perform their hit tune 'Torture' in a video that features a masked dominatrix flailing her whip."[6]

A Plague of Immorality and Disease

Don't tell me that Matthew 24 isn't knocking at the door! In verse 12 of that chapter, it declares that a sign of the Lord's return will be the coldness of people's hearts. One hundred years ago, the divorce rate was less than one out of every three hundred. Twenty years ago, people were alarmed because it was one out of every thirty. At the present time, it is one out of every two, and futurists say that if this continues, it will be perfectly natural and normal for the average couple to be divorced many times during their lifetime. Marriage contracts will be changed with options to renew and other special clauses in them, as if you were speculating on a piece of real estate.

Dr. Edward Cornish, editor of *The Futurist* magazine puts it this way: "In the future, we can see the family disappearing. We can hear people saying, 'Look here! We don't have to live in families. If you want to live with someone, that's fine, but let's not call it a family. We can have children brought up in test tubes, raised by the state. There is no need to have them raised by the family.' "

The Assistant U.S. Attorney General has said: "We know, statistically, that 20 percent of all murders are family-related, and one-third of female homicides are committed by their husbands or partners. We know that reported cases of child abuse have doubled from 1976 to 1981—they have escalated almost 400 percent by 1984. Yet, over 50 percent of crimes of this nature are not being reported because of people not wanting to get involved."

These startling words are coming out of the mouths of experts in every field.

Senator Jesse Helms recently told me in an interview, "Divorce rate, teen-age suicide, spread of herpes, AIDS, sexual-related murders, runaways, the assault on children—all of this is being encouraged through pornographic literature and movies. Their slogan is becoming commonplace—'If you don't have sex by eight, it's too late.' So, I believe these are alarming and appalling indications that we have a very serious problem in the United States."

I know that Jesse Helms is right. And I believe these social problems are indicators that we are definitely on a countdown, a prophetic countdown.

I recently read a report on *chlamydia*. I had never heard of it before, and I am sure the average, sheltered American has not either. However, there are thirty million Americans who have heard of it, better than 10 percent of the population. You see, it is being coined "the sexual disease of the decade." According to the Centers for Disease Control in Atlanta, this new sexually-transmitted disease can result in anything from cervicitis (an inflammation of the cervix) to pelvic inflammatory disease (which scars the fallopian tubes and can lead to abnormal pregnancies). It can also give rise to rectal and throat infections in both sexes and Reiters Syndrome (arthritis involving the eyes, skin, and mouth lesions in men). Mothers can transmit this disease to their newborns, and it is the most common cause of pneumonia and conjunctivitis in babies under six months. Incorrectly labeling this condition as another venereal disease or as a yeast infection could eventually mean the end of a woman's fertility, warns Dr. Atila Toth, Associate Professor of Obstetrics and Gynecology at the New York Hospital Cornell Medical Center.[7]

Dr. Toth estimates that at least 25 percent of all infertility causes can be attributed to chlamydia, which is code named STDs.

But perhaps immorality doesn't have just physical effects. Suicide, especially among teens, has become a serious public health problem in the U.S., to the point that the Federal Center for Disease Control has reported the suicide rate among white male teen-agers rose 60 percent between 1970 and 1980 and is continuing to increase. The past years, the victim may have been your uncle or your father; now it is your son, according to CDC epidemiologist Mark Rosenberg.

Don't think for a moment that professing Christians have been exempt from this plague of immorality. Recently an evangelist friend told me that he had received a letter from a young teen-age couple who wanted him to know that they believed the Bible and would never violate its principles regarding fornication. Therefore, to meet their sexual needs, they were having oral sex. They were only asking the evangelist for prayer that they would not go any further than that because they would not want to do anything that would anger God.

That letter might seem like an isolated case, but sadly it is not. People are confused. Though knowledge has increased, mankind is degenerating to a state worse than animals.

A License Never Allowed to Sodom and Gomorrah

As the *Newsweek* writers aptly put it: "virtually any adult American has a license the Lord never allowed the citizens of Sodom and Gomorrah." The shameful fact is that a significant number of respectable middle-class Americans are pornography consumers. This widespread toleration of pornography has opened the floodgates of child pornography, molestation, and abuse. The notorious McMartin Preschool case in Southern California is but the tip of a monstrous iceberg. At the bottom of that iceberg is the congealed blood of the millions of aborted fetuses whose deaths have polluted our national soul.

The truth is that just as an unbelievably high number of American women suffer physical abuse, so many more youngsters than we would care to think are regularly abused in our society, physically and sexually. About half the homes in America have been touched by divorce and at least experienced single parenthood for a season. With the departure of one of the original parents from the home, the potential for abuse increases dramatically by a depressed parent, a visiting boyfriend resentful of offspring who represent solid evidence of his new lover's former sexual activity with someone else, or a stepparent with similar sentiments.

Our juvenile institutions are more crowded than ever before in spite of the fact that the percentage of our population under the age of twenty-five, the postwar baby boom generation, has begun to move into adulthood and early midlife. A large percentage of the youngsters in our juvenile jails got there after a court was compelled to remove them from a home where they were being abused, often sexually. This separation from an abusive home, however, often only opens the door for angry behavior in a youngster that eventually lands him or her in jail.

The way our society treats its children does not compare favorably with the way children were sacrificed to the god Moloch in ancient Moab. Our nation has made pornography into a multimillion-dollar-a-year business. We are sacrificing human beings on a much more tawdry altar than our ancient predecessors.

The Permissive Pathway of Deception

Things promise only to get worse. A law of human behavior is that repeated abuse—as, for example, of alcohol—makes it increasingly difficult for the user to achieve the desired effect. In the case of pornography, producers find that they have supply their audiences with ever-new thrills lest boredom set in.

Peter McGrath, writing in the *Newsweek* issue on pornography, cites the work of French sociologist Emile Durkheim to help explain this obvious point. In 1893 Durkheim published *The Division of Labor*, in which he asserted that crime was an integral part of all societies because it swerved to unify and create solidarity among the members of the community. "We have only to notice what happens, particularly," wrote Durkheim, "in a small town, when some moral scandal has just been committed ....[People] stop each other on the street, they visit each other, they...wax indignant in common. From all the similar impressions which are exchanged, for all the temper that gets itself expressed, there emerges a unique temper...which is everybody's without being anybody's in particular. This is the public temper."

So, in spite of how it seems to fly in the face of common sense, deviant behavior promotes solidarity. It helps everyone see the outer boundaries that define the community's identity. It is a rare human being who can live successfully without boundaries, and certainly children and animals have to have them clearly defined at all times.

Another sociologist, Kai T. Erikson of Yale, explains that these "boundaries remain a meaningful point of reference only so long as they are repeatedly tested by persons on the fringes of the group and repeatedly defended."[8] That means that it doesn't matter where a society draws the line and says, "We absolutely will not tolerate this." Somebody will step over the line to test the resolution of its drawers (every parent is familiar with this procedure).

This shows the strong delusion our society has been under for more than a century. It is the delusion that by being permissive we can achieve peace and quiet because everybody will have what they want. So, we have become more permissive with our children, and what is the result? They force us to draw the line somewhere by going to greater and greater extremes of behavior, dress, and grooming. Peace and quiet move further from our reach than ever before because true peace and quiet is the result of drawing the line right where God's word says it ought to be and then contending for it without compromise.

A Nation Snared in Ambivalence

To accompany their article on the war against pornography the staff of *Newsweek* had a poll conducted. Two of the questions in the poll were identical to a Gallup poll conducted in 1977. The first of these two asked people to say if they thought there ought to be a national standard, a community standard, or no standard for determining whether a publication or a movie is obscene. Forty-seven percent of those asked opted for a national standard (as compared to 45 percent in 1977); 43 percent voted for a community standard (up from 39 percent in 1977); only 5 percent voted for no standard (down from 9 percent); those who didn't have an opinion also numbered 5 percent (down from 7 percent).

The second question asked if present community standards regarding the sale of sexually explicit material should be made stricter, less strict, or kept the same. In 1977 the largest group (45 percent) wanted them stricter, but in 1985, the largest group (48 percent) wanted them kept as they were.

Clear majorities for banning pornographic publications and

productions were achieved only in the case of materials that depicted violence. Other questions demonstrated that a majority of Americans want to have x-rated material available to view on their home video players. Arthur Morowitz, president of New York's Video Shack chain, says, "When people buy their tape deck, they buy a kiddie movie for their child and an x-rated movie for themselves. It's the standard starter kit." *Newsweek*'s poll showed the 40 percent of all Americans who own a VCR (video cassette recorder) had bought or rented an x-rated cassette during the previous year.

When Peter McGrath finished his analysis of how pornographers test the outer limits of our morality, he wrote:

> As the *Newsweek* poll shows, Americans are ambivalent about pornography. They want access to conventional erotica while suppressing more extreme forms. But there is no going back: the law's acceptance of a hard core that now seems mild made room in the legal shadows for more brutal forms. We *can* refuse to go forward, however. Any outright embrace of those more brutal forms would create a new vacuum on the other side of the borderline—to be filled by material most of us cannot even imagine.[9]

McGrath's analysis is fatally flawed. The poll tells him there is no going back because Americans in vast numbers want porn in their homes. I do not dispute the poll. In fact I'm sure that things are worse than it says. One time a group of overweight people was asked to keep an hourly record of the food that each one ate for two weeks. Then they were placed in confinement for two weeks and fed exactly what they had recorded during the previous two weeks. If their list mentioned a Coke and a burger at three o'clock on Wednesday afternoon, they got exactly that exactly then. Midnight snacks, doughnuts at coffee break—nothing was omitted. Without exception they all lost weight because there was a significant difference between what they wrote down and what had truly passed their lips.

The people who answered the *Newsweek* poll were, I am certain, doing the same thing. For example, only 37 percent admitted to buying or reading magazines like *Playboy,* and a bare 13 percent confessed to reading magazines like *Hustler*. Nine percent said they had rented or purchased an x-rated screen production during the previous year (that's how they calculated that 40 percent of VCR owners did it). I think the true figure is closer to 60 percent.

The flaw in McGrath's argument is in his saying that we can refuse to go forward. How can we refuse to go any further? He doesn't say. He only says that, if we don't, it will be awful. But that's not enough. The pattern of permissiveness and compromise in American society, in all of Western civilization, is set in concrete. The *Newsweek* staff who wrote the main feature article, "The War Against Pornography," concluded it by expressing the hope that their act of having aired the fear and pain of the victims of pornography might "help change the hearts, minds, and habits of a nation that sometimes seems to have lost its shame."

Darkness and Light

When the apostle John had finished recording the things he had heard and seen, an angel told him, "Do not seal the words of prophecy of this book, for the time is at hand. This will happen. He who is unjust, let him be unjust still; he who is filthy, let him be filthy still; he who is righteous, let him be righteous still; he who is holy, let him be holy still" (Rev. 22:10–11).

These are hard words to understand. They do not mean that repentance is useless, but they do point to the inevitability of cultural decline in the last days before the return. Only after we have heard the announcement that the time has arrived for God to judge mankind will we also hear the announcement that goes with that: "She has fallen! Great Babylon has fallen! She made all people drink her wine—the strong wine of her immoral lust!" (Rev. 14:8 TEV).

Nothing short of the power of Almighty God can set the captives free! As I am writing these words, I just put down the receiver from talking with a young lady who told me that for twenty years she has been in and out of mental institutions. She has seen a great number of psychiatrists. She has tried every drug conceivable, every demonic new revelation. She has been involved in every cause imaginable, including attempting to go to Nicaragua to be a freedom fighter.

She called me from a halfway house, having just been released from a mental institution, bound by darkness and demonic powers. She asked me about the possibility of her trying a new form of psychiatry. She said that those who had been treating her diagnosed her as hopeless and recommended institutionalizing her for the remainder of her life.

Psychiatrists have diagnosed hundreds of different things wrong with her; however, they offer no solution.

I told the young lady that her biggest problem was fear. I began reading Scriptures:

> God has not given us a spirit of fear, but of power and of love and of a sound mind (2 Tim. 1:7).

> The LORD is my light and my salvation;
> Whom shall I fear?
> The LORD is the strength of my life;
> Of whom shall I be afraid?...
> Though an army shall encamp against me,
> My heart shall not fear;
> Though war should rise against me,
> In this I will be confident (Ps. 27:1, 3).

As I was reading these Scriptures to her and sharing that the Lord Jesus could set her free from her fear, bondage, and torment, she began cursing and saying that she was not interested in it. She didn't want to be a religious fanatic. The words of matthew 24 rolled through my mind: "...what will be the sign of Your coming, and of the end of the age?...many will come in My name...and deceive many....And then many will be offended, will betray one another, and will hate one another."

What deception! Too long have we sucked at the breast of great Babylon, the mother of all prostitutes and perverts in the world, she who is drunk with the blood of God's people and the blood of those who were killed because they had been loyal to Jesus.

There is still time to break away from the arms of Babylon and find safety in the arms of Jesus. Thank God you can make your decision today to experience God's forgiveness, peace, and *total* deliverance from the powers of darkness.

VIII

False Prophets

"When a man ceases to believe in God, he does not believe in nothing. He believes in anything."

—G.K. Chesterton

Jesus said that one of the signs of His return to earth would be that "Many men, claiming to speak for me, will come and say, 'I am the Messiah!' and they will fool many people" (Matt. 24:5 TEV).

Some of the false messiahs are easier to spot than others. It was about two-thirty in the morning when I found myself walking the quiet streets of Jerusalem in the company of a good friend. My friend is a general in the IDF, Israel Defense Force, and he had invited me out for this unusual walk not long before.

We came to the western wall of the old temple grounds, the *Haram esh Sherif* to the Arabs. As we stood staring in the moonlight at the enormous building blocks that have withstood the torments of the two millennia since old Herod had them laid in place, I heard footsteps coming rapidly up behind us. My friend and I turned to see who it could be.

There before us he stood panting slightly. His eyes were like stars, something strange about them. Before we could say anything he blurted out, "Come with me. My master is the Messiah, the one for whom Israel has been waiting so long! He will restore the Temple. He will bring peace to the world. Quickly, come and meet the Messiah!"

My friend scolded him in Hebrew and he ran off. Then, my friend looked at me and shrugged his shoulders. "There's a new one every week, it seems. Somehow, they always attract at least a few followers."

It would require volumes just to list the names of the false messiahs who have come and gone in the last nineteen and a half centuries. Some are remembered, like Bar Kokhbah who led the great rebellion against Rome in the second century. It was from that insurrection that Masada gained its fame. Most are forgotten, like two men in Illinois in the late nineteenth century. One was named Schlatter and the other Schweinfurth. Each of them attracted a small following. If they have been forgotten, you might ask, how is it that I remembered their names? I didn't. I found them in a book, published in 1930, that mentioned them in passing.

In recent times the most memorable false messiahs seemed to have been those who attracted large followings that became cults of one form or another. Mary Baker Eddy (1821–1910), the founder of Christian Science, made claims about herself on a par with those of Jesus. Today there are about three thousand branches of the church she founded.

Neither Joseph Smith (1805–1844), the founder of the Mormons, nor Charles Taze Russell (1852–1916), the founder of the Jehovah's Witnesses, ever to my knowledge claimed to be the Messiah. But both men, like Mary Baker Eddy, can take credit for having led many people astray. Today Mormons number over 3.5 million; Jehovah's Witnesses, 619,188.[1]

Annie Besant (1847–1933) spent much of her life in India. She began her pilgrimage as an Anglican. From that she moved to atheism, thence to spiritualism, and finally to theosophy. She established educational institutions in India, including the Central Hindu College of Benares (1898) and the University of India (1907). Her greatest sensation came nearer to the end of her life, however, when she proclaimed that her adopted son, a spiritual mystic named Jidder Krishnamurti, was the new messiah. It was a claim he later repudiated. Nothing lasting came of it, but it does stand as a precursor to the popularity of gurus stemming from the time of the Beatles.[2]

In these waning years of the twentieth century, Hinduism has disguised itself as first one thing and then another—Transcendental Meditation, for example—and made significant inroads into American society. One guru or maharajah after another attracts a following, often with roots in Southern California. Carryings-on there and in Oregon have made the newscasts from time to time in recent years. These fellows and women qualify readily as false messiahs because Hindu doctrines of reincarnation and the like allow them to announce that they are Jesus or the Christ in ways that appear somehow innocuous. They serve mostly to lull any vestiges of Christian sentiment in their American converts.

In another vein, Jim Jones made a name for himself by leading nearly a thousand people into suicide in the backwoods of Guyana. Jones had started out as a sincere Christian, but his overactive libido led him into so many compromises with his conscience that it shipwrecked his faith. He started telling his people that he was God. Before too long, he had himself and them believing it.

Part of Jones's transition into false teaching was made with the help of Father Divine. By 1907 Divine had begun to claim that he was "God in the sonship degree." He left the South and moved into New York. His movement made rapid gains in the 1930s–40s as he spoke across the country and published his magazine, *The New Day*.

Jones went to him in the late 1950s to ask for advice about, among other things, how to handle the temptation of women who were making themselves increasingly available to him. Father Divine told him that he was serving the sisters well and ennobling their lives by having sex with them. Scruples about adultery were for men of lower stature, Divine assured him.

Father Divine ran a massive cooperative agency and employment service, providing low-cost meals and lodgings in his "heavens." He imposed an exceedingly strict moral code on his followers, but apparently not on himself. Today his white widow and heir, Mother Divine, leads over a million followers in the U.S. and elsewhere who worship Father Divine as god.

The Reverend Sun Myung Moon, founder and leader of the Unification Church, has attracted an enormous following. His roots are in Korean Christianity. But, at some point in his ministry, he began to announce that he was Jesus come back to earth. In 1984 he was jailed for tax evasion.

The point I want to make from all this is that deception is rampant. Jesus said, "for many will come in My name saying, 'I am Christ' " (Matt. 24:5). In the Greek of the original New Testament, the word for "I" was *ego*. Today we use that word in describing someone who has an inflated opinion of himself. The word Christ derives from the Greek for "anointed." Today, as I travel around, that's what I see a lot of: egos running around our nation proclaiming that the anointing is upon them and that people ought to follow them. But they are fakers who gain their followings by deception—the same deception that first led them astray themselves.

It is astonishing and appalling, but the Bible predicted it and it's happening. "The Spirit says clearly that some people will abandon the faith in later times; they will obey lying spirits and follow the teachings of demons. Such teachings are spread by deceitful liars whose consciences are dead, as if burnt with a hot iron" (1 Tim. 4:1, 2 TEV).

Proclaiming the Values of this Age

In 1982, *Reader's Digest* published an examination of the World Council of Churches. It said, "All in all, the Geneva-based ecumenical organization made clear its preference for social concerns over purely religious ones. It showed that its approach to solving the world's ills owes almost as much to Marxism as to Christianity."[3]

The World Council represents 400 million members of Christian churches. It was founded in 1948 in an endeavor to address the scandal of a fragmented church; but its increasingly aggressive involvement in politics and its financial support of violence have made it a source of division rather than unity in the church. As best as anyone can tell the quest for Christian unity ran head-on into unyielding doctrinal disputes between members.

In addition, the churchmen of the World Council found themselves so often under the scrutiny of the press that their agenda began to be shaped by the values of the secular journalists who were commenting freely about their activities. They wanted desperately to be applauded and to avoid being scoffed at. They quickly learned that to achieve those goals, they needed to appear socially relevant—clear-thinking and practical men free of the cloudy notions of religious sentiment. Piety was scorned in favor of an agenda of social programs.

Thus, when the WCC assembled in Nairobi, Kenya, in 1975, the podium resounded with militantly anti-Western sentiments. Michael Manley, then prime minister of Jamaica, was applauded enthusiastically when he called for people's democracies to take the place of the corrupt capitalist oligarchies of the Western nations. During the eighteen-day conference, the assembly (1) endorsed the WCC's program to combat racism by giving money to political organizations and guerrilla movements; (2) urged the creation of a program to challenge corporations accused of exploiting Third World nations; and (3) denounced South Africa for intervening in the civil war in Angola. With regard to this third item, the assembly passed over the Soviet-Cuban intervention in Angola, which had provoked South Africa's action in the first place, in silence.

The program to combat racism, mentioned above, subsequently gave $85,000 to the Patriotic Front for the Liberation of Zimbabwe, a Marxist guerrilla organization that was fighting to overthrow the white regime of Rhodesia (as it was then known). At the time of the grant, the Patriotic Front already had a bloody record. The deaths of nearly two thousand people, black and white, in Rhodesia were attributed to it. In 1978 troops of the Patriotic Front were responsible for the grisly slaughter of nine white missionaries and their families which included several young children.

By 1981 the World Council's program to combat racism had a budget of a million dollars. Half of that money went to guerrillas who were employing terrorist tactics to overthrow other white regimes in southern Africa.[4] Among them were:

1) The Soviet-backed MPLA of Angola
2) The Marxist FRELIMO of Mozambique
3) The Russian-funded and Cuban-trained SWAPA of Namibia
4) A number of groups in the Western Hemisphere with ties to

the Soviet Union, the IRA, and the PLO.

None of the money was dispatched to dissidents inside or near the Soviet Union. Marxist governments and Moscow in particular customarily receive only the kindest and gentlest treatment by the World Council.

What are we to think of that? Is it that the leaders of the World Council have received special grace to love their enemies in measures unheard of heretofore? Or should we think ill of them and suppose they are submitting to some kind of Soviet blackmail? Perhaps there is a private arrangement by which the delegates of the Russian Orthodox churches are permitted to attend and participate in World Council activities on the condition that the council express no criticism of the Soviet Union.

Whatever the answer to that question, the patience of two member groups of the World Council, the Salvation Army and the Irish Presbyterian Church, gave out. Both of them suspended their memberships in protest against the handling of the program to combat racism. One spokesperson called the grants "racism in reverse."

The World Council held another international assembly in Vancouver, British Columbia, Canada, in 1983. Representatives of 301 Protestant and Orthodox churches from around the globe decided: (1) to oppose vigorously any sort of military intervention, covert or overt, by any government; (2) to call for an end to the supply of arms to Afghan rebels who were fighting the Russians in their country; and (3) to label the deployment of nuclear weapons by any country as a crime against humanity.

In connection with number one above, the delegates accused the United States of trying to renew support for Guatemala's violent military regimes, of trying to resist the forces of historic change in El Salvador, and of trying to militarize Honduras. In connection with number two, the delegates lamented the "tremendous suffering" of the people of Afghanistan, but they refused to attribute any of that suffering to the actions of the Soviet government or armed forces.

I have sadly concluded that the leaders of the World Council of Churches are deluded at best and guilty of treachery at worst. I would not want to be in their boots on the Day of Judgment.

Too many of our churches have sought so earnestly to be relevant that they have lost their balance and gotten themselves into the most awkward sort of situations. In one church the members who were homosexuals staged a demonstration during a worship service. Thirty-two of them stood to their feet and marched to the front of the church to assert their rights. When the entire group was assembled, some of the members of the congregation still had enough of a grasp on reality to be shocked by the sight, and especially by the fact that among the thirty-two stood several Sunday school teachers, two members of the choir, and one member of the pastoral staff.

If Jesus was affronted by the moneychangers in the temple, what must He have thought of the leaders of that church who permitted the flaunting of such sin? Homosexuality is neither an acceptable lifestyle nor is it a genetic necessity. It is perversion. It was the sin of Sodom and Gomorrah for which those cities received the torrent of fire and brimstone. It was part of the reason all Israel assembled at Mizpah and destroyed the inhabitants of Gibeah (see Judg. 19–20). The Mosaic code said, "If a man has sexual relations with another man, they have done a disgusting thing, and both shall be put to death. They are responsible for their own death" (Lev. 20:13 TEV). And the apostle Paul wrote, "Do not fool yourselves; people who are immoral or who worship idols or are adulterers or *homosexual perverts* or who steal or are greedy or are drunkards or who slander others or are thieves—none of these will possess God's Kingdom" (1 Cor. 6:2, 10 TEV, italics added).

What has happened to the church that it can overlook these sorts of clear testimonies? Time and again church boards and pastors are fully aware that a member of the congregation is cheating on his wife or his wife is cheating on him, yet they sit on their hands and do nothing, absolutely nothing. They don't even bring up the matter for prayer. I'm not talking about churches that are devoid of faith; I'm talking about churches where the Bible is honored as the Word of God and where the gospel is preached.

What has happened at the level of the World Council of Churches and at the congregational level and everywhere in between is that we have allowed ourselves to become conformed to the standards of this world. We no longer seem to have prophets who will cry out against the present darkness. Instead, like the World Council they seem to be a part of the darkness.

The age we live in is evil—always has been, always will be (see Gal. 1:4). Jesus calls His disciples to be in the world but not *of* it, to take a stance that places us over against the way things are. If anyone takes that call seriously, he or she will be subject to ridicule as a fanatic or worse. When Jesus promised blessing to those who were subject to insults, persecution, and the telling of all kinds of evil lies because they were following Him, He did it because that is exactly what will happen to anyone who follows Jesus with any measure of serious dedication. In fact, He said, "Woe be to you when all men speak well of you, for so did their fathers to the false prophets" (Luke 6:26). Has your walk with Jesus earned you no enemies, no ridicule? Beware.

What About Hell?

What has happened to preaching and teaching about judgment and hell? When was the last time you heard a sermon that mentioned either one?

Preachers invite their listeners to receive Jesus as their Lord and Savior for a number of reasons. He will make your life better, they say. He will fill you with joy. He will turn your light into darkness. He will heal your diseases and forgive your sins. He will make you prosperous. He will supply all your needs, comfort you in your sorrows, give you strength to face afflictions, and protect you from harm. The list is much longer, and all these things are true.

But how many preachers warn their listeners to flee from the wrath to come? John the Baptist actually had the nerve to challenge the Pharisees who came to him for baptism by saying, "Brood of vipers! Who has warned you to flee from the wrath to come?" (Matt. 3:7). Not very kind of Him, was it?

Or was it? Who loves the more? The one who holds back the truth for fear of offending his listeners and suffering their displeasure? Or the one who does not shrink from declaring the whole purpose of God, even if it does earn him some bruises?

Jesus said something once that often gets overlooked. He said, "But one thing is needed" (Luke 10:42). He said that to Martha after she complained that Mary was neglecting the housework to sit at Jesus' feet to listen to Him. But to boil down all the concerns and weights that life places on us by saying that only one thing is necessary was a radical thing to say. How can we understand it?

The answer to that is simple. All of life must be viewed in the light of eternity. The greatest reality is not what we see here in our solar system or on our planet. What happens here to any one of us encompasses only a few brief years. But what happens in those few brief years determines how we will spend eternity. That was the framework from which Jesus told Martha that just one thing was necessary.

We think of things as being necessary in terms of how intolerable things would be without them. For instance, without money we can't pay the mortgage or the rent. That faces us with the unpleasant possibility of being out on the street or perhaps living with having to accept the charity of a relative or friend. All of us will admit that there are worse things. Being without food long enough means you die. The absence of water shortens the process dramatically.

So, doesn't that make at least food and water necessary? After all, even the apostle Paul said that we ought to be content so long as we are provided with food and clothing. Yes, but God has been known to let His servants go naked. We should not doubt that Jesus hung naked on the cross in spite of the loin cloth with which numberless pious artists have bedecked him.

The key lies in the word *necessary*. As long as the maintenance of the biological existence we call life is the bottom line for us, then lots of things are necessary. But that was not the bottom line for Jesus or for Paul. Nor is it for any authentic follower of Jesus. They know that what the Bible calls *eternal life* is the only life that counts because it is the only indestructible form of life. With that perspective, only one thing is needful.

When Peter was preaching the gospel to the members of the Jewish council, he told them, with reference to Jesus, "Salvation is found in no one else, for there is no other name under heaven given to men by which we must be saved" (Acts 4:12 NIV). Why did He use the words "must be saved"? In normal usage we would say "by which we might be saved" or "could be saved." But once again we're faced with strong necessity. Salvation is not an option. It is the one thing that is necessary. Without it, all of life, both here and hereafter, is futile—completely devoid of meaning. Except for the meaning of hell.

Without salvation men and women are faced with the necessity of spending eternity in the flames of outer darkness where there is only, according to Jesus, weeping and gnashing of teeth. Now that is truly intolerable. Next to that, missing the rent is a breeze, missing a meal is of no consequence, going naked is entirely bearable, and facing death is a slight inconvenience.

> Then I saw a great white throne and the one who sits on it. Earth and heaven fled from his presence and were seen no more. And I saw the dead, great and small alike, standing before the throne. Books were opened, and then another book was opened, the book of the living. The dead were judged according to what they had done, as recorded in the books. Then the sea gave up its dead. Death and the world of the dead also gave up the dead they held. And all were judged according to what they had done. Then death and the world of the dead were thrown into the lake of fire. (This lake of fire is the second death.) Whoever did not have his name written in the book of the living was thrown into the lake of fire (Rev. 20:11–15 TEV).

This is a sobering message to anyone who reads it. Anyone who did not scoff at it would want to know how to assure that his or her name would be found, on that momentous day, in the book of the living. We get a hint of the answer in the remark that tells the lake of fire is the second death. The first death, of course, is the one we earthlings are familiar with. It happens to many people every day. We read about them in the obituary column of our newspapers. Someday our own names will join them there.

Making a special point to call one's being cast into the lake of fire the second death gives us a subtle signal to think about another "second" the Bible talks about—the second birth. Jesus told Nicodemus, "You *must* [there's that word again] be born again" (John 3:7, italics added). When Jesus had first mentioned this to him, Nicodemus asked how it could happen. Would a man have to reenter his mother's womb and start over a second time?

"I am telling you the truth," replied Jesus, "that no one can enter the Kingdom of God unless he is born of water and the Spirit. A person is born physically of human parents, but he is born spiritually of the Spirit" (John 3:5, 6 TEV). Jesus is talking about two births: one physical (of water) and one spiritual (of the Spirit). Today the phrase "born again" has made its way into popular usage in America. Almost everyone's heard about it and has a vague notion of what it means.

The point I want to raise in reciting this familiar story is that when John called the lake of fire the second death, the truth of the second birth was not far from his thinking. Whoever has experienced the second birth is exempt from the second death. Likewise, whoever has failed to experience the second birth will be subject to the second death. The assurance that one's name is written in the book of the living comes as part of the package with the second birth.

At the end of this book I'll explain very clearly and simply how to become born again.

Cheap Grace

Dietrich Bonhoeffer originated this phrase in his book *The Cost of Discipleship*. He argued that though the grace of God is given to us freely to forgive our sins, comfort our sorrows, and heal our wounds, it is not given cheaply. It was purchased at the infinite expense of the blood of Jesus. But the church has made so much of the fact that salvation is a gift from God that cannot be earned it has made conversion almost painless.[5]

Too often we have invited people to receive Jesus with no more intensity than if they were to receive a casual birthday gift. Simply pray and invite Jesus to come into your heart, we say. We mention none of the stern demands Jesus places on His followers. For example, we love to quote Jesus' words, "Do not fear, little flock, for it is your Father's good pleasure to give you the kingdom" (Luke 12:32). But we almost always fail to quote the words He said immediately after that: "Sell what you have and give alms; provide yourselves money bags which do not grow old, a treasure in the heavens that does not fail, where no thief approaches nor moth destroys. For where your treasure is, there your heart will be also" (Luke 12:33–34).

One of the greatest examples of that sort of living in this century was Corrie ten Boom, a little Dutch woman who, in company with her father and sister, harbored Jews in their home in Haarlem in the Netherlands during World War II. Many are familiar with her story through her book, *The Hiding Place.* The Nazis eventually found out what the ten Booms were doing and arrested them. Corrie's father and sister died in prison, but Corrie was spared. She was released from Ravensbruck concentration camp and spent the remaining thirty-odd years of her life as what she called "a tramp for the Lord." Her treasure was in heaven.

I once made a pilgrimage with my family to the ten Boom home in Haarlem. Downstairs in the little watch shop that the family once operated, I purchased a watch which I wear always as a memento of that day. Then we went upstairs and came, at last, to the top floor of the narrow building. There, in the back, was the secret hiding place where the Jews had gone each time the Nazis had come to inquire and search. The children and I actually crawled into the tiny compartment, and there I said a prayer. I asked God to make us all as brave and faithful as the ten Booms had been.

In this century alone, more believers in Jesus have suffered martyrdom than in all the previous centuries put together.[6] On every continent, in every nation, men and women have been deprived of life because of their testimony for Jesus.

Itching Ears

Paul wrote, "The time will come when people will not listen to sound doctrine, but will follow their own desires and will collect for themselves more and more teachers who will tell them what they are itching to hear" (2 Tim. 4:3 TEV). The time has come. At this very hour popular teachers and preachers are assuring the "faithful" that they can be good Christians and enjoy all, or nearly all, the pleasures the world has to offer. There are those who even teach that if you are not rolling in greenbacks, it's because you're not trusting God aright.

After emerging from a season of idealism and activism, America has entered upon a season of self-indulgence and pleasure-seeking. And they have found plenty of preachers who will cater to their tastes, giving them exactly what they want to hear. "God wants you to own an expensive car, an expensive home, and to wear the most expensive clothes. Nothing is too good for you because you are His child."

The Three Stooges

We live in a world of such foolishness, deception, and compromise that it has become the standard, the norm. My philosophy has always been that the shortest distance between two points is a straight line. Get to the point and express what you mean. It is the truth, and only the truth, that will set us free.

As I am writing this, I am thinking of three preachers. When I asked one of them, "What is your greatest goal in life?", he replied, "To live in a million-dollar home and have a Rolls-Royce."

Another preacher expressed to me that his goal was to live without stress and he is succeeding. He has gone years without one moment of stress.

The third, accusing me of being simplistic because I believe everything is either black and white, said, "Between black and white are all the colors of the rainbow. I don't believe that a person is either a saint or an 'ain't,' lost or found. I believe that the real beauty of God can be seen when we do not emphasize absolutes."

As far as I am concerned, these three preachers are three stooges, and God have mercy upon them if they don't repent! No wonder more people have hardened their hearts against the truths of Jesus Christ when they are taught such nonsense! But thank the Lord! The majority of preachers that I know preach the truth and live it.

Heaven help these "teachers" who are leading people into deception! The shame of it is that what they give the people only feels good for a while. It never quite soothes the ache that comes from having lived through the debacle of the Bay of Pigs, the horrors of Vietnam, the shame of Watergate, the humiliation of the Teheran embassy hostages, the frustration of hundreds of Marines dying at the hands of a fanatic in Beirut, and the day-after-day stress that living in the last days of this century brings on us all.

These people, we people, need to hear the truth. We need to find God's answers for our lives. We don't need the deception of accommodation and convenience. We don't need the temporary comfort that these teachers offer.

I'm not saying that God doesn't bless and show favor to His people. He does. But we are in danger of seeing only that and choosing to ignore His call on our lives. We need to make sure we get *all* the sin out.

I'll never forget the astonishment and pain I felt the day I was with a busload of pilgrims in the Holy Land. On that same bus was a man of some reputation who was a very wealthy Christian businessman and served on the boards of many organizations. This, of course, is a sign of a person's high character and godly wisdom having been demonstrated faithfully through the years.

I had not met him before that day, but I knew of him for the reasons I've just explained. So, as we rode along through the Israeli countryside, he suddenly cried out, very loudly, "My God, have mercy on me. I'm a homosexual!" I turned around to see his face buried in his hands, his body shaken by his sobs. Next to him his wife sat in stunned horror.

I did what I could to counsel him. As we talked I found that he had been practicing the sin he had named for a long time. What appalled me the most was that he had been so close to so many religious leaders, teachers, and preachers of the Word of God, and some of them had known about his problem with perversion, but they had evidently chosen to ignore it. These men should have stood as prophets of God to call this man to repentance.

Our leaders too often tolerate—yes, some even foster—hypocrisy within the church of God. I know one particularly wealthy businessman who has contributed generously to various churches and works of ministry across the land. The fact had so endeared him to various preachers and ministers that I had heard only wonderful things about him. He was, according to the reports that had come to my ears, a fine believer of unsurpassed piety and godliness.

You can imagine my chagrin when we met and spent some time talking. A little way into the conversation he said, "Mike, pray for me that God would take the love out of my heart for my wife, and that he would give me a vision for a new wife."

My jaw nearly hit the floor. After I collected my wits I said, "I rebuke you for saying that! You don't need a new wife, you need to repent. God hates divorce!"

I could tell by his response that he was not accustomed to having people contradict him. Later I learned that he had already divorced two wives. The one he was telling me about was his third, but he had claimed to be a devoted Christian all the while. The truth was that his money had made him a middle-aged spoiled brat. Once again I was troubled even more by the realization that so many leaders I knew simply ignored this man's dismal marital history and constant immorality and praised him to the skies as a model of godly living. He had paid them well and he had gotten what he wanted: self-indulgence with an untroubled conscience.

Idols

Our idols have snared us. We have not loved the Lord our God with all our hearts, souls, minds, or strengths. But we have dallied long before the idols of beauty, sexual pleasure, money, power, popularity, and security, to name but a few. And our idols have deceived us.

Perhaps looking at what happened to the church under Hitler will help us to get a perspective on ourselves today. First there were the German Christians who thoroughly supported the ecclesiastical policies of Hitler's regime. The nationalist and racist traditions of nineteenth-century German Protestantism achieved great prominence in the church, often by force, after Hitler came to power. At one extreme these traditions expressed themselves through those who made a pagan religion of German blood and destiny, hostile to traditional Christianity. On the other side were Christian theologians who believed God was calling the church to again be the church of the German people, freed from a dead and alien past. It was a nationalist exploitation of the old liberal theology that had rejected the Old Testament and the Jewish origins of Christianity.

When Hitler's agent for control of the church, Ludwig Mueller, was elected *Reichsbischof* in September of 1933, the Confessing Church began to emerge from such movements as Martin Niemoeller's Pastors' Emergency League and the free confessing synods. The Confessing Church opposed Mueller and erected a structure that helped discredit his regime. It did this by preventing the emergence of docile unity that Hitler was looking for in the churches, but doctrinal differences within the confessing church movement kept it from ever doing more. By 1936 it was too divided to offer effective resistance to the Nazi regime. Even the wing of the movement led by Niemoeller and Bonhoeffer (who was later implicated in the plot to assassinate Hitler and executed) was often inhibited in its criticism of the government by its own conservatism and nationalism and by the political ineptness of its leaders.

Niemoeller's League, formed in 1933, voiced opposition to the Nazi anti-Jewish laws. Niemoeller himself made a brave protest to Hitler in person, but without success. He was imprisoned in Dachau between 1937 and 1945.

The saddest aspect of this story is that, for the greatest part, those who call themselves "religious" in Germany acquiesced to the policies of the Nazi regime, and some, as we have seen, even applauded them. The voice of protest was thin at best. That this acquiescence was achieved through threats and use of violence does mitigate their indifference to the Jewish plight, but only slightly. God is their judge, and He is merciful, but I am glad not to have been in their shoes also.

We must learn a lesson from the church in Germany. We need to recognize the radical nature of the call of Jesus. We need to allow Him to open our eyes to our idolatries and self-indulgences that bloat us and make us deaf to His call in all but the most superficial ways. We need to listen afresh to these words of John:

> Do not love the world or anything that belongs to the world. If you love the world, you do not love the Father. Everything that belongs to the world—what the sinful self desires, what people see and want, and everything in this world that people are so proud of—none of this comes from the Father; it all comes from the world. The world and everything in it that people desire is passing away; but he who does the will of God lives forever (1 John 2:15–17).

If you are a person who proudly abstains from church attendance lest you have to brush shoulders with all those vile hypocrites, I have something to say to you. Sin is sin wherever you find it, in church or out of it, and wherever and however you practice your sin makes little difference. You'll go to hell for your pride just as quickly as the hypocrites will for their hypocrisy.

Surely hypocrisy will receive its special reward. Jesus told of those who would come to Him on Judgment Day and protest that they had cast out demons and performed many mighty works in His name. He assures us that their hypocrisy will nevertheless earn them this judgment, "Depart from Me, you who practice lawlessness" (Matt. 7:23).

Don't trouble yourself about the fate of hypocrites. No one gets away with anything for long when they are dealing with God. If you have tried to hide from God behind the assertion that the church contains hypocrites, stop it. You fool no one but yourself.

Stop and think about it. One of the greatest testimonies to the truth that Jesus is who He said He was, God with skin on, is the existence of so many counterfeits. If the American dollar were valueless, who would try to counterfeit it? If Jesus were only a pleasant myth of the past, why does the world abound with those who claim to be Him in some sense?

Consider this profile: nearly two thousand years ago lived a man who was born contrary to the laws of nature. He was reared in obscurity and was familiar with poverty. He never traveled far from His home. His family was full of insignificant people who lacked prestige and formal education.

When only an infant He troubled a king. As a young lad He puzzled scholars. In the prime of his manhood, people asked about Him, "who is this that even the wind and sea obey Him?" He healed multitudes of afflicted and diseased people, but never charged a cent for His services.

He never wrote a book, but the greatest library in the world could not begin to contain all the books written about Him. He never wrote a song, yet He has furnished the theme for more songs than any other person in history. He never founded a college, but no institution anywhere in the world could claim to have more students than He does. He never marshalled an army, but no other leader has ever brought so many rebels to their knees or taken as many captives. He never practiced psychiatry, but He has healed more twisted minds and broken hearts than all the psychiatrists put together.

The venerable statesmen of Greece and Rome, in whose time He lived, have come and gone. Today they are all but forgotten except by the historians and antiquarians. But Jesus stands as the focus of love, devotion, and worship of more people on earth than any other person who has ever lived. He is the radiant light of a world shrouded in the darkness of deception and sin. His return, which may happen soon, is the blessed and only hope of the entire planet. There is no other hope. He alone is the Prince of Peace, the Mighty Counselor, the Everlasting Father, the great I AM, the Rose of Sharon, the Lily of the Valley, the Bright and Morning Star, the fairest of ten thousand.

Our Lord has said: "I am the light of the world. He who follows Me shall not walk in darkness, but have the light of life" (John 8:12).

IX

The Temple of Doom

"Make war upon those who believe not ... even if they be people of the Book [Jews or Christians]. Make war upon them until idolatry is no more and Allah's religion reigns supreme."

—The Koran

We were flying fewer than forty feet above the ground when we came over the Mount of Olives. We were headed directly toward the Golden Gate in the eastern wall of the Old City of Jerusalem. The door was off the helicopter, and Paul was hanging out with a strap around his waist. He was holding his camera by its tripod.

"Okay, here we go," said the pilot.

I thought of the trouble we had encountered in trying to take this shot. We had needed clearance from the Israeli defense ministry because the area we wanted to film was protected by missiles that are set to fire automatically at any aircraft that approaches too near. We had gotten the clearance. Now I held my breath to see if they had succeeded in deactivating the missiles. But we passed the perimeter in peace.

The helicopter turned suddenly at a sharp angle. The golden dome of Omar's mosque was so brilliant in the sun that it nearly blinded me. As we came beside it, the copter shot straight up into the air like a rocket.

Tears filled my eyes. It was an incredible experience for me to look down on the very spot where the temples of Solomon and Herod had once stood. This was the place, too, where Abraham had been commanded to offer his son Isaac in sacrifice. It is ground so holy that no pious Jew would dare set foot on it.

Sitting today on this site, however, is an elegant Islamic shrine known as The Dome of the Rock, the Mosque of Omar. In accordance with this name, it is a great golden dome that sits above the rock on which Abraham almost sacrificed his son Isaac, and from which, according to a legend, Mohammed ascended one night into heaven for a special visit. Moslem feet patter over these sacred surfaces with impunity. Their donkeys are often tied nearby, occasionally urinating on this ground that no religious Jew would touch with his foot.

As the copter climbed higher, a thousand years of history spun before me. More tears streamed down my cheeks. I turned to the pilot as he veered up over Mount Scopus to the old Jerusalem airport. "You weren't joking about those missiles, were you?" I asked.

"No," he replied. "Jerusalem is heavily defended. Nobody flies over the city without clearance. Close flight over the Temple site is particularly sensitive because Israel's government has pledged to protect all holy sites in Israel—be they Christian, Moslem, or Jew. There are fanatics who would like to blow up the Dome of the Rock and rebuild the Temple. They believe it would usher in the arrival of the Messiah, but Israel knows that it must keep such fanatics in check. If the Dome of the Rock were blown up, it would provoke another war with the Arabs."

Looking back at the site, I thought of when Jesus foretold the destruction of the temple that stood there in His day, the temple of Herod. Thirty-seven years before it happened, Jesus told His disciples that not one stone of it would be left standing on another (see Matt. 24:1–2). His disciples had been dumbfounded in astonishment at this radical prediction. But Jesus' words were carried out to the letter by Roman legionnaires in A.D. 70. The siege of the city had ended in a vast slaughter of the Jewish defenders. Then the Roman soldiers tore down the temple building utterly because of a rumor that its building blocks were cemented by gold. It was unbelievable. No one had ever thought it would happen. Only the great platform that Herod had erected as a base for the Temple was left.

That entire platform has been Moslem property since A.D. 637, five years after Mohammed's death, when the Caliph Omar's troops captured the city of Jerusalem from the Byzantines. The Dome of the Rock was first built on the temple mount at the end of the seventh century. Only for a brief period, about a century, during the Crusades of the Middle Ages, did that Islamic ownership of the Temple mount and the Dome of the Rock lapse. The European knights saw the Dome or, as it is also known, the Mosque of Omar, and mistook it for Solomon's Temple. No one, apparently, ever managed to correct this notion during the time of the Crusades.

But today Jews and Christians alike read their Bibles and know that someday the authentic Temple which was long ago erected for the worship of God will be reconstructed. Jesus said that one of the signs of the approach of his return would be the appearance of what is variously translated as the "Abomination of Desolations," the "Disastrous Abomination," and the "Awful Horror," to name but a few. Whatever it is—it was first mentioned by the prophet Daniel—it will be set up in the Holy Place of the Temple (see Matt. 24:15). Many people believe an individual known as the Antichrist will be involved in this sacrilege.

The prophet Daniel foresaw the fall of the great empires of ancient history—the Babylonian, the Median, the Persian, the Grecian, and the Roman. And he declared, "There is a God in heaven who reveals secrets, and he has made known...what will be in the latter days" (Dan. 2:28).

Today there is an intense fever raging throughout Islam. It is a fever that seeks to reach out and take Jerusalem away from the Jews, to make it an Arab city. The Saudi Arabian government spent over a billion dollars hosting a conference of Islamic leaders to discuss plans to retrieve Jerusalem and its holy place, the Mosque of Omar, the Dome of the Rock.

But, in this plan, they are being drawn into a gigantic snare. That is because the angel of death hovers over this historic site and will surely strike grimly at any who would reach out to seize it. It will be a temple of doom for them.

Today there is no more sensitive piece of real estate on earth than the temple mount, the *Haram esh Sherif* of Islam. Israel reunited Jerusalem in 1967 after it had suffered a division, not unlike Berlin's, for nearly twenty years. The Israelis have always been very careful to acknowledge the sanctity of the holy sites in the city, and that includes the Dome of the Rock and the Al Aksa Mosque, which is built on the temple platform at its southern end.

Tradition has long held that the temple will be rebuilt. The Moslems are nervously aware of this tradition and the prophecies behind it. They are also aware that the traditional assumption about the rebuilding of the temple is that the Dome of the Rock will have to be demolished first, presumably by the Jews (or more accurately, a Jew), to clear the site. And so they guard the Dome of the Rock all the more zealously.

Several years ago an Australian tourist—a Gentile, not a Jew—set fire to the Al Aksa Mosque. When he was captured by Israeli police, he turned out to be mentally unstable. He believed, he told his interrogators, that God wanted him to burn the place down to make room for the rebuilding of the temple. The incident demonstrated the Israeli commitment to protect the holy sites, but it also aroused angry cries from Islamic spokesmen and heightened their anxiety and resentment at the fact that the *Haram esh Sherif* is no longer under Arab sovereignty. However, precisely the same incident could have happened back in the days when Jordanian police patrolled the eastern portion of Jerusalem, which included the Haram. The tourist trade in east Jerusalem was a great boon to the Jordanian economy. They encouraged tourists to visit the Haram and afforded much less protection to it than do the Israeli authorities today. The fact is, regardless of which government has control of Jerusalem and the temple mount, the Arabs have lived with the vague dread that the Dome of the Rock is doomed to destruction.

I have already presented evidence in my book *Jerusalem, D.C.,* that shows this demolition may not be necessary. The fretting may be for naught because the actual site of the ancient temple, Herod's temple at least, may have been at the north end of the platform where no significant structure presently stands. As I concluded in that book, after describing the evidence that supports this hypothesis, if that is the case, then the stage is more set for the return than we might have thought.

The Blood of Abraham

The revival of the Arab people and their sudden rise to international prominence is surely one of the great, but overlooked signs that the return is near. It has been overshadowed by the restoration of Israel, but it is hardly less remarkable and only slightly less dramatic than that event. The sovereign hand of God is at work every day in the world, carefully preparing conditions and circumstances for the final fulfillment of the prophecies He inspired so long ago.

Archaeologists have traced Arab civilization back to around 2000 B.C. on the Arabian peninsula. It was about that time that the biblical patriarch Abraham was living in Canaan, the land God had promised to him. Not long before this, Abraham had been able to subdue nearly all of the local chieftains so that he was living in unchallenged peace.

Only one thing was still robbing him of total contentment. His wife, Sarah, was barren. God had also promised him innumerable descendants, but nothing was happening. Abraham wasn't getting any younger. What good would his victories do him if he had no heirs to sustain his dynasty?

It was Sarah who finally suggested that her own slave girl, Hagar the Egyptian, act as a kind of proxy for her. Abraham could make Hagar his concubine and perhaps father a child through her. However, when Hagar discovered she was pregnant, she became proud and despised Sarah. Sarah complained to Abraham who told her Hagar was her slave and she could handle her any way she liked.

Sarah made life so intolerable for Hagar that she ran away, but God encountered her in the wilderness and told her to go back and submit to Sarah. Then He promised her,

I will give you so many descendants that no one will be able to count them. You are going to have a son, and you will name him Ishmael [which means "God hears"], because the LORD has heard your cry of distress. But your son will live like a wild donkey; he will be against everyone, and everyone will be against him. He will live apart from all his relatives (Gen. 16:10–12).

When Hagar was out in the wilderness, she saw a well, but as Israelis love to joke today, it was not an oil well. It was a well of water. Today, however, oil wells have become more important to Arab culture than the highly-prized oases. Abraham's two sons, Ishmael and Isaac, have come to the forefront of world history and have shaken the industrial world to its knees.

The 1973–74 oil crisis was begun by the Arabs as a hate campaign against Israel, but it ended as the biggest financial bonanza in history. The oil embargo was instituted in response to the Israeli victory against the Arabs in the Yom Kippur War of 1973. They hoped it would compel the United States to stop being Israel's ally. But then something happened that distracted them from their original goal. The price of oil quite naturally shot up overnight. Suddenly the Arabs realized that their oil was as good as gold, and they were overwhelmed by greed.

The cost of a barrel of crude oil jumped from about $2.40 in 1973 to more than $30 in 1980. At one point, it rose as high as $45 before conservation efforts among the free-enterprise nations forced the price lower. Overnight the primitive people of Arabia became fantastically wealthy and began to exercise unheard-of power. Today Saudi Arabia accounts for a third of all oil exports, and oil itself constitutes one quarter of the total volume of all the trade in the world.[1]

Ishmael had awakened to realize that two-thirds of the world's known oil reserves lay beneath his tents. Every man, woman, and child on the face of the earth has been affected. In 1974, the United States paid $3.9 billion for imported oil. That figure jumped quickly to $24 billion. Japan went from $3.9 billion to $18 billion; the United Kingdom from $2.4 to $8.5 billion; West Germany, $2.9 to $11.3 billion. International inflation followed and has never been brought entirely under control. Many nations have been brought to the brink of bankruptcy. Many banks have been taken over that brink. Meanwhile, Ishmael has accumulated vast fortunes which he has forged into a new weapon called the capital investment dollar.

No one in their wildest imaginations would have thought it fifteen years ago, but it has happened. As a consequence, the ancient prophecies of the Bible, that Ishmael and Isaac would stand at the center of world attention, have come clearly into focus overnight. No one would have believed that the nomadic tribesmen that Lawrence of Arabia led into Damascus in 1918 would have joined fashionable society. In fact, their wealth is so enormous that they can tell society what is fashionable in some cases.

One would suppose that wealth and culture would bring stability to Arab society. Far from it. Attempts at democracy among the Arabs have consistently failed, and the monarchies and dictatorships that have prevailed in the Arab states are far from stable. In the last thirty years, twenty-four heads of Arab states have died in office violently.

A Look to the Past Helps Us Understand the Present

After the true child of promise, Isaac, was born to Abraham and Sarah, Hagar and Ishmael were sent away. God comforted Hagar in her exile, and Hagar found an Egyptian girl to be Ishmael's wife. Eventually Ishmael fathered twelve sons who became the heads of twelve tribes: Nebajoth, Kedar, Abdeel, Mibsam, Mishma, Dumah, Massa, Hadad, Tema, Jetur, Naphish, and Kedemah. Those names became attached to their villages and camping places located in the regions east of Egypt between Havilah and Shur (see Gen. 25:12–18). That equates with the western regions of the Arabian peninsula. The historian Josephus first noted that the Arabs were the descendants of Ishmael.

Archaeological evidence points to a hearty Arab culture of several kingdoms centered near what is today Yemen (Havilah) around 900 B.C. Those kingdoms grew wealthy through the export of frankincense, myrrh, and spices.

From about A.D. 300 to 500, those Arab kingdoms went into a decline for which historians have no explanation. Nomadic tribes began to dominate the entire peninsula. After the birth of Mohammed, about A.D. 570, things began to change. Before the middle of the next century, the Arabs, now the passionate advocates of Islam, began to rise to dominate the whole Middle East and North Africa.

That domination continued for almost a thousand years. But, by the sixteenth century, the Ottoman Turks were in control of the Middle East and Arab culture was fast declining. Thus the image of the backward Arab tribesman became commonplace in Europe and eventually in North America.

I got a personal taste of the source of this image in 1983 when I and my family were invited to a feast in a Bedouin village in the Middle East. We entered the tent and sat on the ground in a large circle. Then a cloth was spread out, on which the feast was served up. It consisted of a goat's head encircled by mounds of rice covered with gravy. Carolyn, my wife, must have anticipated how primitive things were going to be because she had found an excuse that precluded her attendance at this feast. So I was there with my lovely daughters.

We were the only Westerners there among about twenty-five tribal leaders. As the feast began the tribesmen passed around a common cup that looked as though it hadn't been washed in twenty years. I shuddered. Then everybody started digging in on the rice and the goat's head. The idea was to pick a bit of meat off the head with one's fingers and consume it with a handful of rice and gravy. I wondered how Lawrence of Arabia had lived through this sort of thing. I was simply unable to participate with any gusto. I tried to pick politely at the rice so as not to give offense.

My daughter Rachel, however, found the whole thing delightful. Despite my discouraging hints, she plucked away at the goat's head gleefully. It was, she assured me, delicious. However, a little later in the day, I found her tugging at my coat. "Daddy," she pled, "I have to go number ten!"

I thought for a minute. Number one, I knew, and number two—but what was number ten? Quickly I realized she had chosen this way to describe the urgency and discomfort she felt in her lower abdomen. The "Egyptian plague" had struck!

That was the light side of our visit. A little while after the feast I saw the Arab who had brought us to this village. He was standing in the middle of a circle of tribesmen who were shouting angrily. I didn't have to wonder what was going on for long because a spokesman soon came over and asked me, "Would you be offended if we killed this man?"

I could hardly believe my ears. "What did he do?" I asked.

"He kept his shoes on after entering the tent of his fathers. It is a great offense. He should not have done such a thing!"

I was a little bewildered. Both I and my daughters had been informed of this custom and had removed our shoes for the feast. Apparently this man had thought to impress me with how westernized he had become by refusing to observe the custom.

"What happens if I'm offended?" I asked.

The spokesman replied, quite matter-of-factly, "If you would be offended, then we would not do it. We must never offend our honored guests. If you would not be offended, then we would surely kill him because he deserves it!"

I looked at him a moment and said, "If you kill that man, I will be terribly offended."

The spokesman went back to the cluster of tribesmen who had encircled the offender and announced my verdict. The issue was settled and nothing more was said about it, but I must admit the whole experience left me a little shaken. It was a taste of that primitive and violent spirit that has become a part of Arab culture.

The old image of the Arabs as backward and of no account in the affairs of the world is passé. It was the result of the short-sightedness of people who failed to recognize that the Middle East was on a prophetic countdown. Ishmael was destined to rise with enormous power as the great clock of history ticks its way closer to the midnight hour.

The Fly in the Ointment of Arab Oil

The great fly in the Arabs' ointment is Israel. Israel's existence is an offense to the Arab sense of pride and bravado. Many Arabs still want to drive the intruding Jews into the sea. After Israel drove back the fourth major Arab attempt to do just that in 1973, (the previous attempts had been in 1948, 1956, and 1967), several Arab countries cut off or reduced oil shipments to the United States and other countries that had supported Israel.

The Arabs have arrived, at this day in the history of the world, at a place near the center of the stage. By a strange coincidence, the Jews were restored to the Holy Land at precisely the same time. The resulting conflict has already shaken every nation on earth, especially the largest and most powerful ones.

The stage for the great culminating battle of history at Armageddon is being set. Arab nationalism has driven the British, the French, and the Americans out of the Middle East. It was precisely the presence or nearness of the armed forces of those countries that had long held the hungry Russians in check. The only significant populations in the Middle East are in Iran and Egypt, and Iran's armed forces are bleeding to death on the Iraqi frontier. There will be little to stand in the way of a Soviet invasion when the day comes—little, that is, except for Israel.

Is it all just a coincidence? Or is it evidence of the strong hand of God Almighty bringing to pass the words He gave long ago to the prophets of Israel?

Jihad—Holy War

Islam is a religion of violence, a thing hated by the God of the Bible. But the Koran instructs the faithful, "Make war upon those who believe not...even if they be People of the Book [Jews or Christians]. Make war on them until idolatry is no more and Allah's religion reigns supreme." The word for this holy war is *jihad*. And it is something, according to Islamic teaching, that will go on until the Day of Judgment.

Until recent years, little was heard in public about Jihad. Arab devotion to Islam seemed to be moderating. Moslems of all sorts, Arabs and non-Arabs alike, seemed able to coexist with non-Moslems on a somewhat relaxed basis. Only in India did there seem to be much trouble, and that was handled by the creation of Pakistan.

In the late 1970s, the cauldron began to bubble again. The revival of Islamic fanaticism was signaled most clearly by Khomeini's successful overthrow of the Shah of Iran, who was perhaps the shining example of Islamic accommodation with the ways of the West.

Since then the cauldron has boiled over time and again. Jihad has been born again. The United States is one of its chief targets, as demonstrated in the embassy hostage crisis in Teheran and the bombing of the Marine barracks in Beirut.

In Lebanon, after the Israelis successfully dispersed the PLO operatives who had so long plagued northern Galilee from bases inside southern Galilee, they finally decided to withdraw. Why? Because Moslem extremists had taken over where the PLO had left off, but with multiplied vigor and viciousness. A *Los Angeles Times* photographer took a chilling sequence of pictures in Sidon, Lebanon's largest southern city, the day after the Israeli withdrawal. Those photos showed of a group of gunmen dragging a pajama-clad man, suspected of collaborating with the Israelis, from his house. He was dragged through the streets, thrown into the trunk of a waiting car, driven off, and never heard from again.

Nor is this extremism confined to the Middle East. Southeast Asia has felt its heat as well. In Indonesia, the world's most populous Islamic country, Moslem fanatics have rioted, set fires, exploded bombs. In Malaysia, where Moslems comprise a majority of the population, a hard-line Islamic political party is demanding that the multiethnic nation become an Islamic state. Philippine government troops in Mindanao have been put on the defensive by Moslem separatists who have received encouragement and support from Khomeini. Even heavily Chinese Singapore lives in fear that its Moslem minority may reignite the racial rioting of former years.

If this Iranian-style fanaticism with its sinister hatred of the United States manages to take hold, our government could be faced with the existence of hostile regimes in a region that has long been friendly to America and that represents vital military, economic, and political importance.

As an example of the nature of this released genie, a *mullah* (Moslem teacher) in Malaysia denounced television as an instrument of infidel propaganda. He urged his students to destroy their family TV sets. If their parents dared to interfere with this holy act, he told them it would not be a sin for them to behead them.

This same fanaticism was aired on American television sets early in 1985 in a report on the Iranian suicide squads being trained to clear minefields for the upcoming (and subsequently failed) offensive against Iraq. The motivation to volunteer for such duty lay in the assurance of the mullahs that death in such an endeavor guarantees one immediate entrance to heaven. Each recruit wore a "key to heaven" around his neck. The training consisted of a brief series of pep talks by religious spokesmen. In the TV report, one of the recruits broke down in tears as his group was boarding their bus for the front. He refused to get on, and perhaps since the cameras were rolling, was permitted to stay behind. What the foreign TV crew did not see were the younger recruits for this duty. Children as young as six have been known to be in these suicide squads. On the field of battle they are tied together just before they begin their march across mine-infested territory.

The Israeli government secured TV footage of the following and tried to encourage one of the U.S. networks to air it, but it refused. The footage was of teen-aged Syrian girls dancing to the beat of demonic music in front of Syria's president, Hafaz Assad. As they danced the girls were grasping live snakes in their hands. They waved them about wildly and fondled them as the rhythmic music increased its pace to a frenzy. At the climax of the dance, they began tearing the snakes apart with their teeth. Soon they were spitting out bits of flesh as blood dripped from their chins. The purpose of this grotesque affair was to commemorate and celebrate the initial victories of the Syrian army against the Israelis in the 1973 war. The snakes represented the Jews who had been killed in those battles.

Islam's adherents number more than seven hundred million people. The population of the world is approaching five billion. That means one in every seven people on earth worships Allah. They constitute the majority population in fifty-seven nations.[2] More than two million live in the United States. The effect of such an enormous group of people, once aroused to a fanatical pitch such as we have seen examples of already, could be devastating. The ghost of Hagar has come to haunt the whole world.

The True Pathway to Peace in the Middle East

Sitting before me as I write this is an invitation. It says that the largest gathering of Arabs in the U.S. will occur in Washington, D.C., and they'd like me to speak at the conference at which they say Jimmy Carter and Tom Brokaw of NBC news have also been invited to participate. If I accept, I'll have twenty minutes to express my views. I guess they invited me because they know my opinions about the Middle East are based upon the Bible as a fundamentalist, and they feel that there is sufficient ammunition on the other side to satisfy themselves that my views would be countered.

It makes me think of the time I was invited to participate in the "World Conference on Peace in the Middle East" sponsored by the United Nations. I asked the official who was inviting me and who and what sort of people would be attending this conference. He told me there would be delegates from roughly a hundred different liberation organizations.

Liberation is such a nice word. It sounds so right and noble and true. When I think of liberation, I think of a whole roomful of people singing "I'm So Glad, Jesus Set Me Free." Or maybe I think of Patton's Third Army arriving at the Dachau Concentration Camp on April 29, 1945. They liberated thirty-two thousand survivors.

But, somehow, I knew it would be different at the U.N. conference. These delegates wouldn't be singing about Jesus, and they wouldn't want to celebrate the liberation of any Jews from concentration camps. If anyone had asked me how to describe the organizations represented at the conference, I would have said they were terrorists. Of course, no one asked me.

I'd like to poll the secretaries of state who have served this nation since George Marshall held that post under Harry Truman. I'd like to ask them to name the most stubborn and unmanageable foreign affairs problem they had to deal with. I'll bet that the Middle East would win hands down. Even suave old Henry Kissinger, the man who managed to carry the Paris negotiations with the North Vietnamese to a conclusion, couldn't seem to make anything happen in the Middle East.

If these fellows had only read their Bibles they would have wasted a lot less time. Nothing is going to cool the Middle East. It is a cauldron that will boil and spill over ever more nastily until the return of Jesus.

Manachem Begin once let me in on a hot story. He had just met with Sadat in Alexandria. Sadat had told him that Egyptian intelligence had confirmed that the government of Saudi Arabia was in serious danger of being overthrown. It would happen in a revolution not unlike the one that dethroned the Shah of Iran.

The story was just about to be aired on national network news, but it was tossed out at the last minute because congress was just about to vote on the sale of AWACS planes to Saudi Arabia. Any news that said the Saudi regime was in trouble, that the government in Riyadh might soon resemble the government in Teheran, had to be quashed. Otherwise, congress might balk and not approve the sale, a defeat the president's advisors did not want to face.

Saudi Arabia—and this is common knowledge—is the most vulnerable country in the entire Middle East. Ironically it is also the wealthiest. It is vulnerable, first, because its population is tiny, about nine million people in over eight hundred thousand square miles of territory. Almost as many people live in New Jersey, which has less than eight thousand square miles. Saudi Arabia could afford a great army, but it simply doesn't have enough young men to make one up.

It is vulnerable, second, because the monarchy is a tenuous affair, not unlike the governments of the other Arab countries. The monarchy is especially vulnerable to reactionary Moslem fanatics like those who overthrew the Shah. It is for that reason that they dare not appear too friendly with the United States. After all, the Shah was a friend of the United States—look what happened to him! But that leaves them to face the Russian threat by themselves. So, in the face of invasion or insurrection, they have little to fall back on.

I believe the Bible tells us that many of the Arab countries will align themselves with Russia in a great move to eradicate Israel. It will be the greatest mistake they ever made, for it will put them in direct opposition to God Himself. The Arab people desperately need to recognize and receive Jesus as the Lord of Lord and King of Kings.

God Loves Ishmael

Yet God is no respecter of persons. He loves every one of His creatures, the Arabs and the Jews included. One night I was sitting with an Arab by the Sea of Galilee. The Arab's name was Shamir abu Jad. I listened to him talk for two hours about how much he hated the Jews. He was aligned with a Palestinian terrorist organization.

Near the end of the two hours, he turned to me in some embarrassment. "Excuse me," he said. "I haven't let you speak a word. I don't know anything about you."

I smiled and said, "My friend, I used to be a black belt karate instructor."

His eyes widened a bit. "I never want to make you mad at me," he said. Then he began asking me lots of questions about karate.

I answered them in a friendly manner. Suddenly I leaped to my feet, went into a karate stance, gave a karate shout, and announced, "I love the Jewish people and Israel!"

He threw his hands over his head in surprise.

I broke into laughter. I laughed so hard that tears started rolling down my cheeks.

Then Shamir stared at me in puzzlement.

I reached out and embraced Shamir. I told him how I had accepted Jesus as my Lord and Messiah in 1966. I told him Jesus had given me the peace that passes understanding. Then I said, "Shamir, let's pray together."

We went back to my room and started praying at about ten o'clock at night. Shamir asked Jesus to come into his life and to give him the same peace I had. Then we went on praying together. We wept and besought God on behalf of all Arabs to pour out His Spirit on them and to work a miracle of peace and healing in the Middle East. I believe God in His mercy, in spite of the evil intentions of the vast majority of these governments and Moslem fanatics, will answer that prayer by pouring out His Holy Spirit upon everyone who truly calls upon His name. I believe that a great number of Arabs will come to believe in Jesus. This in no way contradicts a single prophecy of the Bible. In fact, there is a wonderful prophecy in Isaiah 19:18-25 that ought to encourage us to do evangelism among Arabs. Isaiah says that someday many Arabs will acknowledge the one true God.

We are on a countdown to Armageddon, and that is why we must do everything we can to light a candle rather than curse the darkness. That is what God wants of us. He loves the Bedouins and their goats' heads. He wants to bless them. God has even shown that to me in a personal way.

I was on a trek through the Sinai desert with my friends Jamie Buckingham, Gib Jones, and Angus Sergeant. Jamie is a writer, Gib is a photographer, and Angus is a physician. Our trip was something of a pilgrimage and an attempt to do some serious wilderness living.

One day, deep in the desert, we came upon a Bedouin tent. A sobbing woman came out to us. She brought a little girl with her. As they drew near, we could see that the child had a terrible abscess on her head. It looked bad enough, but it had been made worse by attempts to cauterize it with hot pokers.

Angus was explaining to the woman, through an interpreter, that there was nothing we could do. This sort of thing required surgery, which was impossible out in the desert in such dirty circumstances. I felt overwhelmed by the love of God for this child and its mother. The pain I felt for the child was as if she were my own offspring.

I reached out to place my hand on the little girl's head, but one of my companions said, "Don't, Mike. It will offend the Moslems."

But I couldn't stop. The urgency and pain I felt were too strong. With my hand resting gently on the child's head near the abscess, I cried out, "Lord Jesus, touch this precious little one and heal her!" That was all. I felt no surge of power, no trembling in the child, and there was no visible sign that the abscess was affected at all. Had I done the right thing? I was confident I had. But who could know for sure?

We resumed our trek and went deeper into the desert. That night we camped at an oasis. The next morning Angus Sergeant, the physician in our group, was troubled about his failure to have helped the little girl. Finally he announced, "I must go back there and do what I can. She'll die if that thing isn't removed. I'll just have to trust the Lord that she won't die from whatever bacteria get into her because I couldn't operate under sterile conditions."

So, our party turned around and went back to that lonely Bedouin tent. When we finally got there, Angus went inside the tent itself. I, of course, was curious to see if my prayer had done any good. I didn't want to get in the way, so I tried to wait patiently outside, but I couldn't wait long. After a few minutes, I walked over to the tent, bent down, and peeked inside.

The first thing I saw was Angus sitting on the dirt floor. He was crying like a baby. In his hand was a cup, another one of those Bedouin utensils that looked as though it hadn't been washed in twenty years.

Then I saw the little girl and her mother. The light in the tent was dim. Were my eyes deceiving me? It looked like the abscess was gone!

Right then, Angus lifted that cup. "Lord," he wept, "I don't know what's in this cup of tea. There could be many diseases. But I will not offend this lovely lady. You healed this little child, and you can keep me from what's in this cup." He drank it all and smiled gratefully at his hostess.

Before long everyone was outside in the light and we got a good look at her head. Where the abscess had been was a fresh patch of healthy skin. Angus had not even touched the child. It was all God's doing. Gib, who had taken photographs the day before, took some more. It is the most thoroughly documented and verified miracle of healing with which I am personally familiar.

Jesus is the source of peace for the Middle East. His power alone is sufficient to meet the deepest needs of the people of this or any region.

But we need to see also that strong demonic spirits are at work in that region in a peculiar way. Among them are spirits of violent hatred, savagery, and seething anger. The ultimate goal of their ferocity is Jerusalem and the great platform Herod built two thousand years ago for his temple. There the final catastrophic events of history will transpire. The great Dome of the Rock will be a temple of doom for all who rise up against God and His purposes for the earth.

X

The Mystery of Israel's Rebirth

"I spread my wings and keep my promise."
—Motto of British Fourteenth Bomber Squadron as
they flew over Jerusalem in 1917

Frederick the Great of Prussia (1712–1786) was known as "the enlightened despot" because he worked hard to establish efficient government for his people even though he was convinced they were incapable of governing themselves. He once said, "My people and I have have come to an agreement which satisfies us both. They are to say what they please, and I am to do what I please."

The title also was fitting because he liked philosophy and included Voltaire, the French writer and skeptic, among his friends. Frederick admired Voltaire so much, in fact, that he began to have doubts about his own faith. He was a staunch Lutheran in the old Prussian tradition, and his doubts troubled him a great deal.

One day, so the story goes, he was holding court with some of his advisers. The existence of God came up as a topic of conversation, and finally Frederick spoke his heart. "I am tired of these philosophical arguments. I would to God that someone would show me some firm evidence that He exists."

At this, one of his older advisers, a man who had kept silent during the previous discussions, spoke up, but only briefly. He said, "The Jew, your majesty."[1]

A Dream

It all started with Abraham. After the judgment on the Tower of Babel, God seemed to turn His back on the rest of mankind and to focus his attention on one man from Ur in Babylonia. He was a

---

descendant of Noah's son Shem; he was a Semite. He lived in the center of intractable idolatry, Babylon. There the traditions of mighty Nimrod had almost erased the memory of the Creator God.

That memory had to be restored, and the sin of man had to be dealt with. Could it be done? How?

Locked in the heart of God from long before the creation lay a deep mystery. That mystery was the plan God had conceived to restore His creation. By calling Abraham to leave Babylonia, God revealed the first stage of that plan.

> The Lord said to Abram [his name was changed later], "Leave your country, your relatives, and your father's home, and go to a land that I am going to show you. I will give you many descendants, and they will become a great nation. I will bless you and make your name famous, so that you will be a blessing. I will bless those who bless you. But I will curse those who curse you. And through you I will bless all the nations" (Gen. 12:1–3 TEV).

The odyssey of the Jews is one of the most incredible phenomena of history. They were a tiny nation of farmers and fishermen who lived in a little slot of land between the two great and ancient contenders for control of the Middle East. To the north and east flowed the Tigris and the Euphrates, which nurtured a series of Mesopotamian empires. To the south and west flowed the majestic Nile, sustainer of successive Egyptian dynasties.

The Promise of a Messiah

Israel's star has shone very brightly in the galaxy of nations at different times in history. The eleventh century, before the birth of Jesus, was one of those times. At that time David came to the throne after the death of Israel's first king, Saul. David succeeded in unifying the tribes under his leadership. He established his capital in Jerusalem, a city which was not associated with any one of the tribes in particular. Then he soundly defeated the formerly ascendant Philistines. Before he was done, his domain extended north and east to include Syria, east across the Jordan to the edge of the Arabian desert, south to the site of Aqaba (then known as Ezion-geber), and thence west to the Mediterranean. Philistia retained a small stretch of land along the south coast, and the Phoenicians held on to the coast of Lebanon.

It was a golden age the Jews would never forget. When the dark days came during Solomon's reign and idol worship became prevalent in Israel, God started sending prophets to warn and comfort the people. They warned that God would judge their sin by bringing conquerors out of the north to destroy Israel's kingdom that had begun so well under David. They gave comfort by promising that God would one day raise up another one like David, an anointed one—a Messiah—who would restore the kingdom to Israel and rule from Jerusalem. He would, in fact, so exalt Jerusalem that all the nations, the *goyim,* would come from the four corners of the earth to acknowledge the God of Israel as the one true God of all creation.

God's secret plan, the plan that had begun to come to light when He called Abraham out of Ur in Babylonia almost a thousand years before the time of David, was becoming a little clearer. But that moment of light faded quickly. Little happened in the succeeding centuries to build hope, but amazingly the hope was kept alive in the hearts of faithful Jews.

When Jesus arrived on the scene, the mysterious nature of God's plan became more evident, to some at least. But to many Jews, and particularly to the leaders of the Jews, Jesus was not suitable to be the Messiah. To many of the common people He did not fit with their expectations of a warrior king who would drive out the despised Roman occupiers. To the leaders He was a threat to their establishment. So He was crucified.

That's when the deepest aspect of God's mysterious plan came to light. The Resurrection changed everything. In fact, the world has never been the same since.

During the latter part of the first century, Jewish resistance to Roman authority erupted violently and was even more violently subdued. A second rebellion in A.D. 137, led by Simon bar Kokhbah, was the last straw. The land was renamed Palestine, and the Jews would not rule it again for nearly two thousand years.

The Dispersion

Under normal circumstances a people subjected to the sort of slaughter and dispersion that was visited on the Jews by the Roman empire would have gradually become extinct. Many of the ancient tribes, in fact most of them, failed to sustain themselves into modern times. But somehow the Jews were always different. They wandered across the world for two millennia without a homeland of their own. Always they were visitors, aliens.

Nowhere at any time were they entirely and unreservedly welcomed by their hosts. Instead they were subject to persecution and harassment. Yet they survived and always managed to exercise an influence and power in society that seemed to have little to do with their numbers, and nothing to do with their advantages. Scholars, scientists, philosophers, artists, jurists, physicians, entertainers, and many others of similar ilk have found numerous Jews among their colleagues.

The story of the Jews was precisely the answer Frederick the Great needed that day. It is an absolute miracle that they exist today at all. No people on earth have suffered more than the Jews. For example, I have already mentioned the slaughter visited upon them during Titus's campaigns between A.D. 67 and 70. The great Roman general had come to subdue the Jewish rebellion that had fiercely driven the regular Roman garrison troops out of the territory.

All of Jerusalem was laid waste with the exception of Herod's palace, which served as a barracks and headquarters for the Roman Tenth Legion, which became a permanent occupying force there. One of the leaders of the rebellion, Simon bar Biora, was taken back to Rome to be hanged next to the forum. Thousands of Jews were sold into slavery in the aftermath of the campaign.

Further bloody slaughter was visited on rebellious Jews in Mesopotamia and Egypt in the four decades after the destruction of Jerusalem, but nothing would compare to the carnage that resulted from the Bar Kokhbah rebellion. It was a response triggered by the Emperor Hadrian's prohibition against circumcision. By A.D. 131, Bar Kokhbah had enlisted nearly four hundred thousand troops. In a series of fierce battles the Roman garrison troops were again driven out of the country. For almost three years the Jews held Jerusalem and ruled themselves, but then Julius Severus arrived in Judea with five legions of battle-hardened troops. By A.D. 134 they had retaken Jerusalem. Bar Kokhbah himself was not captured and killed until A.D. 136.

The revenge of the Roman army after its victory was terrible. Some of the leaders of the rebellion were skinned alive prior to their execution. Massacres during the fighting had been common. Now the survivors were either sold into slavery or allowed to starve. Burial was not permitted so that heaps of corpses decomposed in the streets and fields.

I call this ghastly series of events the Roman holocaust. In it we see the hand of Satan. He thought he had blocked the purpose of God when Jesus was crucified, but that was because he has no grasp of God's mind and he cannot solve the mystery of His plan. The Resurrection had taken him by surprise. The Roman holocaust was a reprisal after the fact.

The Nazi Holocaust

If the Roman holocaust came after the fact, the Nazi murder of six million Jewish men, women, and children—the greatest single atrocity in the history of mankind—was Satan's biggest play before the fact. The prophecies that had pointed to Jesus' resurrection may have been laced in mystery, but the prophecies that foretold the restoration of Israel were plain for anyone to see. As often happens, Satan overplayed his hand so that the Nazi holocaust actually *served* to help open the door for the emergence of a Jewish state after World War II. That does not mitigate the cruelty, the incredible horror, or the enormity of what happened across Europe between 1933 and 1945.

It was an event of such immeasurable moment that we are compelled to search out its significance continually, never to be satisfied that we have fathomed it. I have already pointed to it as a precursor to the refounding of Israel, never again to be called by the hated name of Palestine, the name assigned by the avenging Romans (evidently as a Latinate rendering of *Philistia*).

I believe that the meaning of the Holocaust extends beyond its role in the establishment of the Israeli state. The Holocaust stands by itself as a great signpost of the end of the age.

Because he knew after the Balfour Declaration of 1917 that his days were extremely limited, Satan found a unique servant in Adolf Hitler. If any great head of state in modern history has been demonized, it was he. Hitler relied heavily on astrologers and fortunetellers. His hatred of Christianity was almost as deep as his hatred of Judaism. He understood, more clearly than many German churchmen, the close affinity between Judaism and Christianity. He knew that authentic Christianity can never divorce itself from a sincere love for the Jewish people and a deep gratitude to them for their special place in God's plan. Thus Hitler revealed himself to be a willing tool of Satan in attempting to thwart God's purposes.

Israel Becomes a Modern State

The story of the rebirth of the nation of Israel stretches back through the centuries of anti-Semitism that the Jews endured when they were away from their homeland. Modern Zionism (a deliberate movement to achieve a homeland for the Jews in the Holy Land) was surely born late in the nineteenth century in the heart of a secularized Austrian Jew named Theodore Herzl (1860–1904). Herzl, working as a journalist, was assigned to cover the trial of Captain Alfred Dreyfus (1859–1935), a Jewish French soldier who had been accused of spying for the Germans. The charges had been trumped up in a wave of anti-Semitism in the French military establishment.

Standing in the streets of Paris outside the courthouse, Herzl heard the crowds chanting in French, "Death to the Jews." In that moment he recognized that genuine assimilation was impossible. No matter what advances European civilization had made or would make, it would never take the Jews fully into its bosom. The Jewish people needed a state of their own if they were ever to be truly free.

Herzl set to work on the book that would create Zionism, *Der Judenstaat* (The Jewish State). It was published in 1896 and immediately began to attract a following. In 1897, Herzl presided at the first Zionist congress in Basel, Switzerland.

Herzl died in 1904, but he had done his work. In the meantime, others carried on his work. Chaim Weizmann was a Russian Jew who was a British citizen and a chemist. His contribution to the British war effort (1914–1918) brought him into contact with important government officials.

Weizmann was an ardent Zionist. He was also an unsurpassed lobbyist. His skills and great personal charm were able to win the sympathies of a number of his friends on the British War Cabinet. After a good deal of behind-the-scenes maneuvering, which included a message of support from President Woodrow Wilson, the Balfour Declaration was issued. It certified British government support for the "establishment in Palestine of a national home for the Jewish people." The date was November 2, 1917.

Hovering Birds

As he approached the Holy City General Allenby was concerned. Although this was a great moment of triumph, less than six weeks after the Balfour Declaration, Allenby was worried that the Turks and their allies, the Germans, might resist. Should he shell the city and risk damaging some of the holy sites? He wired the war office in London for advice. They told him to use his own judgment, but that was what he was seeking to avoid doing. He wired the king himself at Buckingham Palace. George V wired back, "Make it a matter of prayer." Evidently he did and he hit upon an idea. He had pilots drop leaflets on the city to urge peaceful surrender.

The Germans and Turks evacuated the city on December 9. They left behind them the city's mixed population of Jews, Arabs, and Europeans to whom the leaflets from Allenby had come as welcome news. Apparently the British would not massacre them.

Jerusalem's civilian mayor, Haj Amin Nashashibi, decided to take Allenby up on the offer. He borrowed a white bedsheet from an American missionary and walked out of the city by way of the Jaffa Gate toward the southwest, the direction from which he understood the main body of the British troops was coming. He and his associates had not gone far when they encountered two startled British scouts, Sergeants Hurcomb and Sedgewick of the London Regiment. By pointing to their flag and employing the few words of broken English the mayor had at his disposal, he managed to make his intentions clear to them.

General Allenby's capture of Jerusalem fulfilled a twenty-five-hundred-year-old prophecy by Isaiah: "Like birds hovering overhead, the Lord Almighty will shield Jerusalem; he will shield it, and deliver it, he will 'pass over' it and will rescue it" (Isa. 31:5).

"Like birds hovering..." Isaiah could not have described aircraft more aptly considering the time he prophesied (eighth century B.C.). So, like hovering birds, the little biplanes were used by the Lord to defend Jerusalem. It was, in fact, protected, rescued, spared, and saved in accordance with Isaiah's words.

Four hundred years of Ottoman oppression of the city was ended without the firing of a single shot or any damage to even one of the holy places. Adding to the sense of mystery and evidence of God's hand guiding events was the fact of the motto of the Fourteenth Bomber Squadron whose planes were used to drop those leaflets. Their motto was, "I spread my wings and keep my promise."

After the war, Palestine was given to the British by a mandate of the League of Nations. There followed a season of stepped-up Jewish immigration, but Arab rioting in opposition to the Jewish settlers caused the British to begin limiting Jewish immigration.

After World War II, the situation had become so volatile that Britain threw the question of what to do about it into the lap of the United Nations. After a torturous series of debates, the U.N. finally voted for partition—dividing the available territory into two separate countries, one for the Jews and one for the Arabs. The British got out as quickly as they could and left the Jews and the Arabs to settle it between themselves.

On May 14, 1948, in the midst of unimaginable political and military chaos, David ben-Gurion gathered his cabinet in the art museum of the city of Tel-Aviv to proclaim the independence of the State of Israel, and within hours President Harry S. Truman extended American recognition to the new state.

The story behind Truman's role is remarkable. Truman had

been persuaded, against the advice of the state department, to receive Chaim Weizmann, the chemist who had secured the Balfour Declaration in 1917 and who was now about to become the first president of Israel. Truman's old friend and business partner, Eddie Jacobson, was a Jew; they had suffered bankruptcy together and had repaid all their creditors in full. He had come to the White House and tearfully urged the president to break precedent by seeing Weizmann. Jacobson's most convincing argument apparently had been to compare Weizmann with Truman's favorite hero, Andrew Jackson.

On March 18, 1948, five days after Jacobson's appeal, Chaim Weizmann called on the President of the United States at the White House. Two months later, when the ben-Gurion government declared Israeli independence, the United States extended official recognition to the new nation within eleven minutes of the declaration. A year later, the leading rabbi of Israel visited Harry Truman and told him, "God put you in your mother's womb so that you could be the instrument to bring about the rebirth of Israel after two thousand years."

In less than two years of desperate fighting against the invading armies of five of its Arab neighbors, the Israelis had made good their claim on the land. In an event unique in history, the descendants of an ancient people reclaimed their homeland and established it as a sovereign state after 2,536 years of almost uninterrupted foreign subjugation.

A Dead Language Comes Alive

Through the heart of Jerusalem runs a large street called ben Yehuda. Whenever I visit Jerusalem, I often go jogging in the early morning hours down Ben Yehuda Street. I must know every shop that lines it.

The street got its name from a man whose story is one of the most amazing and romantic I know. He was Eliezer ben Yehuda, the man who almost single-handedly restored Hebrew to the family of modern spoken languages.

In his youth Eliezer had been diagnosed as having tuberculosis. As he faced the possibility of a shortened life, his sharp mind fastened upon an idea that has gained him a measure of immortality.

His idea—perhaps it would be better to call it a vision—was born out of the fact that the Jews of eastern Europe and Russia had long spoken Yiddish, a language that employs the Hebrew alphabet, but which is actually a mix of German, Hebrew, Aramaic, French, Italian, and some of the Slavic languages. It is a language that bespeaks the dispersion of the Jews among the nations of the world. In more recent years it has even drawn expressions from English, and of course, it has contributed many to it.

The knowledge of Hebrew had been preserved among the rabbis and scholars down through the ages. Jerome (ca. A.D. 345–419) was the great translator of the Old and New Testaments of the Bible from Hebrew and Greek into Latin. He studied and mastered Hebrew under rabbis in A.D. 373. Luther studied Hebrew under a rabbi before translating the Bible into German in the sixteenth century. By the time of the King James translation of the English Bible, early in the seventeenth century, Hebrew was widely known among Christian biblical scholars. But, of course, like Latin and ancient Greek, it was only studied and read. Even among the Jews it was seldom spoken because it was considered sacred and therefore not to be used casually.

Eliezer ben Yehuda was caught up in the spirit of Zionism. He was certain that his people would be restored to their homeland. After all, had not the holy Scriptures held forth that promise for nearly twenty centuries? When that day came, Yiddish would no longer serve the people. For one reason, Yiddish was a fluid language that differed from place to place, throughout the world, and the Jewish people spoke about seventy other languages in addition to Yiddish. Something was needed that would unite them. Eliezer knew that something was the Hebrew language.

Hebrew had already been enjoying a renaissance among certain writers. The most notable of them was a contemporary of ben Yehuda named Shalom Jacob Abramovich. Abramovich helped develop a modern Hebrew literary style that was both precise and natural.

Ben Yehuda went to live in Israel, or as it was still called at that time (late in the nineteenth century), Palestine. It was there that he began to promote the idea of reviving Hebrew as a spoken language. He was opposed as advocates of change always are. Pious Jews objected on religious grounds. To the rest it seemed like a pipe dream. There was plenty of work to do draining swamps and trying to turn this wasteland into productive farmland. Who had time to learn to speak Hebrew?

Ben Yehuda was not discouraged. He knew such a change would take time to accomplish. In the meantime, he was joined in the land by his betrothed, Deborah. With her, at least, he could insist that Hebrew and not Yiddish be spoken. Deborah dutifully obliged and became the first mother to talk to her babies in Hebrew in many centuries.[2]

Eliezer and Deborah lived together for only ten years (1881–1891) when she died of tuberculosis. The saddened widower carried on his mission in the remaining years of his life by working as a journalist and compiling an exhaustive and definitive dictionary of modern Hebrew. He died in 1922 and thirty thousand Jews followed his body to the grave.

I believe the revival of Hebrew as a spoken language is one of the heralds announcing the nearness of the return. It is a miracle in our day.

Operation Magic Carpet

Among the stories of how the Jews have been restored to their ancient homeland, one of the most notable is known as Operation Magic Carpet. Fifty-four thousand Yemenite Jews were airlifted to Israel in the 1950s.

Jews had lived in Yemen, a fanatically Moslem country, for centuries. They had existed under hard conditions. They were desperately poor and usually treated as second-class citizens. They were helped to endure their hardships by the hope that had been kept alive among them that someday God would take them back home to Israel.

After 1948, they began to hear a rumor that something too good to be true had happened: the state of Israel had been reborn. The scattered Jews all over Yemen started to dispose of any property they possessed. Then they began the long, hard desert trek to the Port of Aden, then under British control. They remarked among themselves, "Have not the Scriptures told us that God would bear his people on eagles' wings?"

So it was that the government of Israel dispatched transport aircraft to Aden (Yemen), and the small, fine-boned Yemenite Jews saw the eagles that would bear them home at last. The aircraft were able to bear many more persons than had been estimated at first, because these people were so small and light. Their body weights were well below average after their long treks across the desert. Many of them weighed no more than sixty pounds. Overnight, it seemed, the population of little Israel grew by fifty-four thousand.

Returning to the land was not so easy for some others. In 1947 the Jewish underground bought an old steamer in New York named *The President Warfield*. They renamed it *Exodus* and sailed it to France where they picked up forty-five hundred Jewish refugees who wanted to get to Palestine, which was at that time still under British mandate. The *Exodus* got within twenty-two miles of the coast of Israel when they were intercepted by British destroyers which rammed the old steamer, raked it with machine gun fire, and then sent in an armed boarding party. Many of the hapless refugees were killed.

The *Exodus* was towed to port in Haifa. Its surviving passengers were transferred to departing ships and taken back to Europe. Most of them experienced the final cruelty of returning to the wretched refugee camps in Germany from which they had only lately escaped.

Happily this was one of the last incidents of its sort. The following year the British departed, the Israelis won their independence in a fierce war with five Arab nations, and never again has any Jew been denied entry to Israel.

Prophecy to the Land

Long ago Ezekiel (see Ezek. 36:1–15) prophesied that the land would become verdant and fruitful in the latter days after having been turned into a wasteland by its enemies. In *Innocents Abroad* Mark Twain described Palestine in the nineteenth century as desolate and swampy, barren and mosquito-ridden. Today

Israel blossoms like a rose. The promise of the Bible is that once Zion has been rebuilt, *then* the Messiah will return in glory.

Since 1948 over 140 million trees have been planted in Israel. Thousands of acres of swampland have been drained, and more thousands of acres of desert have been irrigated. The land could only support some few thousand people a century ago. Now Israel's population slightly exceeds four million. Ezekiel prophesied that "I, the Sovereign Lord, am going to take all my people out of the nations where they have gone, gather them together, and bring them back to their own land. I will unite them into one nation in the land, on the mountains of Israel" (37:21–22 TEV).

The fulfillment of this ancient prophecy in our day is a miracle and a sign of the nearness of the return. That is why it makes me all the sadder that our American government still refuses to recognize Jerusalem as the capital of Israel. I have written about this in my book *Jerusalem, D.C.*

During the time that Menachem Begin was prime minister of Israel, I met with him on eleven occasions. On one of those occasions, we discussed the question of Jerusalem. Begin explained to me that the Camp David Accords, which he and Sadat had signed along with President Carter, had not mentioned Jerusalem. "Only letters were exchanged among us. Everybody stated his view about what should happen to Jerusalem, but we reached no agreement."

On another occasion I asked him to talk about the Israeli settlements in Samaria and the hill country of Judea that have caused so much controversy in the press. Part of that controversy has happened because the United States and the Arabs argue that Samaria and the hill country of Judea, which includes Bethlehem, are occupied territories that rightly belong to Jordan or the Palestinians—nobody is quite sure who they belong to.

Begin told me about an encounter he had had with President Carter. "He said something very negative. He told me the settlements were illegal. But I showed the president a list of names—Bethlehem, Shiloh, Hebron, Bethel. I asked him if the governor of Pennsylvania would be allowed to proclaim that no Jews would be allowed to live in Bethlehem, Pennsylvania? He told me the governor would not be allowed to do that because it would be an act of racism. Then I asked him if I, who am the governor of Bethlehem of Judah, should forbid Jews to live there? He had no answer for me."

The Miracle of Modern Israel

Israel has become probably the third strongest military power in the world. That's a big claim for a country about as big as New Jersey that struggles with staggering inflation. But according to expert strategic estimates, only the United States and the Soviet Union are more powerful militarily. In a war between the superpowers, Israel could tilt the scales one way or the other.

I have discussed Israel's feats against Soviet hardware in the 1982 Lebanese campaign. One top Israeli general told me that his country had not used the majority of its advanced equipment. They had withheld them in order to maintain their classified security status.

But some of their latest developments did get unveiled. The Russians employed eight of their most advanced tanks in 1982. These tanks were called "invincible" because the armor was considered impenetrable. Israel, however, had developed a new armor-piercing projectile which their standard Chariot tanks (anti-tank tanks) could fire. This projectile would penetrate eight feet of steel. The information concerning these tanks was top secret. As a result, every one of the new Soviet-made tanks was knocked out of action by this new weapon.

I also had the opportunity to interview the man who has pioneered laser technology in Israel. He told me they already have laser equipment that can be used on the field of battle by planes and tanks. Even back in 1972 they had the capability of using lasers for warfare. The gentleman I mentioned earlier who had invented the laser in Israel told me in 1972 that one laser was perfected that had a three-mile depth and a one-mile range. Any enemy tank operator who would come within the perimeters of the laser would have the nerves in his eyes burned out. The tank operators were using infra-ray lenses, and the lasers would automatically destroy the nerve of the eyes, targeting these eyes through the infra-ray lenses. The same gentleman told me that Israel has never used this incredible weapon. He also told me that Israel was holding most of its advanced weapons in reserve.[3]

The prophecies that relate to the prowess and success of Israel after its restoration to the land in the last days can be found in Ezekiel 5:5, Amos 9:15, Leviticus 26:27–45, Deuteronomy 28:36–68, Isaiah 40–60, and Ezekiel 37–39. I will not elaborate on them here. They speak for themselves. But I do want to comment on Isaiah 19:16–18. These verses speak of a war between Judah and Egypt, and of how the Egyptians will be in fear of the Jews. They were fulfilled after the clashes between Israel and Egypt in 1956, 1967, and 1973. The humiliating defeats that the Israeli army and air force delivered to the Egyptian forces were one reason President Anwar Sadat sought to achieve a negotiated peace between the two countries.

Also in fulfillment of prophecy, God protects Israel. Jeremiah wrote, "I will gather them out of all countries where I have driven them in My anger, and in great wrath, I will bring them back to this place, and I will cause them to dwell safely" (Jer. 32:37). We are moving rapidly closer to the return. Keep your eyes closely glued on Russia. In my book *Let My People Go,* I tell the incredible story of the three million Jews who are not allowed to leave the Soviet Union. Many of them have been put in insane asylums and injected with drugs trying to destroy their minds because of their fanatical love for the word of God and their persistent desire to go to Israel. I believe we will see the judgment of God fall upon Russia. You can be assured of one thing: the return of the Jews to the land is a sign of the return of the Lord. No power under heaven, be it Russia or whoever, will stick its finger in God's eye and try to hinder His prophetic plan.

He Is at the Door

Jesus told us to learn a lesson from the fig tree: "When its branch has already become tender and puts forth leaves, you know that summer is near. So you also, when you see all these things, know that it is near, at the very doors" (Matt. 24:32–33). Then He added a startling comment: "Assuredly, I say to you, this generation will by no means pass away till all these things are fulfilled" (v. 34).

How are we supposed to understand that? To answer that question we have first to decide what He meant by the phrase "this generation." There has been a lot of disagreement on how to interpret this. Did that mean the generation of people of which Jesus Himself was a part? I don't think so. We need to let the context of the verse help us interpret it, and the context talks about a fig tree. "This generation" is the generation of people who see the fig tree putting forth leaves from tender branches.

That brings us to ask, what is meant by the fig tree? Here we need to resort to symbolism to help us unlock the mystery, but the symbolism is not difficult or obscure. The fig tree stands for restored Israel. The leaves of the fig tree are common ornaments on government buildings in Israel. I challenge you to order breakfast anywhere in Israel without its being served with some figs.

In the Bible the majority of references to the fig tree are symbolic. It appears often as an illustration in stories and parables. Jothan used it about the trees (see Judg. 9:10–11). Jeremiah told a parable concerning the exiles (see Jer. 24, compare 29:17) which employed the fig tree. The fig tree was often a symbol of peace and prosperity (see 1 Kings 4:25; 2 Kings 18:31; Joel 2:22; Mic. 4:4, Hag. 2:19; Zech. 3:10). It was also employed in prophecies of impending national distress (see Jer. 5:17; 8:13; Hos. 2:12; Joel 1:7, 12; Amos 4:9). The fig tree has always been a symbol of the nation of Israel. If you were trying to get the four most important symbols of Israel, they would indeed be the Star of David, the menorah, the olive branch, and the fig tree.

From these things we must conclude that Jesus' use of the fig tree in talking about the end of the age was not casual. For those who had ears to hear, it meant that Israel itself would be the key sign of the imminence of the return.

Here, then, is how I interpret Jesus' remarks about the fig tree and "this generation." The generation of people who see the blossoming of the fig tree (Israel's rebirth and establishment in the family of nations) is the generation that will see the completion of "all these things" (the signs of the end recorded in Matthew 24). The generation of people that saw the blossoming were born between 1925 and 1935. Their lifespan will be roughly seventy years according to the Bible and the actuarial charts. Some of them will live much longer, but the Lord will have returned before their generation passes away, I believe.

The Bible warns us against fixing days and hours (see Matt. 24:36), but we are exhorted to recognize the season. Most of all, we must live in daily expectancy. The rebirth of Israel, then, is a sign that the return will occur within the lifetimes of some of us now living. But nothing stands in the way of its happening tonight or tomorrow. If ever a generation of people had reason to believe they were living in the days immediately prior to the return, the glorious appearing of the King of Kings and the Lord of Lords, it is our generation.

> Listen to this secret truth: we shall not all die, but when the last trumpet sounds, we shall all be changed in an instant, as quickly as the blinking of an eye. For when the trumpet sounds, the dead will be raised, never to die again, and we shall all be changed. For what is mortal must be changed into what is immortal; what will die must be changed into what cannot die. So when this takes place, and the mortal has been changed into the immortal, the scripture will come true: "Death is destroyed; victory is complete!" "Where, Death, is your victory? Where, Death, is your power to hurt?" Death gets its power to hurt from sin, and sin gets its power from the Law. But thanks be to God who gives us the victory through our Lord Jesus Christ! (1 Cor. 15:51–56).

XI

The City of Armageddon

"If the Israelis threaten us, we will wipe them out within two days.
I can assure you our plans are made for this eventuality."

—Soviet Ambassador Anatoly Dobrynin

I sat in a circle of men, young and old, all of whom were blind.
I looked at them all through my tears. Strangely, as I sat there, I
remembered something a general once told me. "Mike," he said,
"if America turns her back on Israel, the Soviets will come. And
Jerusalem, the city of peace, will become the city of Armageddon."

These men with whom I was sitting had all been soldiers. For
each of them, Jerusalem had already become, in some measure,
the city of Armageddon. "Why," I asked them, "were you willing
to pay such a price as losing your sight for Jerusalem?"

Moisch sat in the circle. He was a handsome veteran of the
1967 war. That was the war in which Jerusalem had been recaptured from Jordan. It was Moisch who answered first. "Mr.
Evans," he said, "Jerusalem is our soul. A man cannot live without a soul. For thousands of years we prayed—my parents, my
grandparents, my great-grandparents, and their great-grandparents, and I—we prayed that we might return to Jerusalem, our ancient Holy City. Without Jerusalem, before Jerusalem, we were
all blind. But now we have Jerusalem. I may not have eyes, but
that was a price worth paying for so rich a prize. Now my people
can see with their own eyes the fulfillment of the ancient prophecies of the Bible."

Another veteran, a man in his thirties, spoke in turn. "You have
to understand. This is serious business. These Russians have been

involved in every war we have fought. Provoking them, arming, instigating—they want to turn this into an Armageddon, but they would have to take more than our eyes before we would let them have it. They would have to take our arms and legs before we would stop fighting for Israel."[1]

That night in my room I made a call to an old friend, Menachem Begin. He asked me to meet him at the Waldorf Astoria before he met with President Reagan. Israel was in battle, and he was weary. The battle, as I mentioned earlier in the book, was more against Soviet technicians and strategists, Soviet MiGs and Soviet SAM missiles and terrorist organizations from throughout the world than with the PLO or Moslems. Israel's capture of those incredible caves, six to eight miles deep, loaded with Soviet weapons, was one of the greatest discoveries of our time. They captured over one hundred different Russian weapon systems—so much equipment that it took Israel over two months, using 150 ten-ton Mack trucks and one thousand Israeli soldiers to haul the equipment back into Israel. This was, without question, an incredible picture of the Soviet Union's true intentions to turn Jerusalem, the city of peace, into the city of Armageddon.

I invited several people to go with me that night to meet the prime minister at the Waldorf. Among them were Ben Armstrong, the president of the National Association of Religious Broadcasters; Forest Montgomery, the attorney for the National Association of Evangelicals; Bobbie James, the first lady of Alabama; and Anne Murchison, the wife of the owner of the Dallas Cowboys. I'll never forget what happened when Anne sat down beside the prime minister. She started to speak, but no words passed her lips. Instead, tears flooded her eyes. Her tears of compassion were for a weary old man with the weight of the world on his shoulders. She buried her head in her Bible and wept. Menachem Begin patted her hand and then he began to weep also.

At last she spoke. She looked up and said, "Mr. Prime Minister, do you know why I am crying? It is not I, but God who is weeping through me. He loves you and your precious land and people so much."

Then she continued reading:

Thus says the LORD,
"You are Mine.
When you pass through the waters,
I will be with you.
And through the rivers,
they shall not overflow you.
When you walk through the fire,
you will not be burned,
Nor shall the flame scorch you.
For I am the LORD your God,
the Holy One of Israel, your Savior" (Isa. 43:1–3).

Still weeping Begin replied, "I am so very thankful for the Christian friends we have. We live in difficult times...we must do everything in our power to resist it. We believe, all of us, in divine providence. And we believe in the Book of books. This is the reason we sometimes have great moral strength, even to withstand pressure from the mighty ones. The friendship between Christians and the Jewish people is a new phenomenon of our time. It is indeed the beginning of the redemption of Israel."[2]

Later, shortly before we left, we gathered about the prime minister to pray for him. I asked Anne to lead us. "O God, send down Your holy angels to strengthen this nation and these people. I pray, Lord, that You would put a wall of fire around the nation of Israel. Be the glory in her midst. Protect and guard this nation. Give Your wisdom to this dear man, and strength, and healing. We pray for the peace of Jerusalem."

Jerusalem has experienced so little peace. A worried prime minister had little peace in a world that wanted him to give up Jerusalem. Soldiers with blind eyes had little peace because of Russians' endeavoring to move against Israel and Jerusalem. Colonel Gissin, the spokesman for the Israel Defense Force in Jerusalem, had little peace. He told me how vulnerable Israel is to attack. Russian missiles in Jordan and Syria sit in a semicircle around Jerusalem, only minutes from their targets.

In 1984, the same year that I sat in Jerusalem with some of the blinded veterans of Israel's wars, I also had opportunity to meet and talk with General Mordechai Gur. Gur commanded the paratroopers who figured importantly in the capture of Jerusalem in

1967. He was the chief of staff of the IDF. I asked him, "What was it like in 1967 when you captured the city?"

He said, "First of all, remember that Jerusalem was divided. Israel held the new city on the West. East Jerusalem was in Jordanian hands. Walls and fences separated the two halves. The Jordanian garrison was strong and their positions well fortified with bunkers, trenches, and mine fields.

"Jerusalem was probably the hardest battle we ever fought. That was because we would not allow ourselves to incur civilian casualties or to damage the holy sites if it were at all possible. So, it was difficult fighting. We fought at very close range, between sixty and eighty yards. You can throw a stone that far. Artillery and bombs are no good when you're that close to the enemy. It was an infantry fight only. Tough.

"We went across the line at two-fifteen in the morning on Monday; and it was ten o'clock in the morning on Wednesday when I announced to the government, 'The Temple mount is ours!' So, in all, it took less than forty-eight hours....

"It was the greatest experience of my life. I was born in Jerusalem. It had been the center of our nation for thousands of years. I remember well what I wrote in my diary that day: 'What will my family say when they hear that Jerusalem has been liberated?'

"We were dirty and exhausted, still in shock from having lost so many men. But everyone was rushing to the Wailing Wall. Near the wall there was a big, impulsive celebration, excitement, singing, praying. Two rabbis argued. One said the appropriate prayer was one of thanks to God for the victory. The other said they should deplore our losses. So...they did both at the same time—one thanking and one wailing. Then they all sang *ha' Tikvah [The Hope*, Israel's national anthem].

"I watched all of this with my own eyes. I was still in my position, commanding the operation. As a soldier, I watched the civilians rushing to the wall as the flag of Israel was flying over the Western Wall."

Big Night on the Town

I am going to call him Jacob. He is a general in the Israeli army with whom I have become acquainted in recent years, and I now count him among my friends. But he is entitled to a measure of privacy, so I'll call him Jacob.

Jacob turned out to be an unusually warm and personable man who obviously enjoyed talking about Israel, the Bible, world events, Jews, Christians, the Patriarchs, Jesus—he loved to talk and think about things. He was very suave, too, a real man of the world by his demeanor.

As our interview was drawing to a close after several hours of talking, he looked at me with an impish twinkle in his eye. "Mike," he said, "do not deny me. I am coming to your hotel tonight at eleven o'clock to pick you up. Be ready to go because I'm going to show you the biggest time of your life!"

"Well, uhh,..." my tone of voice reflected my reluctance.

"Come now, you will never be the same after tonight. I assure you."

"I don't doubt it, but..."

He chuckled, "You must trust me."

"Of course," I replied. What could he have in mind? My pulse raced.

"What you are going to do and see tonight will blow your mind!"

I tried to smile and act nonchalant. "Really?" I said.

"I guarantee you, you are really going to experience something."

I didn't want to offend the general; but to stay on the safe side, I invited my associate, L. W. Dollar, to join me. I told L. W. that if things got bad, we would excuse ourselves and go back early.

That night he arrived at the hotel promptly at eleven and rang my room. We were both dressed casually in the usual Israeli style. We zoomed off in his car. He still hadn't told me where we were going, but we were headed away from the hotel district.

Before I knew what was happening, we were pulling up in the small parking are adjacent to Zechariah's tomb, one of the city's ancient monuments. Jacob got out of the car, then reached in the back seat for something. I got out on the passenger side. "Come on!" he said.

We walked over to the tomb, exquisitely lit for night viewing.

Jacob had a Bible in his hand. He opened it. "Let us read some of the words of this great prophet," he said, and commenced to read aloud:

The LORD Almighty gave this message to Zechariah: "I have longed to help Jerusalem because of my deep love for her people, a love which has made me angry with her enemies. I will return to Jerusalem, my holy city, and live there. It will be known as the faithful city, and the hill of the LORD Almighty will be called the sacred hill. Once again old men and women, so old that they use canes when they walk, will be sitting in the city squares. And the streets will again be full of boys and girls playing" (Zech. 8:1–5 TEV).

"Jacob!" I exclaimed, "those words are being fulfilled in these very days!"

"It is true," he replied. "It would have seemed impossible not very long ago, but now it is within reach."

We recited prayers and psalms there. Then we got back in Jacob's car and drove on the Absalom's tomb where we did much the same thing. Next on the agenda was the Pool of Siloam; after that, David's tomb.

It was two in the morning by the time we were approaching the Western Wall of the temple mount. Jacob went and awakened the gatekeeper to let us in. He led me down into the excavations that archaeologists have made by the wall. He showed me the layer of ash from the burning of the Temple by the Romans in A.D. 70. Deeper down was evidence of a secret passageway that the levitical priests may have used, perhaps as an escape route. In one area they had uncovered natural rock. Could it have been part of the rock of Moriah on which Abraham prepared to sacrifice his only son, Isaac, to God?

As we walked and looked, we also paused as we had at the other places to read the Scriptures and to pray. It was back on the pavement in front of the traditional site of prayer below the Wall that we were approached by the man I mentioned earlier who urged us to come and meet his master who was the Messiah. As I said, Jacob rebuked the man so that he fled back to wherever he had come from and left us in peace to contemplate this, the most hallowed site of all in Judaism.

After that we walked through the streets of Jerusalem the rest of the night. It was about five-thirty in the morning when we arrived back at the hotel. Jacob had been saying, "I do this at least once a week, sometimes more often—it is my entertainment, my night life." He laughed, "I do this instead of going to a movie."

"You're not kidding, are you?" I observed.

"No, it is truly important to me. I have been in a lot of fighting, and I know that God has spared my life. One time I was in a tank that took a direct hit. It literally blew up. I still don't know how I survived that, except that I know it had to be God's hand of mercy to me.

"So I know every street, every alleyway, every hill, every valley, every rock of this city—this holy city. It is the greatest privilege of my life to be able to live here and to worship God here as I have just done with you."

"Thank you for taking me along. It was an honor and a joy to share this night with you," I said.

"Mike, I could tell that you love the God of Israel and the Bible as I do. I knew you would understand. You see, I know God has a plan for my life and for this whole nation, and above all, for Jerusalem—for this is where the Messiah will come. I pray every day that He will return soon. I always think, maybe it will be today!"

Turning a Corner

I think that what I encountered in my Israeli friend, Jacob, is not so rare anymore as some would think. Israel has passed through troubling times of late. Besides the pain of the desperate fighting and heavy casualties of the Yom Kippur War in 1973, there has been the disappointment of the Peace for Galilee campaign in 1985. Added to those things is the drain on the quality of daily life created by the ever-present threat of terrorism; for example, teachers who take their students on outings do so with firearms slung on their shoulders.

Other factors may even contribute more heavily to throwing Israeli life out of joint. Inflation rates and economic conditions in the country have been nearly disastrous for several years. Part of this is attributable to the staggering cost of national defense in Israel. Then there are the Arab portions of the population whose birthrates exceed those of Jewish Israelis by a significant margin. Especially in Samaria (more often called the West Bank by the Western press), which was captured from Jordan in the 1967 war, an enormous number of Arabs—a majority of Samaria's population—continues to live. The government in Jerusalem is faced with the dilemma of what to do with them. They consider Samaria an integral part of Israel's territory, but most of its residents hold Jordanian citizenship. A great number of those Arabs living in Israel do so because of the economic benefits.

In spite of what the media says, the Lebanese people did not rejoice when Israel left. Quite the contrary, those living close to the borders wept because of the marvelous care they had received from the Israelis in their hospitals, employment, and food.

How much do these sorts of problems—chronic terrorism, skyrocketing inflation, the Arab population explosion—weigh on the Israeli psyche? Think with me, for a moment, about how they compare with other sorts of problems, usually of a strategic or tactical military nature, that have faced the Israelis in the past. Wiping out the Egyptian air force in 1967 was hard, but it could be and it was done. Rescuing the passengers of the Air France flight, highjacked on its way to Israel, from the airport in Entebbe, Uganda, in 1976 was not easy, but it was possible. Taking out the Iraqi nuclear reactor in 1981 went off without a hitch. Overcoming sophisticiated Soviet antiaircraft missile systems in the Bekka Valley in Lebanon in 1982 was entirely within the realm of possibility. All these things won them admiring headlines around the world.

The Israelis wish they could solve their economic and sociological problems with the same effectiveness. But no amount of technological expertise, no amount of derring-do by Israeli pilots or commandos, no amount of foreign aid from the United States, and no amount of political acumen are going to do it. The nation is staring straight into the eyes of cruel problems that are not yielding, even in the face of their finest efforts and their supreme sacrifices.

What happens to you and me, on a much smaller scale of

course, when we are faced with apparently insoluble problems? From time to time, each of us finds ourselves in such a situation. Israel has, you have, and I have; we have all been humbled. Even the hardest man in desperation will cry out to god for strength. It's that simple.

A Close Shave

Israel's victory in the Six-Day War of 1967 was an incredible event. I remember it well. I was sitting in a barber's chair in Philadelphia that June morning. The radio was playing some restful music, as I recall. But suddenly: "We interrupt this broadcast to bring you a special bulletin. Early this morning, Middle Eastern time, hostilities broke out between Israel and three of its Arab neighbors—Egypt, Jordan, and Syria. U. N. peacekeeping forces in the Gaza Strip and the Sinai Peninsula only recently completed their evacuation as demanded by Egypt. Egyptian forces closed the Gulf of Aqaba to Israeli ships two days ago.

"At this hour we have sketchy reports of Israeli air raids early this morning. However, the Israeli government has ordered a blackout of all news, and our correspondents in Cairo, Amman, and Damascus have been unable to verify rumors of the raids. An official joint communique from Cairo and Amman indicates deep penetration of Israeli territory by Egyptian and Jordanian forces. Stay tuned to this station for further information as soon as it becomes available."

The music resumed playing on the station, but my barber didn't resume clicking his scissors. "Well," he said, "looks like this may be it for Israel. If all those Arabs go at 'em at once, they won't have a chance."

"I think it's the other way around, my friend," I replied.

"What do you mean by that?" his scissors were clicking again now.

"I mean I don't think those Arabs have a chance because God Almighty is going to fight for those Jews. You watch, when the dust settles, the Jews will have Jerusalem all to themselves."

"Hmmm," he paused, "guess we'll have to wait and see."

We didn't have to wait long. The rumors about the Israeli preemptive air raids proved entirely correct. The communique proved entirely false—pure Arab bravado in the face of disaster. The Arab air forces had been almost totally destroyed on the ground. After that the Israeli army devoted its main attention to the Egyptian thrust across the Sinai. It was one of the largest tank battles of history. Without air cover, the Egyptians never had a chance. They were slaughtered.

The battle in the Sinai was going so well, in fact, that an entire brigade of paratroopers was rerouted to Jerusalem. That was Mordechai Gur's brigade. The city was in Israeli hands in two days, thanks to the fact that Israeli armor was able to block reinforcements going to the Jordanian garrison in the city. Meanwhile, other Israeli units systematically pushed the Jordanians out of Samaria and back across the Jordan.

In the north, Israeli units captured the critical Golan Heights that overlook the Sea of Galilee. For years Syrian artillery and rocket fire from those heights had harassed Israeli settlements in the area. By this time the troops in the Sinai had pushed the Egyptians back across the Suez. Israel had captured territory including the Sinai peninsula that was three times greater than its own size prior to the war. And it had all taken only six days.

It was an event unparalleled in military history. Hilter's *blitzkrieg* strategy had never enjoyed comparable success. The whole world was dazzled. It was the David and Goliath story all over again. Israel's elation knew no bounds. But, as I've already explained, that elation has not been sustained in recent years. Something different is happening in Israel today. To understand this different something, we need the help of the ancient prophet of Israel, Ezekiel.

Ezekiel's vision of the restoration of Israel was of a valley full of dry bones (see Ezek. 37). First those bones had to be brought back together; then sinews were laid on them. Then came the flesh and the organs; and at last, skin covered them over. But the job was not finished. They still needed the breath of life, the Spirit of God, before they could stand upright and truly live.

That gives us a pattern for understanding God's work in restoring Israel. It started out on a purely physical level—a political state with a parliament, a government, a post office, an army, and sewer systems—but devoid of the Spirit. The final stage, the ultimate stage of Israel's restoration, will come when God breathes His Spirit into His people; and they come to believe in their Messiah, Jesus.

Jerusalem, the Miracle City

I have visited Jerusalem more than twenty times. My favorite time to walk the streets there is early in the morning, around five o'clock. Then you can hear the voices of Jerusalem first rising, and you realize that this city is not just ancient stones and stories. It is real life. It has a soul. But still the ancient stones of this marvelous city seem to whisper stories of bygone centuries.

Jerusalem has the sad honor of being considered the world's most hated city. More wars have been fought at her gates than at the gates of any other city in the world. No spot on earth has known the heartache, the tears, the bloodshed Jerusalem has known. It has changed hands twenty-six times and been leveled to the ground five times.[3]

The city of peace has been besieged by tyrants. It has been inflamed by riots within. It has known treachery and intrigue at its lowest and meanest. Its walls and streets have been splashed with blood generation after generation.

While it is hated, Jerusalem is also loved as no other city on the earth. Hundreds of thousands of Jews have kissed the earth on which the city stands. So, Jerusalem is precious to God and man, and it is the emblem of spiritual beauty.

Many cities have stirred men either to great deeds or to desperate acts, but no city has so perpetually stirred the heart of mankind as has Jerusalem. Its soldiers have fought like madmen. Its poets have written like angels. Its pilgrim-citizens have plowed through the blood and fire of hell to sustain its holy existence.

Jerusalem is one of the smallest cities in the world. But its place in the history of the world and the imagination of mankind is almost unlimited. Jerusalem is the center of the earth. Here east meets west. Here three great continents—Europe, Asia, and Africa—touch in more ways than one.

Jerusalem has been, for many, a city of tears. The Word of God says yet more tears will flow in its streets. I believe Russia will be destroyed on the mountains of Israel. Ezekiel prophesied that long ago (see 39:4). He called Russia *Gog,* an ancient name rich in symbolic meaning. Russia will invade Israel. The great initial battle will be fought on the plain of Esdraelon near Megiddo. There the hand of God's wrath will fall on the Soviets.

The Lord told Ezekiel that after many years Russia would come into "a country where the people were brought together from many nations without fear of war. He will invade the mountains of Israel, which were desolate and deserted so long, but where all the people now live in safety" (Ezek. 38:8).

This is one of the most stunning passages describing the re-gathering of Israel at the end of the age in all of the Bible. Surely the Jews were brought back from the sword: that sword killed six million of them in Europe during Hitler's Holocaust—one million of those who perished were children. Israel is the only modern nation that has been brought back from the sword. They were also brought back out of many nations: more than eighty nationalities are represented in modern Israel's population. The land to which they returned was truly desolate and deserted: the Israelis have given the land a new birth. When they started to re-enter Israel in the last century and during the early years of this century, they were met by as desolate a piece of real estate as anyone might imagine. They drained swamps, started irrigation projects, reforested the hillsides, and planted the land for the first time in centuries.

God told Ezekiel that Gog (Russia) would start thinking up an evil plan to invade a helpless country where the people live in peace and security in unwalled towns that have no defenses. When Ezekiel wrote that, no such place existed anywhere. Every town had walls or some means of defense. In Israel today there is no wall around any village. The Israelis are a people at rest. After centuries of exile, living in lands where they were regularly persecuted, they have come at last to a place of rest. They have their own flag and their own government.

There is only one great body of Jews in the world still languishing under the persecutor's lash. These three million children of Israel who are in pharaoh's bondage in Russia long to be freed from oppression, prison, mental institutions; and they are, indeed, going to experience freedom, because God's word is true.

Jeremiah's prophecy must soon come to pass:

The Lord says, "The time is coming when people will no longer swear by me as the living God who brought the people of Israel out of the land of Egypt. Instead, they will swear by me as the living God who brought the people of Israel out of a northern land and out of all the other countries where I had scattered them. I will bring them back to their own country, to the land that I gave their ancestors. I, the Lord, have spoken" (Jer. 16:14–15 TEV).

This prophecy means that Russia, the northern land mentioned by Jeremiah, must give up the Jews living inside her borders. The time has come because the return is imminent. When Jesus spoke of the destruction of Jerusalem, He said that those Jews who were not killed by the sword would be taken as prisoners to all countries. He added, Jerusalem would be trampled over by the Gentiles until their time is up (see Luke 21:24). Their time was up when Jerusalem was captured by Israel in 1967, with one exception. One last vestige of Gentile control still remains in Jerusalem: the old temple mount. That is where the Mosque of Omar, better known as the Dome of the Rock, and the Al Aksa Mosque are located. It is protected by the Israeli government as the exclusive domain of the Moslems. When that Gentile rule of the Temple mount is terminated, it will be heaven's signal that the era of the Gentiles is finally and utterly past. It will be time to usher in the new age that will be inaugurated by the second coming of Christ.

Jerusalem, the city that has changed hands more than a score of times down through history, is a key factor in the interpretation of biblical prophecy. Its administration by Israel tells us to lift up our heads and realize that our Savior's return to earth is near. There are other Bible prophecies that tell us a world leader will rise in the last days who will try to unify the entire world. He will make his headquarters in Jerusalem. He will be the ultimate false Messiah; and he will be at the head of a revived Roman Empire, represented in our day by the European Common Market (see Rev. 13; Dan. 7).

I have in my possession two documents that were given to me in January, 1981. One is called The European Declaration and the other is called The Luxembourg Agreement. Both of these documents have been issued by the Common Market. Both of them include demands that Israel restore into Arab hands all the lands that it has won in its various wars, especially Jerusalem and Samaria and the hill country of Judea. The Common Market supports demands for the establishment of a Palestinian state in Samaria and Judea.

Serious students of prophecy see this stance of the Europeans against Israel and Jerusalem as a sign that the battle of Armageddon may be looming. In the next chapter I will spell out in clear detail why that is the case. But for now, suffice it to say that the powers of hell will rage until the City of Shalom, the Holy City of Jerusalem, becomes the city of Armageddon. Israel's only hope, our only hope, in the face of this great threat is the Blessed Hope of the return of our Lord Jesus. That is a sure and certain hope that will never betray those who embrace it.

XII

My Warning

"The next decade may well become the most violent in the past 4,000 plus years...since the chaotic days of Noah."

—Cliff Harris, Climatologist

Speaking the truth is hazardous. If you do it too often, people will begin to call you a sensationalist, a fanatic, a preacher of doom whom they don't need to take seriously. But what about the truth? Does it cease to exist because people overlook it? Does it disappear if they ignore it long enough? Lots of people who have cancer do that. When some little problem, like a sore that won't heal, comes along, they ignore it. Psychologists call it denial. But it doesn't work. If they stay in denial long enough, the cancer has time to grow to the point that a doctor can offer them no hope for recovery.

Mankind is doing essentially the same thing with the signs of the times in which we live. Our planet has a number of sores that aren't healing, but most people choose to ignore them. What can we do about it? they ask. To ask such a question is to acknowledge that they are ignorant of the Bible's message to all of God's creatures.

I talked with the vice chairman of one of the largest banks in the world. I said, "You're in a good position to see what's going on in the world of finance. Tell me, what kind of prediction would you make about the future from your perspective?"

"Mike," he replied, "things are so bad that the only thing I'm willing to predict is that the return of Jesus Christ is near."

The amazing thing about that incredible statement is that in 1984 alone seventy-five banks went bankrupt. Much of America's wealth has been loaned out to nations and governments that are, by any standards, bankrupt. We keep loaning money to countries just so they can make the interest payments on the money they owe us!

"Could you imagine how long a bank would last that kept loaning you the money to make your payments on the loan they gave you to buy your house?" the banker asked me.

"Not long," I replied. "I couldn't afford to do it!"

"Nobody can. And those who think they can are only kidding themselves. They are merely postponing disaster. That disaster, when it comes, will be God's judgment on this nation."

Neither that banker nor I are prophets. One doesn't need the gift of prophecy to read the Bible and then compare what it says with what is happening today. According to my understanding of events, the times in which we are living are the beginning of the end—and the beginning of the end is already partly over.

Billy Graham once said that if God didn't judge America for its sins, He would have to apologize to Sodom and Gomorrah. God is giving us a first warning before that judgment starts in earnest, just as He gave warning to Sodom and Gomorrah. Only one family, the family of Lot, heeded that warning and fled in time. The rest of the citizens of those infamous twin cities had laughed the warning off. They loved their sins too much. That night homosexual lovers snuggled comfortably into bed together throughout both cities. But, by dawn the next morning, they and their beds were only ashes. And so were the beds and bodies of those in the city who were not homosexuals, but who had turned a blind eye to the perversion for so long.

Long ago Jeremiah wrote:

The Lord said to his people, "Stand at the crossroads and look. Ask for the ancient paths and where the best road is. Walk in it, and you will live in peace." But they said, "No, we will not!" Then the Lord appointed watchmen to listen for the trumpet's warning. But they said, "We will not listen." So the Lord said, "Listen, you nations, and learn what is going to happen to my people. Listen, earth! As punishment for all their schemes I am bringing ruin on these people, because they have rejected my teaching and have not obeyed my words" (Jer. 6:16–19 TEV).

I had dinner one evening with one of the wealthiest men in the world. He was a true billionaire. I told him I had heard a story about another billionaire who had lost everything, almost overnight. "Could that possibly be true?" I asked.

"Yes," he replied.

"How could it happen?"

In answer to that he told me several incredible stories of the various ways very wealthy men had lost all their money. As I listened to him I had not a glimmer of what was about to befall him. In fact, within a matter of days after we talked, eleven of his own companies were forced to file Chapter 11 and, ultimately, bankruptcy.

Changes come unexpectedly only on those who are unprepared. What is astonishing is how the majority of people move through life as if they were part of some enormous herd. They give no thought to their course or their destination. They merely follow the steer in front of them, and the trail boss brings them to watering places and grazing lands. That's all that counts. Only too late do they discover that they have been led to slaughter. That is how Satan herds the sons and daughters of this present evil age.

God is good to us and forgiving, full of constant love to all who pray to Him (see Ps. 86:5). He sends His messengers and prophets, men like Aleksandr Solzhenitsyn and Billy Graham. They and others warn us that God will not overlook our x-rated society with its filth, smut, pornography, violence, homosexuality, prostitution, and perversion. Hundreds of thousands of children in this country do not know the identity of their true parents because they were conceived in immorality and shuttled off to an adoption agency as tiny infants.

One evening we ate dinner in the French Quarter of New Orleans where I was holding a crusade. Out on the streets literally hundreds of homosexual couples strolled arm-in-arm along the sidewalks. They often kissed and made other public displays of affection, many of which would have been shameful even if they were exchanged between a normal heterosexual couple. Overhead an enormous billboard displayed a picture of the Statue of Liberty. Beside this venerable symbol stood a bottle of whiskey.

The caption announced that this particular brand of liquor was "the spirit of America."

A Mardi Gras mentality has swept our nation. Consequently, we live in a society and a world that is speeding toward judgment. We have made idols of materialism, humanism, pleasure, and ease. Those were the things that brought the downfall of Sodom, Nineveh, Tyre, and Rome.

Why, then, are we in North America so blind to the warning signals, deaf to the sound of the trumpet? Our prosperity has deceived us. The last really tough times in this country were from 1929 until 1939. Most of the people alive in America today are not old enough to remember what it was like to live through those days, and so we assume that such things will never happen.

We need to repent of that kind of shortsightedness. We hear of earthquakes in Guatemala, famines in Africa, terrorism in Europe and the Middle East, and we naively think that we are exempt from such things. Anyone who has the temerity to stand up and warn us that those things are about to befall us will suffer ridicule and rejection. People who love lies also hate the truth, and they hate anyone who speaks the truth.

Instead, they love those who tell them what they want to hear. They even vote for them in elections and send them to Congress and the city council. If one of them mentions God or uses a phrase like "God bless you" or quotes a verse from the Bible, then people flock to him and sing his praises twice as loudly.

But our nation's leaders need to repent of using their offices to gain power and wealth. They need to repent of lying to their constituents. They need to repent of their immorality, lust, and perversion.

Many otherwise religious people need to repent of their pride and self-righteousness. These are sins that stink more foully in the nostrils of God than many of the practices of pagans.

The time has come to look up and recognize that we are being herded to slaughter by Satan. Then we can turn aside and join the flock of the Good Shepherd who calls us and waits for us with open arms. Then we can say with David:

The LORD is my shepherd;
I have everything I need.
He lets me rest in fields of green grass
   and leads me to quiet pools of fresh water.
He gives me new strength.
He guides me in the right paths,
   as he has promised.
Even if I go through the deepest darkness,
I will not be afraid, LORD, for you are with me.
Your shepherd's rod and staff protect me.

You prepare a banquet for me,
   where all my enemies can see me;
      you welcome me as an honored guest
         and fill my cup to the brim.
I know that your goodness and love
   will be with me all my life;
and your house will be my home as long as I live (Ps. 23 TEV)

God's promises are full of tenderness, love, and mercy for those who turn to Him with tears of repentance.

The Prophetic Track Record of the Bible

With the foregoing as a background to help us understand the setting and nature of biblical prophecy, let's try now to get some measure of the accuracy with which these people prophesied. What we see will show us why their writings were included in the Bible to be preserved there for all time to come, and especially to help us understand the days in which we live at the end of the twentieth century.

The Beginning of the Prophetic Tradition

Moses was a prophet, and bands of prophets were a regular part of Israel's life from that time on. We read their mention in the times of Samuel and the early united monarchy (under kings Saul, David, and Solomon). But it was after the kingdom was divided that the prophets seemed to come into their own. That was because the true religion of the Lord was waning. None of the kings of the northern kingdom were devoted to the Lord. Even in Jerusalem from where David's descendants ruled, very few of the kings supported and sponsored worship of the Lord as King David once had.

So, the promulgation and preservation of the true faith fell more and more on the shoulders of the prophets. It was in this setting that Elijah came to prominence. He and his successor, Elisha, stood steadfastly against the encroachment of Baal worship that King Ahab's wife, Jezebel, tried to import to Israel from her hometown of Sidon in Phoenicia (modern Lebanon). We read at length of their adventures of faith in the books of the Bible called Kings and Chronicles.

Amos was the first prophet in the Bible whose message was recorded in a separate book which was named for him. Although he came from a town in Judah, he preached to the people of the northern kingdom of Israel, about the middle of the eighth century B.C. It was a time of great prosperity, notable religious piety, and apparent security. But Amos saw that prosperity was limited to the wealthy, and that it fed on injustice and oppression of the poor. Religious observance was insincere, and security more apparent than real. With passion and courage he preached that God would punish the nation, but it is doubtful that he lived to see the fulfillment of his prophecies with the fall of Samaria to the Assyrians in 722 B.C.

Most of Amos's prophecies against Syria, Philistia, Tyre, Edom, Ammon, Moab, and Judah were fulfilled either within his lifetime or no more than a century after his death. His one prophecy of things in the distant future spoke of the restoration of the kingdom of David. " 'The days are coming,' says the LORD, when...I will bring my people back to their land. They will rebuild their ruined cities and live there" (Amos 9:13–14). This was first fulfilled through the Edict of Cyrus, the Emperor of Persia in 538 B.C., roughly two hundred years after Amos died. It was fulfilled again in the twentieth century following the Balfour Declaration in 1917.

Jonah was contemporary with Amos. Hosea's life and ministry began slightly later and extended slightly longer. During the latter part of his ministry, Isaiah and Micah both prophesied. Because these men were grouped so closely together, they are known as the eighth-century prophets.

It was not until the second half of the next century, the 600s, that another group of prophets appeared whose utterances were recorded. They were Jeremiah, Zephaniah, Nahum, Habakkuk, and Ezekiel. Their job was twofold: to warn Jerusalem and the surrounding territory of Judah of the judgment of God that was coming from the north from Babylon and to interpret the catastrophic events that accompanied the fall of Jerusalem in 587 B.C.

So we see that God sent two clusters of prophets: the first came in the century prior to the fall of the northern kingdom to the Assyrians in 722 B.C.; the second came in the century before the fall of the southern kingdom in 587 B.C. The final group of prophets whose writings have come down to us, Haggai, Obadiah, Malachi, Joel, Zechariah, and Daniel, were clustered in time between 550 B.C. and 450 B.C., when the Jews were allowed by the Persians to return to Jerusalem to rebuild the temple and the walls of the city.

I want to take an example from each of these three groups to give a sampling of the sort of prophetic accuracy both in the short run and the long run that they were capable of. It will help us to take them seriously when we read their predictions about the things that are going to happen in our generation.

Isaiah, Prince of Prophets

Many of the things Isaiah said and wrote during his long ministry (740–690 B.C.) have come down to us in the music of Handel's *Messiah*. One of Isaiah's most often quoted prophecies, about the day when men would pound their swords into plowshares and their spears into pruninghooks, is engraved on a large slab outside the main entrance of the United Nations General Assembly building in New York City.

In 702 B.C., the fourteenth year of King Hezekiah's reign in Jerusalem, the Assyrians captured the fortified cities of Judah, leaving Jerusalem within Hezekiah's domain. The Assyrian emperor, Sennacherib, sent his chief official, backed by a large military force, to demand the surrender of Jerusalem (see Isa. 36 and 37).

The chief official stood just outside the walls of the city and shouted his intimidations in Hebrew. He painted a sorry picture of their hopeless situation, surrounded with no one to help. If they were depending on their God, he shouted, hadn't Hezekiah already earned the wrath of his God by tearing down the altars and shrines in the land? (This was a serious flaw in the Assyrian official's thinking. Hezekiah had introduced sweeping reforms to *restore* the worship of the Lord as prescribed in the Scriptures. Thus the elimination of the various altars and shrines of idols had earned him the blessing of God.)

It is hard to say how readily the people of Jerusalem noticed this flaw in the Assyrian's argument, because in spite of the flaw, it seems to have sent an understandable wave of fear throughout the city. Hezekiah himself thought the situation looked desperate, but he kept his head and called on Isaiah to discover what the Lord had in mind in this predicament.

Isaiah came back with comforting news. Hezekiah could relax because the Lord was going to take care of the Assyrians. The emperor was going to hear a rumor of trouble back in his own capital, Nineveh. So, he would withdraw from Jerusalem to return home where he would, in turn, suffer assassination. Incredibly, tiny Judah and Jerusalem were spared just as Isaiah had said, and in very short order.

Looking at the longer term, Isaiah prophesied that Hezekiah's descendants would fall captive to the Babylonians. They and all Jerusalem would be exiled to Babylon (see Isa. 39:5-7). It happened, precisely as Isaiah had said it would, 144 years later in 586 B.C.

Looking a little further into the future, Isaiah also prophesied that Babylonia would be overthrown in its turn. Its destruction by the Medes and the Persians would be so thorough and enduring that he likened it to that of Sodom and Gomorrah (see Isa. 13:17-22).

The fulfillment of that prophecy makes a fascinating story. Babylonia, according to Isaiah (who said this was the Lord's appraisal) was the most beautiful kingdom of all (see Isa. 13:19). It was accounted one of the seven wonders of the ancient world. Its walls stood 150 feet high and were wide enough at the top for five chariots to run abreast along the parapets.

The Medes and the Persians laid siege to the city in 538 B.C. But the Babylonians were so unconcerned that the emperor, Belshazzar, was holding a drunken orgy in the palace right in the middle of the siege. This party is mentioned by Daniel because it grew so drunken and blasphemous that the hand of God wrote a message of judgment in the plaster on the wall of the banquet room. That sobered everybody up! Belshazzar had to summon Daniel to discover the meaning of the words; and almost as soon as they were interpreted, they were fulfilled. This is how it happened.

The Euphrates River ran through the center of Babylon. It entered under the wall on the north side of the city and exited under the wall on the south side. Median engineers had gone upstream and found a location to erect a dam. Once it was complete, their army had opportunity to sneak into the city through the openings in the walls through which the water had been formerly pouring. They entered and took control of the city on the very night of Belshazzar's feast. As Daniel had told him, Belshazzar had been weighed in the balances and found wanting. Therefore, the Lord was taking his kingdom from him and dividing it between the Medes and the Persians.

Jeremiah, Prophet of Doom

Jeremiah was born about sixty years after Isaiah died. By that time Manasseh's notoriously evil reign had all but sealed the doom of the southern kingdom, Judah. Jeremiah took up Isaiah's prophecy that the Babylonians would capture Jerusalem. He predicted the duration of the Babylonian captivity at seventy years (see Jer. 25:11). The foundations of the new temple in Jerusalem were laid in 520 B.C., sixty-six years after the people of Jerusalem were taken to Babylon. Within four years of that foundation-laying, the Babylonian captivity was effectively over for most of the Jerusalemites and their descendants born in Babylon. Jeremiah, who was despised and ridiculed during his lifetime, was enshrined in Israel's halls of honor because he had spoken God's hard words in a hard time.

The Gospels and the Acts

It was Jesus Himself who first directed His disciples' attention to the time when He would come in glory. This would contrast to His appearing in lowliness and weakness during His first coming.

Two men in white stood by the disciples as Jesus was ascending and disappearing out of their midst forty days after His resurrection (see Acts 1:11). They reminded the disciples that this same Jesus would come back in the same manner He had departed— that is, through the air.

The Writings of Paul

You might be surprised to know that references to the return occur in every one of Paul's letters! Thus, his writings are very prophetic. In 1 Thessalonians, probably the first letter he wrote and therefore the oldest document in the New Testament, he returns repeatedly to the theme of the Lord's return and the hope it holds out for all believers. This hope is based on two things: first, the dead will be raised when Christ returns; and second, the faith of all believers, living and dead, will be vindicated before a scoffing world.

One of the most graphic descriptions of the retur is

There will be the shout of command, the archangel's voice, the sound of God's trumpet, and the Lord himself will come down from heaven. Those who have died believing in Christ will rise to life first; then we who are living at that time will be gathered up along with them in the clouds to meet the Lord in the air. And so we will always be with the Lord (1 Thess. 4:16–17 TEV).

The Revelation

As with the rest of the New Testament, references to the return in this last book of the Bible are too numerous to mention. At the very end of the book we find these words that should express the desire of every believer: "He who gives his testimony to all this says, 'Yes indeed! I am coming soon!' " (Rev. 22:20 TEV)

Yes, the Bible is true. One of the reasons the Bible has stood the test of time is the incredible accuracy of its predictions. Roughly two-thirds of all the prophetic utterances in the Bible have already come to pass. Those that remain in waiting have to do with the end of history as we have known it. It is time now to examine some of the themes of end-time prophecy and to see how things are shaping up for their fulfillment.

Chairman Mao

History is filled with dominant personalities. Each age has had its Caesar, its Charlemagne, Genghis Khan, Catherine the Great, Napoleon—the list is endless. In the twentieth century, the number of such leaders has multiplied, and we've seen the impact of each multiplied through the revolution in communications that is the earmark of our era.

A great wind is stirring from the accumulated pressures of living together on this planet. It is a wind that whispers, "Something, someone, unusual is needed to deal with the impossible problems facing us. We need a dictator for the whole world, or at least for as much of the world as we can bring under one umbrella."

Think of the conditions that catapulted Hitler into power in 1933. Germany was hit by an economic depression quite as bad as the one in the U.S. (where we elected a man who accrued more power to the presidency than had ever before been imagined for that office). Millions of Germans were out of work. Small businesses were collapsing. Banks were failing. Anarchy, lawlessness, and moral decadence prevailed. People were desperate to find a way out through the establishment of order and discipline. Hitler told them a comfortable lie: it could be remedied by ousting the Jews who were responsible for it all. He promised to take decisive steps to make Germany great again, and he was swept into power.

Today these same conditions can no longer be confined within the borders of nations. Decadence, symbolized by the entertainers idolized and lionized by the adolescents of the western Hemisphere and beyond, has seized our vitals. What happened in Germany to bring Hitler to power is so overshadowed by what is happening in our world today that it seems almost insignificant. But of course, the murder of millions of people could never be insignificant.

Arnold Toynbee, one of the most eminent historians of this

century, once said, "By forcing on mankind more and more lethal weapons, and at the same time making the world more and more interdependent economically, technology has brought mankind to such a degree of distress that we are ripe for the deifying of any new Caesar who might succeed in giving the world unity and peace."[1]

Long ago the Bible (see Rev. 13) talked about the Antichrist who would come and deceive the nations of the world. He will mark the epitome of all that the world extols. He will be powerful, amoral, cunning, ruthless, vigorous, relentless. He will perform wonders and miracles to make the whole world stand in awe of him. In fact, they will begin to worship him just as men began to worship Caesar centuries ago.

He will literally seduce all the nations and achieve the appearance of a truly unified and efficient government for the entire planet. The book of Revelation calls him "the Beast." He will control the world more through economics than through military power. No one, for example, will be permitted to buy or sell anything unless they bear on their person his mark—possibly the infamous numerals, 666.

People have long speculated over the meaning of that number which divulges the identity of the Beast of Revelation. Numerals did not exist either in Hebrew or in Greek (the language in which Revelation was written). Consequently both of these languages attached numerical values to the letters of their alphabet. Thus the number of the beast is the sum of the separate letters of his name. Of the countless explanations, the most probable is *Neron Caesar* (in Hebrew letters). Spelled without the final "n," *Nero Caesar* (which is how it would be spelled in Latin—the spelling with "n" is according to Greek conventions) would total 616 which would account for the variant reading of 616 found in a few ancient manuscripts. This points to a dramatic reincarnation of just such a man in our own age another man similar to Mao—a great Caesar to lead the world beyond the collapse of parliamentary democracy.

Nero (A.D. 37–68) is remembered for his mistreatment of Christians and his neglect of government affairs while he pursued a musical career. When he succeeded Claudius as emperor in 54, he had Claudius's son, Britannicus, poisoned and buried him in haste and secrecy. He had his interfering mother killed in 59. In A.D. 62 he arranged the murder of his wife so that he could marry another (divorce was out of the question apparently, because his first wife had been Claudius's daughter and therefore represented some potential for rivalry). When a fire burned part of Rome in 64, Nero blamed the Christians for it and had them put to death cruelly. He committed suicide in 68 when he discovered that the palace guards were plotting with members of the Senate to overthrow him.

Because of his scandalous ways, the greater realities of Nero's fourteen-year reign are overlooked. He was a good administrator with excellent advisers in the philosopher Seneca and the soldier Burrus. He brought peace to Britain after a revolt there, sent a fleet to protect Roman shipping on the Black Sea, and he selected superb commanders for wars in Armenia and Judea.

We see in him the model for the coming world ruler. He will be a cruel and immoral man who is culturally refined, even gifted. He will have the finest advisers and make shrewd decisions.

The Market Is Good

In Daniel (2:24–45) we read of Nebuchadnezzar's dream in which he saw a giant statue, bright and shining and terrifying to look at. Its head was made of finest gold, its chest and arms were made of silver, its waist and hips of bronze, its legs of iron, and its feet partly of iron and partly of clay. In the dream a stone broke away from a cliff, struck the iron and clay feet of the statue, and demolished the whole thing. Then that stone grew and became a mountain that covered the whole earth.

This was a vision, as Daniel explained it, of five empires that would rule the world in succession, beginning with Nebuchadnezzar himself as the head of gold. But the fifth empire, represented by the feet of iron and clay, would be a division of the former iron empires. Its leaders would try to reunite it by intermarriage, but the attempt would fail. At the time of those rulers, Daniel said, the God of heaven would establish a kingdom that would never end. It would never be conquered, but would completely destroy all the former empires and then last forever.

To Jews living in the last two centuries before the arrival of Jesus, the giant statue had clear meaning. It spoke of the succession of the Babylonian, Median, Persian, and Greek empires. Alexander the Great's Greek empire had been the strongest (legs of iron), but it had been divided among his generals. They had held it together for a while, but by 311 B.C., it had broken into a group of successor states. The Ptolemies (descendants of the general named Ptolemy) ruled Egypt. The Seleucids (descendants of the general named Seleucus) ruled Syria.

The Maccabean revolt in Judea in the middle of the second century B.C. managed to establish a brief period of independence for Israel. Many Jews hoped that this kingdom—the Maccabean, or Hasmonean, as it was more commonly known—was the fulfillment of Daniel's prophecy about the establishment of the kingdom of God that would last forever. But the dynasty declined until its ruler was an evil man who was hardly even a Jew, Herod. His friend Marc Antony, the great Roman general, had put him in power in Judea.

Jewish hopes for the Hasmonean dynasty had fallen on hard times. Surely, if Daniel's prophecy were going to be fulfilled, something had to happen soon. Messianic expectations ran high throughout the Jewish community. Herod was even visited by some strange stargazers from the east looking for a king. The baby born that winter in Bethlehem went unnoticed by most people.

Those who did notice Him were told He would come again in glory at the end of the age. That coming would mark the final fulfillment of Daniel's vision of the stone which destroyed the giant statue. That statue seemed embodied from head to foot, finally, by the vast Roman Empire which vastly overshadowed the former five empires.

Thus it is that we see the Roman Empire being revived, more along economic lines (which is as the book of Revelation hinted) than according to the old military pattern of the former Caesars. This modern revival is embodied in the European Economic

Community, better known as the European Common Market, whose policies toward Israel I mentioned briefly in the previous chapter.

Since its inception in the 1950s the community has grown steadily. With the admission of Denmark, Ireland, and Great Britain in 1973, it surpassed the United States in production of steel and motor vehicles. This increasing economic power gives the community some international political influence. Vigorous competition from Japan and low-cost manufacturers in the Third World, as well as frequent squabbles with America, are pushing the Ten, as the community is also known, toward closer cooperation.

So effective has the European community grown, in fact, that the Soviets have refused even to recognize it. "The Soviets never liked us," says one expert in Brussels (EEC headquarters). "They prefer a Europe split into nation states they can play off against each other."

A British "Eurocrat" at EEC headquarters views the community as an instrument to achieve political stability "north and south of the Alps" by tempering left-wing radicalism and neutralism and pushing member countries toward compromises. Left-leaning regimes generally fall in line with community attitudes on domestic and international issues.

Quietly and unobtrusively the old empire is being reborn. When the time comes, it will be ready to install a modern-day successor to Nero Caesar on the throne. He will be hailed as a true match, at last, for the Stalins, Khrushchevs, and Gorbachevs of the East—someone who can lead us to "peace" at last.

Red Hot China

In the book of Revelation we read a fascinating prediction that the River Euphrates will be dried up "so that the way of the kings from the east might be prepared" (Rev. 16:12). They will probably be at the head of the army of 200 million soldiers mentioned in Revelation 9:16. This army will wipe out a third of all mankind at the Battle of Armageddon.

An army of such size probably could be recruited only in the Orient, perhaps from China, possibly from India. Bible students have long understood the prophecies to speak of a great conflict between the kings of the east and the invaders from the north which Ezekiel describes. This would mean fighting between Chinese and Soviet troops.

Just a few decades ago that would have sounded odd to Western ears. The Communist takeover of China seemed to create an enormous and sinister "Sino-Soviet bloc." Today, with the heightening of Sino-Soviet tensions, we can see that such a move would be entirely plausible.

China has long backed the Arabs in their conflict with the Israelis. For a long time this backing was expressed by support for the Palestine Liberation Organization. However, in recent years the Chinese have recognized that this has hampered relations with conservative Arab regimes, like the ones in Oman and Jordan. So they have worked to establish more cordial relations with the regular governments of the Middle East and Africa. In 1976, after Anwar Sadat broke with Moscow, the Chinese entered into a treaty with Egypt. As things stand now, a Chinese move into the Middle East to counter outright Soviet aggression in the region would make a lot of sense. The Bible hints that this is exactly what will happen.

He Is Coming Back

After Jesus rose from the tomb He remained with His disciples for forty days. Then He was taken up from their midst to be seated in the place of all authority in heaven and on earth. As He was ascending that day, the disciples were asked, "Men of Galilee, why do you stand gazing up into heaven? This same Jesus, who was taken from you into heaven, will come in like manner as you saw Him go into heaven" (Acts 1:11).

We have come this far looking at some of the more prominent signs that tell us the day of the return is much closer than we might have thought. That day will come suddenly and it will startle most of the people on the face of the earth. It will be a day of light and gladness for those who are ready. For those who are not it will be the Day of Judgment.

I am not going to get into the arguments that abound concerning the timing of Jesus' return. The purpose of this book is *not* to speculate, but to *awaken*. The Bible tells us clearly to be ready, to live our lives in light of the return, as men and women who know we will have to give account of ourselves. No one knows the day or the hour of the return; Jesus assured us of that. But the Bible is filled with prophecy that tells us how to interpret the times in which we live. We are living in the last of the last days.

XIII

Truth or Consequences

"What can the world or any nation in it hope for if no turning is found on this dread road? This is not a way of life at all. It is humanity hanging from a cross of iron."

—Dwight D. Eisenhower

Do you feel your life is disconnected? On November 2, 1985, the *Washington Post* News Service released an article that declared at least 15 percent of all U.S. teenagers aged sixteen to nineteen are unlikely to become productive adults because they are already "disconnected" from society, according to a committee of business, education, and political leaders. The chief "disconnectors," it says, are drug abuse, delinquency, pregnancy, unemployment, and dropping out of school. Almost 2.4 million youths—up to half the high school population in some major cities—fall in that group, and the number is growing, according to the study conducted by a business subcommittee of the Education Commission of the States.

So many people in this world have no purpose or reason for being. They don't know who they are or where they are going. They behold the violence in this world, and it terrifies them. It needs to if they do not have peace with God.

According to FBI statistics, in 2,697 cities with a population of under ten thousand the murder rate has increased 28.4 percent since 1970. In the large cities, the increase is 17.8 percent. This information was published in a book called *God's Prison Gang* by Chaplin Ray. He went on to say that three mathematicians at the Massachusetts Institute of Technology, who made a study of homicide, put the problem in perspective: "An American child born in 1976 is more likely to die by murder than an American soldier in World War II was to die in combat." The chaplain went on to say that according to "Dr. Donald T. Lunde, assistant professor of psychiatry and law at Stanford University, who's also made a study of murder, 'More Americans were homicide victims between 1970 and 1974 than died in the Vietnam War.' "

If that was the case in the seventies, what is it now? No wonder people are filled with fear. There is reason to have fear if you do not have peace with God.

We have described so many things in this book that are signs of the times, but let me just take one second to mention another statistic about AIDS. According to *Time Magazine,* October 28, 1985, the United States has the largest number of cases in the world. To substantiate that fact, the *Dallas Morning News* reported on August 16, 1985, that AIDS is found to be the number-one killer of New York men aged thirty to thirty-nine last year:

> AIDS was the number one killer of New York City men between the ages of 30-39 last year and the second-leading cause of death among women aged 30-34, health officials said. Statistics gathered by the city Health Department show that more men in both the 30-34 and 35-39 age groups died last year from acquired immune deficiency syndrom than from homicide, sucide or cancer.

What are you going to do with all these startling facts? What are you going to do with this catalog of bad news? Can you ignore it and hope it will go away? It will not, but it is pointing to something that is the greatest and best event of all times. It only will be the best event for those who are ready for it and will take the signs of the times we live in seriously.

In an earlier chapter I mentioned a day when I flew over Mount St. Helens and saw the black smoke belching from its mouth. It's almost humorous; because as I am working on this chapter right now, the pilot just mentioned on the loudspeaker that we should look at Mount St. Helens: it is still belching smoke. I have just left Seattle on my way to Dallas.

As I turned my head after staring out the window, the story of old Harry Truman who used to live there, came back to me—that man wouldn't take Mount St. Helens seriously in spite of all the warnings he had received. Harry was what the Bible calls a scoffer. He had no use for God or anyone else who might try to tell him what to do.

Those in that area who knew Harry said he was a nasty old man, and Harry wasn't afraid of anything. To our modern ears that sounds like a wonderful thing to say about someone. But it's not. Harry proved it's not. His lack of fear identified him as a fool.

The Bible says that the first step in becoming wise and conversely, leaving foolishness behind, is to fear the Lord. Some people get nervous when they hear the phrase "the fear of the Lord." They want to explain it away. It's a reverence and awe, they say. We really shouldn't take it the way it sounds.

I believe it is time that we had the fear of the Lord. Jesus said, "Do not fear those who kill the body but cannot kill the soul. But rather, fear Him who is able to destroy both soul and body in hell" (Matt. 10:28). Hell is a real place, and God's wrath is real. Those who harden their hearts and refuse to accept God's merciful sacrifice, Jesus, will be eternally separated from God. The Bible says that there will be wailing and gnashing of teeth. That is truly something to be afraid of.

When you and I stand in the presence of our Holy God—and we all have a divine appointment with Him we will keep—it will only be through the merciful name of Jesus and the forgiveness that was provided at Calvary's cross that we can enter into God's presence as righteous. Woe be unto the man or woman who stands before the holy throne of God in his own righteousness. No terror on this earth could be compared to the words that God Almighty will say to him.

Welcome to a Loser's World

This book has been devoted in part to cataloging the shape of the world. As one expert on food production put it, "Forget about using the word *crisis*. The correct word now is *climax,* meaning a final and irreversible shortage. The earth is no longer a sustainable society." Anyone who attempts to collect information about our planet is likely to come to similarly dreary conclusions.

Here is just a partial listing of the signs of the times that indicate the nearness of the return of Jesus Christ. May these evidences encourage you to receive Christ as your personal savior if you haven't done so already:

1. Matthew 24:5—An increase in deception
2. Matthew 24:6—An acceleration of violence
3. Matthew 24:7—An acceleration of national wars and strife within countries
4. Matthew 24:7—An acceleration of famines
5. Matthew 24:7—An acceleration of plagues
6. Matthew 24:7—An acceleration of earthquakes
7. Matthew 24:7—An increase in moral breakdown, betrayal, and hatred (see II Tim. 3)
8. Matthew 24:12—A deterioration of marriage (the love of many waxing cold)
9. Matthew 24:29—The incredible threat of nuclear warfare as also described in the book of Revelation
10. Matthew 24:32—The miracle of Israel's rebirth
11. Matthew 24:37-39—A spirit of total apathy
12. Matthew 24:48—An increase in the number of people skeptical about the Lord's return

Many things have gotten away from us. Species of wildlife are disappearing with greater regularity than at any time in the past three thousand years. Desperate efforts are underway in California to preserve the California condor from extinction. These losses, as grievous as they are, serve primarily to illustrate and symbolize the way in which we humans mistreat this planet we have been given to live on. Our selfish exploitation of our resources makes us feel as though we are winners, but the facts are coming to the surface at last. This is a loser's world, and whoever lives only for this present evil system, which the Bible simply calls "the world," is a loser.

Big Bucks

The Greek word from which we derive our words *pharmacy*

and *pharmaceuticals* means "to practice magic arts" or "to mix poison and practice sorcery." Drug abuse has become so widespread in the United States that the sales of cocaine have placed it among the top five money-making forms of business in the country.[1]

The drug of choice among Americans and people throughout the world is still alcohol. The consumption of alcohol has created the largest health problem in the United States when measured in terms of morbidity. It is the fourth largest cause of death, after heart disease, cancer, and stroke.[2]

Most of the drugs that people take are some kind of narcotic. The purpose of narcotics is to dull pain and induce sleep. Alcohol and heroin are the prominent narcotics.

An increasing number of people is using cocaine. Cocaine is not a narcotic, but a stimulant, just as are amphetamines. They produce talkativeness, hyperactivity, dilated pupils, restlessness, loss of appetite, and the like. According to official estimates, five million Americans use cocaine, and 25 million have tried it.[3]

Whether people use narcotics or stimulants, they have this in common: they are running away from life. That is a pattern that repeats itself in all sorts of behavior wherever we go. In 1983 more than 29,000 people succeeded in committing suicide. Experts estimate than nearly half a million youngsters attempt to commit suicide every year. Mental illness in some form affects about 20 million Americans, of whom about six hundred seventy-nine thousand require hospitalization each year.[4]

Something has gone seriously wrong, and the sorts of statistics I've just reviewed point to a widespread flight from reality in response to that wrongness. None of these flights has achieved anything except more suffering. No one has found a way out, because there is none. We need to look at the handwriting on the wall and learn what it says before it's too late.

The Best Kept Secret

There is a source of peace in the face of all this. I refer to Jesus. By His sacrifice on the cross He purchased peace for us, and He gives that peace to all who come to Him humbly asking for it.

Corrie ten Boom, the lady to whom I referred earlier in this book who harbored Jews in her home during the Nazi occupation, had a saying: "Look around and be distressed, look within and be depressed, but look to Jesus and be at rest." You can truly be at rest if it is well with your soul.

I remember a night when I left Houston in a Cessna 210. My dear friend and pilot, Bill Knight, was flying me back to Dallas at 11:00 P.M. In the plane was an associate, Sy Rickman, and my producer, Paul Cole. We had a lot of our camera equipment with us because we were showing a new prime time special which we had just finished entitled "Israel, America's Key to Survival."

We had a full load and a fifty-mile-an-hour headwind. We had not been flying more than twenty to twenty-five minutes when we got close to a town called Hillsborough. All of a sudden I could smell gas. The plane began choking out, we had no internal or external lights on the plane, and we were losing altitude. Without God's intervention what I am describing would be written into a book of statistics on plane fatalities, because the cylinder broke lose on the single-engine plane. The vibration was tearing the entire engine to pieces, including ripping off the gas line.

Being a mechanic, Bill immediately told us what was happening. He said, "There is no way we can land here, and there is not a lift runway for twenty-one minutes. We *have* to make it to Waco."

That seemed totally impossible. How can a plane in that condition with a fifty-mile-an-hour headwind and a full load fly an additional twenty-one minutes, especially when losing altitude? I know of no other way except through the power of prayer. I began praying, commanding Satan to take his filthy hands off that plane and trusting God to touch us.

Sy Rickman was interceding that the angels of the Lord would undergird us. He kept saying the same prayer over and over. The amazing thing was that as he was praying that prayer, that plane kept flying. It seemed as if any second it was going to go out and we would fall into the pitch darkness. But it didn't.

Nineteen minutes. Eighteen minutes. Seventeen, sixteen, fifteen, fourteen, eleven, ten, nine, five, four, three, two...The plane kept flying. As we started heading toward the field in Waco, Bill choked the engine down because he knew that the air speed would immediately cause the leaking gas to ignite.

We glided down over the runway, and when we got out of the plane, we noticed that half of the oil was on the ground. The remainder of the oil had fallen out in the air when the engine starting disintegrating. You could shake the engine in your hand because it was so torn apart when we landed. There was no way humanly speaking that engine could fly and stay together for that length of time.

We got in a cab, and I took everyone home that evening. I considered it one of the cheapest taxi fares I ever paid—almost a hundred dollars—due to the circumstances.

An amazing thing happened the next morning when my secretary, Joyce, called me and said, "Mike, Judy Blanchard called and wanted to know where you were at 11:30 last night."

I asked Joyce, "What do you mean?"

She said, "Well, Judy woke up from a sound sleep and felt as if the Lord was telling her gently to get on her knees and pray for you. He let her know you were in a crisis and that she should pray for the angels of the Lord to undergird you. For thirty solid minutes she prayed to that end."

What a joy it was to tell Judy that the exact moment she began praying, the engine started coming apart. When she felt the release to stop praying, we had landed safely in Waco. Further, the gentleman sitting beside me had been praying the exact same prayer she had for almost thirty minutes.

Yes, Corrie ten Boom was right: look to Jesus and be at rest. God did not promise that we would not have storms, but He *did* promise that He would give us peace and be with us.

XIV

A Local Call

"I believe the world is coming to an end. I just feel that science, technology, and the mind have surpassed the soul—the heart. There is no balance in terms of feeling and love for fellow man."

—Barbara Streisand

We had just left New York City heading south. As I sat in the bulkhead aisle seat in the first-class section, I noticed the gentleman sitting next to me glance down at my Bible and immediately throw his paper up in front of his face to avoid me. I knew sooner or later his paper was going to have to come down. He tried to act as if he were reading every word of *The New York Times* on business, world events, science, technology, and what have you. But I knew better—the eyes are a window to the soul—and I could see through his eyes pain, hurt, and fear.

After about thirty-five minutes, he finally put the paper down. I looked at him and said, "I want you to know that I know it's not well with your soul. You are hurting inside, but God loves you very much and cares about you as a person. He *does* know your name." Tears filled that gentleman's eyes.

Later he told me that he was the general manager for one of the most famous baseball teams in the nation. His story was one of divorce, emptiness, frustration, anger, alcohol, and drugs.

He said, "Mike, you say that God loves me and knows my name, that I am special to Him. But I have been involved in one of the most filthy orgies imaginable only last night in New York City. You are right. I've been running and I'm empty and lonely. Nothing satisfies me. Money doesn't; success, fame, sex. I don't have any peace in my soul."

I said to him, "You know, it's not complicated. God is closer than you think." Before that flight ended, that gentleman received the Lord Jesus Christ as his personal Savior.

If you haven't experienced Jesus already, before this chapter is over, I pray that you will reach out and be transformed by the love of God, that you might say, "Indeed, it is well with my soul."

A Broken Phone

It was a frustrating experience; it was getting to me. I was in the Netherlands and I needed to call home to my office back in the States. What better time, I thought, to use my new telephone credit card? I looked closely and, sure enough, there was even an international code for me to use.

That was the last pleasant thing that happened. I dialed the number (according to my recollection of the instructions), but all I got was silence on the line. I tried again. Same response, or should I say, lack of response. Then I looked more closely at the instructions. It *seemed* that I was doing it the way they said. Again I tried. Nothing. I kept trying for twenty times, and each time my exasperation went up another notch.

Finally I decided the phone must be broken and I slammed it down in frustration. It took awhile for me to admit it to myself, but of course the phone was not broken. It was I who had failed to understand the instructions, probably because I was too impatient to sit down and read them slowly and carefully.

It's that way with a lot of us whenever we come up against something new. We know that dealing with this new thing, be it a phone or whatever, is going to take some time. We don't want to be slowed down, so we search for some kind of shortcut that almost inevitably takes more time than the long way we were trying to avoid.

It's like that when it comes to having a relationship with God. We know instinctively that such a thing will not be inconsequential! We know it will change our lives.

First and foremost, that change will have to do with sin. None of us thinks of himself or herself as a sinner. We see ourselves as entitled to do whatever it is we want to do. No matter what we do, we have a good reason. People ought not to blame us for the things we do; they ought to understand and feel sorry for us.

Looking at another side of this phenomenon, William Bright, the founder of Campus Crusade for Christ, reports a fascinating piece of information. In all his travels and interviews with many of the leading academicians in our nation, he has never talked privately and candidly with one who did not admit in the final analysis that he rejected faith in Jesus Christ because he knew Jesus would require him to give up something he was unwilling to give up. The problem of faith, then, has never been an intellectual problem. It always has been a moral question.

That day in my hotel room in Amsterdam, I had to admit that I had a problem, and that it was not a broken phone. Instead it was my own obstinacy and impatience. That's what I had to do if I was going to get through to my office. It is also what each of us has to do if we are going to get through to God.

Don't Hang Up

One day I was flying on a plane from Los Angeles. The man sitting next to me and I began to get acquainted. He wanted me to know how important he was. He had once been employed by one of our nation's former presidents. He was a powerful and influential man.

Finally I looked him in the eye and said, "You have a hole in your soul."

"A what in my where?"

"A hole in your soul."

"My shoes are new. You must be talking about my soul. Does your lapel pin have anything to do with this?"

"Yes."

"So, tell me, what does 'seventy times' [my lapel pin said 70 x 7] mean?"

"Peter," I replied, "once asked Jesus how often he had to forgive a brother who repeatedly sinned against him. He asked specifically if he had to do it seven times. 'No, not seven times,' answered Jesus, 'but seventy times seven.' "

"A fella'd have to be pretty patient to forgive some cuss who kept it up for 490 times," my fellow passenger observed.

"Yeah," I replied.

"So, what did you mean about a hole in my soul?"

With that I began to share some more from the Bible and to explain the deep need each of us has to know God. Before the hour was over tears had come to this man's eyes. He began to confess his use of drugs and alcohol, the failure of his three marriages, and the lack of any plan or direction in his life. Shortly after that, he prayed quietly with me there on the plane and asked the Lord to come into his life and make a new person of him.

Jesus said, "I have come that they may have life, and that they may have it more abundantly" (John 10:10). My friend on the airplane came to faith because he wanted to have eternal life in heaven, but he also wanted—and knew that Jesus could give him—direction in his life here on earth, a plan for living that would work.

Filled with the Holy Spirit and power, Jesus went about everywhere doing good and healing all who were under the power of the devil. He told His disciples that they, too, would be endowed with the Holy Spirit to do the same sorts of things He had done (see John 14:12).

Billy was one of my closest friends at college. It broke my heart to see him because he was always wearing hip-high braces, which he had worn most of his life. All of his pants had holes in them because the braces were not strong enough to support his weak legs.

You see, Billy was suffering from multiple sclerosis, the mysterious disease that destroys the white matter of the brain and spinal column. It can cause paralysis of the legs and partial loss of vision. The disease had first struck Billy when he was just a toddler. That day in his dormitory he was wearing leg braces that went up around his hips. In the eyes of the law he was a totally disabled person and was receiving compensation as such.

I began to pray very soon after my arrival at Billy's room, and I read Billy a Scripture in Isaiah 53. It talks about the Lord:

He is despised and rejected by men,
A man of sorrows and acquainted with grief.
And we hid, as it were, our faces from Him.
He was despised, and we did not esteem Him.
Surely He has borne our griefs,
And carried our sorrows;
Yet we esteemed Him stricken,
Smitten by God, and afflicted.
But He was wounded for our transgressions,
He was bruised for our iniquities;
The chastisement for our peace was upon Him,
And by His stripes we are healed.
All we like sheep have gone astray;
We have turned, every one, to our own way;
And the LORD has laid on Him the iniquity of us all (Isa. 53:3–6).

After reading this marvelous prophecy about Jesus, I continued praying. I told Billy that there was no way in the world that I could heal him, and that I had never seen a mighty miracle, but I knew that God could do miracles.

I had such a burden for Billy that I continued praying, not for ten minutes, or twenty or thirty or one hour, but for over two and one-half hours. Another young man, who is now a pastor, was in the room. We were both in agony praying over Billy because of his pain.

Then, suddenly, the power of God poured through Billy's body. "Praise God!" he shouted. "I'm healed!" With that, he started unfastening his braces. He threw them off and then literally tore off his orthopedic shoes and ran barefoot out of the room. I followed to watch him dancing around on the lawn outside like a little child. It was a marvelous and wonderful thing. To the day of this writing, fifteen years later, he remains completely whole and healthy.

Not everyone I pray for is healed so dramatically. I can't heal anyone, but I serve a God who can and does. That it doesn't always happen for everyone the same way is discouraging. But the times when it does happen, like the time with Billy, give us hope and encouragement not to hang up. The God who created us is good and loving. He is not bent on our destruction, but on our salvation.

No, I don't have all the answers, and there are certain situations in life that I don't understand. I will just have to wait till I get to heaven and ask the Lord about them. One situation I will have to ask about is the lovely little boy named Ross Kingston Byrd.

At the age of four this beautiful young man fell into a swimming pool and bumped his head. He has been in a coma now for four years. I don't understand that situation, but I do know this: God is a good God, and I'm going to keep praying and believing. I will keep looking to Jesus with that lovely picture of Ross on my desk.

Call Collect

My first experience with God was dramatic. I was only eleven years old. I was home in bed, sound asleep. Shortly after two o'clock in the morning, something awakened me. Then I had a vision of Jesus. Jesus was standing in the clouds with his arms outstretched. Beneath him, I saw graves opening and people coming out of them to go join Jesus. I sat in my bed and wept uncontrollably.

That was twenty-seven years and four and a half million miles ago. That was ten books ago and four prime time specials ago.

Let me take a moment to tell you about the young man who had the glorious vision.

That young man had a speech impediment for eight years, a nervous stomach, and did not attend high school. His father was very abusive, and if it hadn't been for the grace of God that young man would never have accomplished anything. He left home at seventeen with his father cursing him all the way down the road.

I know that young man well, because I am he. It was a glorious experience with the living God that brought me to a total commitment. I acknowledged my need to be forgiven of my sin, and asked the Lord Jesus to come into my life to be my personal Savior.

"But God demonstrates His own love toward us, in that while we were still sinners, Christ died for us" (Rom. 5:8). He loves us, and He has a glorious plan for our lives. But we all have a long way to go; it will not be over with until we are in His presence. We will only get there through His pardon and forgiveness. In no other religious system can we find this. As Isaiah prophesied about the Messiah long ago:

> The LORD says,
> "It was my will that he should suffer;
> his death was a sacrifice to bring forgiveness....
> My devoted servant, with whom I am pleased,
>   will bear the punishment of many
>   and for his sake I will forgive them" (Isa. 53:10–11 TEV).

It was after that that I discovered the startling secret: I could do nothing to earn this forgiveness. It was a free gift. The apostle Paul wrote: "For it is by God's grace that you have been saved through faith. It is not the result of your own efforts, but God's gift, so that no one can boast about it" (Eph. 2:8–9 TEV).

Did that leave me with nothing to do? No indeed. If one ignores a gift or in some way neglects or refuses to receive it, he cannot possess it. So it was that Peter invited his Jewish listeners on the day of Pentecost: "Repent, and let everyone of you be baptized in the name of Jesus Christ for the remission of sins; and you shall receive the gift of the Holy Spirit" (Acts 2:38). At a later date, Paul urged the jailer at Philippi, "Believe on the Lord Jesus Christ, and you will be saved—you and your household" (Acts 16:31). Later that same night, the jailer and all the members of his family were baptized. So, we received God's gift by means of faith, and repentance, and testify to it with baptism.

Faith

Start with faith. That's how it all began with Abraham, who "put his trust in the LORD, and because of this the LORD was pleased with him and accepted him" (Gen. 15:6 TEV). So, today, we can do the same. But we place our faith in Jesus Christ who died to take away our sins. We bring no good work on our part in an attempt to earn God's favor. Rather, we must come "empty-handed." Only what God has done *for* us counts. That is why we must trust and put our faith in Christ and his sacrifice for sinners.

Faith is a subject that has filled volumes. It is something that will grow steadily. The person who grows in faith will find quickly that its essence is not intellectual assent to the idea of the existence of God or the truth of the doctrines of the Bible; it is much more. It is a personal trust in and reliance on God Himself. In this sense, it stands as the foundation of the peace of God.

Repentance

Repentance, turning away from sin, is first of all a matter of changing one's mind. The most easily noticeable sin of most of us in the twentieth century is unbelief. So, in the very act of saying a prayer such as one that will follow shortly, a person indicates that he has changed his mind about God and Jesus. He or she has moved from unbelief to belief. That is an act of repentance.

Repentance, like faith, does not simply stop there, however. It is an ongoing matter. It happens day by day as we begin to see more and more things from God's point of view and change our minds about those things.

Repentance can mean setting aside time each day to read the Bible and to pray. It can mean getting out of bed Sunday morning and getting to church to worship God. It will surely mean a clear break with evil practices, everything from adultery to cheating on income tax. When John the Baptist preached, he preached repentance; and when his listeners asked him, he had clear instructions for them: they were to share their clothing and food with the poor. He also told the tax collectors to cease their fraudulent practices, and for soldiers to stop extorting from the populace (see Luke 3:10–14).

Baptism

Finally, there is water baptism. If you become a Christian, you will want to be baptized as an expression of your faith. Of course, not everyone is baptized in a church. I know of people who have been baptized in swimming pools, in the ocean, and in lakes and streams!

This accords with Paul's remarks to the church in Rome: "If you confess that Jesus is Lord and believe that God raised him from death, you will be saved. For it is by our faith that we are put right with God; it is by our confession that we are saved" (Rom. 10:9–10 TEV). And, of course, Jesus said, "I assure you that whoever declares publicly that he belongs to me, the Son of Man will do the same for him before the angels of God. But whoever rejects me publicly, the Son of Man will also reject him before the angels of God" (Luke 12:8–9 TEV).

Baptism is not merely a setting in which to confess one's decision to follow Jesus. It is an act that expresses that we are buried under water as evidence we share in Jesus' death and burial. When we are raised out of the water, we show that we are raised up in the power of His resurrection to live a new life. Thus, in baptism we illustrate that Christians are set free from the power of sin. Paul also speaks of baptism as the means by which we are circumcised, "not with the circumcision that is made by men, but with the circumcision made by Christ, which consists of being freed from the power of this sinful self" (Col. 2:11 TEV; cf. v. 12; Rom. 6:1–14).

To sum it all up by referring to my illustration of the frustrating phone call: the phone is not broken (our sin is the problem); don't hang up (God's power is greater than any problem we face); it's a local call, and if you have to call from a booth, you can call collect (the price has been paid by Jesus).

The secret is to know that we can do nothing to earn God's gift. It is precisely that: *a gift to be received*. It is not a merit badge you can earn by accumulating points. It is a pardon and a ransom to free us from our sins.

When you take the steps to receive God's gift of life in Jesus, you will be ready for the return. Before that great and final day, you can experience personally the coming of Jesus into your own life through the Holy Spirit. When the Holy Spirit enters your body you are born anew. In that moment, you are made ready to meet the Lord in the air when He comes. While you remain on this hectic and troubled planet, you have the peace of God that passes understanding.

Make this very moment the time of your decision. If you wish, you may use this prayer: "Lord Jesus, You died on the cross for my sins, according to the Word of God. I need a Savior and I cannot save myself. I acknowledge that I am a sinner, and I ask You to come into my life as my personal Lord and Savior. I truly repent and believe that You took my place on Calvary. I am sorry for my sins, and from this moment on, my life is Yours."

If you have never done it before, accepting Jesus is the most sensible thing you could do. You will not be alone. Countless others have trusted Christ also. Two people who stand out in my own mind who are looking for the return are country singers Johnny Cash and Jeannie C. Riley. Here's what they have to say:

Johnny Cash

"Matthew 24 is knocking at the door. I wrote a song by that title. I personally think from the way the world looks.... the signs of the times are pointing to the return of Jesus Christ; and I say, 'Welcome back, Jesus.' I don't think I would really care to live a life on earth if I didn't have the hope of Christ and the resurrection.

"I would advise non-Christians to read the Bible and learn about the prophecies of the return of Christ. If you don't believe in Jesus Christ, then you need to study the prophecies, because Jesus was raised from the dead and His divinity has proved itself for centuries by the lives of the people that have been changed, the beautiful, strong lives of those that have been turned around at the mention of His name.

"The return is the ultimate hope. The amazing thing about it all—not only is Jesus Christ going to return to this earth, and it could be very soon—but He can return to a life, transforming that person to the power of God's peace in one split second."

Jeannie C. Riley

"I would tell a non-Christian not to be looking at a religion or a doctrine or anything. Keep your eyes off people, but be looking for a person. The person is Jesus Christ.

"You know, His Holy Spirit in our hearts is as personal as you can get. I think this is where the world misses its relationship with Christ. Some people think it is going to be another theological thing they are supposed to try. It will be a set of rules to read and do...and maybe they can achieve salvation if they try hard enough. But it's just a personal thing to invite Jesus Christ into our hearts. He is so wonderful and so beautiful we want to share Him with others.

"Get your eyes off of religion and get them on Jesus."

That about says it all. If you have accepted Jesus Christ as your personal Savior, I want you to sit down and drop me a line today. I want to send you, at no cost to you, a lovely Bible and some material on how you can grow in Christ. Just write to me personally in care of Mike Evans Ministries, P.O. Box 709, Bedford, Texas 76021. When you write, take a moment to include a paragraph about yourself. That will help me pray for you more specifically.

I also want to encourage you to begin attending a church that believes the Word of God. When I respond to your letter, I'll try to recommend one you can attend in your area.

Again, feel free to write to me today. I believe with all my heart that you can be equipped to be a prophetic voice declaring that America must repent because Jesus is going to return. In order to help you be a modern day John the Baptist, let me send you our complete Return packet, including a Return pin, bumper sticker, and other items that will equip you to be a Return partner. This material will help you share your faith with others. You need only enclose $1.50 for postage and handling.

Above all, light a candle rather than curse the darkness. You are indeed a part of prophecy, even in the reading of this book: "And the good news about the Kingdom will be preached throughout the whole world so that all nations will hear it, and then, finally, the end will come" (Matt. 24:14 TLB).

Notes

Chapter Two

1. *Dallas Times-Herald*, April 15, 1985.

2. According to Yaacov Meridor, who was a top minister in the Israeli government under Begin.

3. From a personal interview with Jack Anderson.

4. General Bartholomew was interviewed at NORAD.

5. Norman Myers, *GAIA: An Atlas of Planet Management* (New York: Doubleday, 1984).

6. Myers, *GAIA*.

7. Michael Doan, "As 'Cluster Suicides' Take Toll of Teenagers—," *U.S. News & World Report*, Nov. 12, 1984, 49.

8. Doan, *U.S. News & World Report*, Nov. 12, 1984, 49.

9. Myers, *GAIA*.

10. "Superbugs: A New Biblical Plague?," *Parade*, Sept., 30, 1979.

11. Myers, *GAIA*.

12. Larry Ward, ...*and there will be Famines* (Ventura, Calif.: Regal, 1973).

13. Claudia Wallis, "AIDS: A Growing Threat," *Time*, Aug. 12, 1985, 40-42.

14. "Violence from the 'Ring of Fire,'" *U.S. News & World Report*, June 2, 1980, 31.

15. *Reader's Digest Almanac & Yearbook, 1985* (New York: Random House, 1984), 413.

16. "Life in America: Influence of Family is Declining," *U.S.A. Today*, Dec., n.d., 1983, 1.

17. Kurt Anderson, "Crashing on Cocaine," *Time*, April 11, 1983, 23.

18. Myers, *GAIA*.

19. The *Wall Street Journal* published a story called "Profits or Prophets."

20. Mike Evans, *Israel, America's Key to Survival* (Plainfield, N.J.: Logos, 1981).

21. Arkady Shevchenko, "Breaking With Moscow," *Time*, Feb. 11, 1985, 52.

22. From a taped interview with Jack Anderson.

Chapter Three

1. From a taped interview with Dr. Von Hake.

2. John Wesley White, *WW III* (Grand Rapids: Zondervan, 1977), 46-50.

3. *Global 2000 Report to the President: Entering the Twenty-First Century*, Vol. I (New York: Penguin, 1982).

4. *Time*, May 26, 1980, 20.

5. Billy Graham, *Approaching Hoofbeats: The Four Horsemen of the Apocalypse* (Waco, Tex.: Word, 1983).

6. Myers, *GAIA*.

7. Myers, *GAIA*.

8. Ward, *...and there will be Famines*.

9. Ward, *...and there will be Famines*.

10. W. R. Goetz, *Apocolypse Next* (British Columbia: Horizon House, 1980).

Chapter Four

1. From a tape made with General George Keegan (retired), former chief of Air Force intelligence.

2. *World Book*, 1985 ed., s.v. "World War II."

3. Graham, *Approaching Hoofbeats*.

4. From a taped interview with Dr. Crawford.

5. From a taped interview with Dr. Kupperman.

Chapter Five

1. From a taped interview with newspaper columnist Jack Anderson.

2. Mike Evans, *Israel, the Middle East and the Great Powers* (Jerusalem: Shikmona Publishers, 1984).

Chapter Six

1. Ronald Reagan, "Text of President Reagan's Address to Parliament on Promoting Democracy," *New York Times*, June 9, 1982, A16.

2. Roger Rosenblatt, "What the President Saw: A Nation Coming Into Its Own," *Time*, July 29, 1985.

3. George J. Church, "Exploring the High-Tech Frontier," *Time*, March 11, 1985, 20.

4. Church, *Time*, March 11, 1985, 20-23.

5. Douglas MacArthur, *Reminiscences* (New York: McGraw-Hill, 1964).

6. The *Bulletin of Atomic Scientists*, Jan. 1981, cover.

Chapter Seven

1. "No Bodies Found in Hunt for Human Sacrifices," *New York Times*, June 23, 1985, 10 h.

2. "California: Devilish Deeds?" *Newsweek*, Sept. 16, 1985, 43.

3. "The Occult Blossoms into Big Business," *U.S. News & World Report*, Nov. 7, 1983, 83.

4. "Occult Blossoms...," *U.S. News & World Report*, Nov. 7, 1983, 83.

5. Peter McGrath, "The War Against Pornography," *Newsweek*, March 18, 1985, 58-62.

6. McGrath, "The War Against..." Newsweek.

7. Annette Cornblum, "Chlamydia Epidemic: The Campus Bug that Wrecks Your Love Life," *Harper's Bazaar*, June 6, 1985, 74.

8. Kai T. Erikson, *Wayward Puritans* (New York: Wiley & Sons, 1968).

9. McGrath, "The War Against..." *Newsweek*.

Chapter Eight

1. *Reader's Digest Almanac & Yearbook*, 1985.

2. J. D. Douglas, ed., *The New International Dictionary of the Christian Church* (Grand Rapids: Zondervan, 1978), 124.

3. Joseph A. Harriss, "Karl Marx or Jesus Christ?" *Reader's Digest*, Aug. 1982, 130.

4. Hariss, *Reader's Digest*, Aug. 1982.

5. Dietrich Bonhoeffer, *The Cost of Discipleship* (New York: MacMillian, 1983).

6. David Bryant, *In the Gap: What It Means to be a World Christian* (Ventura, Calif.: Regal, 1984).

Chapter Nine

1. Mike Evans, *Israel, America's Key to Survival*.

2. *Reader's Digest Almanac & Yearbook, 1985*.

Chapter Ten

1. Evans, *Israel, America's Key to Survival*.

2. *World Book*, 1985 ed., s.v. "Modern Hebrew Literature."

3. From a taped interview with Yaacov Meridor.

Chapter Eleven

1. Mike Evans, *Jerusalem, D.C.* (Bedford, Tex: Bedford Books, 1984).
2. The interview with Prime Minier Begin was taped.
3. Evans, *Jerusalem, D.C.*

Chapter Twelve

1. Hal Lindsey, *The Late Great Planet Earth* (Grand Rapids: Zondervan, 1970), 91.

Chapter Thirteen

1. *Time*, April 11, 1983, 23.
2. *Time*, April 11, 1983, 23.
3. *Time*, April 11, 1983, 23.
4. *Reader's Digest Almanac & Yearbook, 1985.*